In The Cold Distance

DUANE FINLEY

Copyright © 2017 Duane Finley

All rights reserved.

ISBN: 0-9992993-0-1
ISBN-13: 978-0-9992993-0-2

Chapter 1

In The Cold Distance

The skyline of Indianapolis wasn't more than five miles in the rear view before the feeling that this entire endeavor had been a mistake began to set in. Both city and state put a strict no travel advisory into effect the night before, but with this proposed journalism project hugging strict timelines there was no room for error, Mother Nature induced or otherwise.

Several months earlier a thought locked into my head and became a spinning axis of possibilities in the days to follow. I had been working with fighters on a one-on-one basis for the past six years, and throughout that time found myself fascinated in what had drawn them to such a rigorous, and for the most part, unforgiving career. Granted, with my position as a feature writer for one of the most prominent news sites in mixed martial arts, I'd had plenty of interview time with a massive number of fighters, but the answers I sought weren't the type that come down the line in a ten minute phone interview.

I wanted to know what brought these men and women to not only buck the natural human instinct of avoiding conflict, but to seek something greater within throughout the process. That was the question I needed to answer and I was willing to find that resolution at any physical and mental cost.

I knew I needed to put myself in their comfort zones because only then and there would the true elements of the stories in question begin to surface. And while this sounds easy enough, anyone who has worked with professional athletes in any media capacity will back me up, they are a guarded and sensitive bunch. It may not seem typical of the men and women fans tune in to see pummel one another for paychecks and championship straps, but rest assured this is the unspoken truth that pulses through those who compete underneath the bright lights.

Another important aspect to note is that fighters by their nature are difficult to lock down into any type of schedule. Sure they are going to make it to fight night, and the majority of them hit the contracted weight that will allow them to compete and take home their full purse, but corralling combat sports athletes for anything other than training or fighting is a Herculean task unto itself.

This is what made shoving out from Indianapolis, despite every bit of instinct and the warning of well-trained meteorological experts, the only option. I had reached out to form a powerhouse lineup of champions, former champions, and potential contenders alike. I knew if I didn't hit the travel marks I'd laid out the course to hit though, I could very well be driving into the void with absolutely no return.

Being from the Midwest, it's in my nature to drive through snowstorms. I had been doing it all of my life, as did my father and his father before him. Growing up in such conditions creates a resilience that cannot be found any other place in the country. Not only do we deal with buckets of snow falling from the sky, but the sub-zero temperatures that make such conditions life threatening.

While the original plan was to head west on I-70 toward St. Louis, the weather reports from the night prior were adamant this was no route to be traveling. Therefore the only course of action available was to head down I-74 West toward Champagne, Illinois, and just minutes into the drive it became clear this was the right choice.

At least to me it was, but the large chunk of man riding shotgun was in the silent grips of disagreement as per his facial expressions. This is a good time to explain a little bit about my navigator on the trip: Ed Jones, or "Butta" as he's affectionately called in fight circles. Long before he was frozen in terror in the passenger seat of a 2005 Altima, Butta went toe-to-toe with a cancer that very well could have taken his life. The sickness had depleted much of his bulky frame back then, and from his personal retelling of the period he battled cancer there were numerous moments he wanted to tap out and give up.

It was in those instances of self-pity when UFC heavyweight and Butta's dear friend Matt Mitrione stepped in and demanded he fight. Mitrione demanded Butta stop focusing on the negatives of his situation, and start taking his illness to task. One year later and Butta looked healthier than ever, but this still didn't stop his constant verbal explosions from blasting into my right ear.

"That's forty-eight cars and semis I've counted since we left," he said as his big lumbering hand pointed to the windshield at the twisted and stalled vehicles stuck in the snow-packed ditches just beyond the fringe towns of the Circle City.

The first rule in any situation is to keep your passenger calm, but feeling how frequently the back tires of the car slid and skid on the pavement below, I wasn't sure how my poker face was holding up. The only thing I knew for certain is that he was happy I was the one driving and not him. Here was a man who had faced up to and defeated a disease that nearly took his life, and there is no doubt that the big guy was doing his best not to envision meeting a snowy and frozen demise near seventy miles from the Illinois border.

In order to keep Butta calm I tasked him with reaching out to the would-be subjects of this road trip experiment. I'd spent the weeks leading up locking down dates and times, and even though I was confident my correspondences were going to be enough, having Butta thumb out a few text messages was a good way to bring the brink of danger vibe shooting through the car down several notches.

The plan was to drive far enough west that the snow storm began to give, then turn south to head down to the opposite side of St. Louis. In the conversations we'd had during stops for gas and fill up on a warm meal, fellow truckers and travelers assured us that everything west of St. Louis would be clear sailing. Those words were invigorating to say the least, but traveling at just a clip above 25 mph wasn't going to make our arrival into those parts come in any rapid-fashion.

With that in mind, I simply kept my hands locked in a firm grip on the wheel, and let Butta continue counting ditched vehicles as the miles slowly ticked away. There are a lot of things you notice when you are driving that slow, and the most prominent on that first day was just how long the winter sun takes to set. We both watched as the purplish-pink glow continued to slide closer to the western horizon as if it had been spinning on black ice itself, and just when it dropped low enough to make it's escape for the day, it cast a neon pink hue across the rock-solid sheets of ice that had filled the spaces were crop fields once occupied.

It was a beautiful site to see, but served as an ominous calling card for the hours of travel ahead.

On the initial plan, we were slated to hit St. Louis around the four hour mark, but traveling at a turtle's pace behind a stream of cautious drivers had already doubled that amount. By the tenth hour we were just crossing over into Missouri, with St. Louis still far enough away to keep us from getting excited about it. In fact, the darker things got around us, the more and more paranoid Butta became.

"If we just make it to St. Louis we can pull over for the night and call it a day."

"We were supposed to make twenty hours of driving ground today," I replied. "If we stop there then tomorrow is going to be absolutely hellish to get through."

From his expression it was clear he understood what I was saying and the math I was rolling out to him made sense, but this did not stop the fear from showing through on a man who was physically large enough to topple most things human and non-human alike. Shortly after talking my co-pilot off the ledge, I placed a call to then UFC lightweight champion Anthony Pettis. "Showtime" was still a long ways from making his return to the Octagon, but several new endorsement deals and wanting to let his fans know what he had been up to prompted the champ to agree to do the interview.

When the idea first popped into my mind I figured I'd be sitting in my home office talking to Pettis about all things recovery and the bright future he would be looking to resume later in the year, but as the Milwaukee native talked about self-branding and a talent-rich division he knew would be eagerly awaiting his return, Butta's projection of death by freezing began to set in, because it was in that moment I noticed the cast iron guardrails that typically line the interstate and protect travelers from shooting off into the ravines and rivers were gone.

Only knit sweater-thick darkness outside in the cold distance.

After traveling a few miles further on I-70 West I embraced the fact that no more travel would be worthwhile on the first day. Even if things cleared up drastically there would be no way we could power through another state because it had taken us twenty hours just to crack the three-hundred mile mark. Once I informed Butta of my intention to find a hotel for the night, his entire demeanor changed and suddenly it was as if he had just entered the car from a fresh night's sleep.

His newfound energy managed to boost morale between the two of us, and when a sign appeared on the right hand side of the interstate showing lodging locations, I knew our dreadful opening leg would be coming to a close. A quick hit of the signal and a turn of the wheel took us up an exit ramp to a town that looked as if it hadn't seen a drop of life for the past twenty years. Google maps showed there were two places in the exit ramp town that rented nightly rooms, and we caromed toward the first roadside inn with high hopes.

Those hopes were quickly dashed when a huge "No Vacancy" sign was found plastered to the door. Not wanting to waste time or see the rest of our positive energy fade, Butta quickly pulled up the coordinates for the other possible local, but to no great surprise the Knights Inn was also at full capacity for the night. Upon receiving the second rejection I began to head back toward the interstate to keep moving down the road, and that is when the cool facade Butta held together for the past twenty-one hours shattered into pieces.

"Hey man, why don't we just pull into this Burger King parking lot?" he yelped.

"Why would we do that?"

"I don't know, man," he snapped in a gruff tone. "Just to talk about things for a minute."

By talk I knew he meant stall because the last thing Butta wanted to do was get back onto the interstate and increase our chances of sliding off into a bottomless black chasm where a painful and lonesome death surely awaited us. It was just that cold out, and at no time during our drive did we see rescue or emergency vehicles combing the highways for stranded passengers in the more than one hundred-fifty trucks and cars we saw meet an unfortunate fate on the drive.

Rather than take the chance of getting into a heated argument with my enormous and terrified friend, I assured him that stopping in a parking lot would only decrease our chances of finding somewhere to sleep for the night, and to trust that I would continue to drive at the safe and measured pace that had allowed us to reach that point.

A big exhale came from Butta and I could hear his giant hands gripping the door handle over and over again.

There is something that happens to a man between fifteen to twenty-two hours of driving, and the visual impact was extraordinary. Normal highway driving at night allows a stream of oncoming beams to snap a driver in and out of focus, but we were simply floating out into a void where either the wind or the hidden ice beneath our tires could have forced an ill-fated mishap.

Perhaps it was in those moments of discourse and uncertainty that being a father came into play, because the job of getting this car and the passengers in it to a safe place for the night became the only job that mattered. It wasn't a road trip to interview the biggest names in MMA anymore, it was survival, and I say that with the least amount of hyperbole I can muster.

Fortunately for us, six miles and twenty-five or so minutes down the road, there was a hotel shining brightly atop an upcoming exit. The yellows and blues bent and twisted through the blustering snow the way I imagined a lighthouse fixed at the point of the rocky shores of the Atlantic beckoned sailors into port. We were going to survive the night, and this brought a peace of mind that pushed the stresses of deadlines and schedules far into the distance.

After checking in and dragging a bit of luggage up to the room, I found Butta on the thin green carpet floor cranking out a series of push-ups. He was undoubtedly happy to be alive and launched into a seemingly endless stream of how everything would be okay on the trip.

"We will get there at a good time tomorrow and we won't miss a thing," he said excitedly. "I'm sure all the fighters will understand what we went through today, and this will be nothing but a funny story when we look back on it years later. It's only twenty-two hours, man. You can do that cold, brother."

Just the thought of twenty-two hours seemed like Mt. Everest at that very moment, and the adrenaline pumping through my body only made things all the more complex. Adrenaline is fascinating. When you are gripping the steering wheel and your eyes are locked in like a shark angling in on its prey, the central nervous system does the strangest things. Unfortunately for me, such magical and primal powers did not come with an off switch, so the cycling hormones only served to zap an already exhausted frame and turn my brain into a pile of tapioca pudding.

I didn't even have the strength to lift my hand in his direction and crashed down on the bed. I certainly didn't have the energy to join him in an impromptu calisthenics session. Instead, I grabbed a pillow, placed it over top of my head, and reached for my phone to text my wife that I had survived the great polar vortex and had taken refuge with Butta at a semi-decent hotel in Nowheresville, Missouri.

In her mind, these projects and all the chasing of dreams unseen that I had done in the fourteen years of our relationship were all necessary, but nothing she would ever admit she even tried to understand.

"I love you D," the screen laminated from under the blanket.

"I love you too ….."

Chapter 2

Everything on Ice

There is some great and dark romanticism between the common man and combat sports. The act of watching two competitors step into a cage or ring to engage in a technical yet brutal battle of wills has inspired some of the greatest minds to ever put pen to paper. Norman Mailer and Bob Dylan are the first that come to mind, but the fact of the matter is we are drawn to the spectacle of the fight because it is so far beyond the limits of the normal human condition, but there is still some ethereal element within us that has always been there.

UFC President Dana White is fond of saying, "Everyone understands fighting because it's in our DNA." And while it's highly doubtful a genetic scientist could ever isolate the "fight gene," there is some semblance of truth that resonates in the charismatic front man's words.

When the scope is turned upon the fighters involved, that is when things get a bit more interesting and complex. For years boxing has produced example after example of men who captured the public's attention for their ability to pulverize anyone standing in their paths. Thanks in large part to the rise of the documentary medium and the expansive lens of entertainment to the truly bizarre, the world has been given unprecedented access to the life of the most notorious boxer of the last generation Mike Tyson.

One would be hard pressed to find an individual who lived during the late 1980's and early 1990's who didn't at least have some recognition of the name Mike Tyson. At the peak of his fame, "Iron" Mike was everywhere, from Nintendo games to commercials blasting across television during prime time, and mainstream American culture immediately fell in love with this unstoppable wrecking machine from Brownsville, New York.

After the hitting the mat against Buster Douglas, the rape indictment, and the prison sentence, it looked as if Mike's star would fade. But people were willing to put all of those things aside just to watch this ferocious destroyer of men step back into the ring to do his thing.

While fascination of that caliber was beyond my scope of interest, the first thing on my mind as I woke that morning in Missouri was the task at hand. I removed the pillow from the top of my head to see a fired up Butta packed up and ready to go as he began to spill morning weather reports to me in rapid fire fashion.

As I listened to him talk I couldn't help but associate his demeanor with someone who had gotten his way but was determined to assure you everything would still work out.

The 300-pound slack-jawed trucker who had told us the ice let up immediately west of St. Louis was absolutely correct, and we nearly shed a collective tear when clean iceless pavement began to roll under our wheels. The speedometer cracked 70 mph for the first time since pushing out of Indianapolis the day before, and a new sense of hope sparked through the car.

Still shaking off the morning cobwebs I asked my companion for one of his attention deficit disorder pills to help me blast into the enormous stretch of highway that rested between the Missouri state line and Albuquerque, New Mexico. While Butta wasn't fond of sharing medications of every sort, and believe me when I say he came equipped with plenty (the way a man still in the final stages of cancer recovery often does), he knew the twenty-two hours of driving and the four hours of sleep between picking him up at his doorstep and where we were heading was a rough combination.

"Don't you be speeding all over the road here, man," Butta said sternly as he handed me a round orange pill. "I take these because I need them, and from the way I see you concentrating all the time I don't think you do. Just be careful."

I gave Butta a look that said this was not my first rodeo. I mean…being a career writer, sleep is something you hear your friends talk about, and caffeine pills, jazzy drinks, and stimulants of any and all flavors are never out of bounds.

After a moment of contention he made peace with the exchange, then settled his husky frame into the passenger seat to relax as I waited for the small dizzy spell that comes with uppers to come and go before I could settle in. Moments later the big man was out like Michael Spinks, and the Nissan Altima transformed into a mobile office rolling at 85 mph. There were calls to be made about appointments that needed to be reconfirmed, and the miles and scenery of the day all became a blur outside of the window to my left.

I was happy to learn the schedule I had initially set was still intact, and even more so to learn that the live blog I was running on the trip for Bleacher Report was picking up steam. My adventure was rolling in real time, and social media platforms such as Twitter and Facebook were abuzz knowing that Butta and I had come out on the other side of the polar vortex. The boost from the energy surrounding the trip carried me long into the day, and time didn't snap back into context until I saw the orange sun set just over the view of my knuckles gazing out in the wide open expanse of North Texas.

By this time Butta had fallen back into his sixth nap of the day, and it was then I started to think about Dylan, Woodie Guthrie, and Jack Kerouac, who all found something magical in the road and the push to head west. The darkness was moments away from falling, and rather than lament the rugged roadside textures I could no longer see, I immediately embraced the stars above that were suddenly visible in a manner I had never before witnessed. The celestial bowl above was magnificent, and I couldn't help but to think those great names that had floated through my mind miles earlier had been awestruck by the same flickering glimpse of inspiration that had traveled at light speed to reach them.

The Altima kicked up some loose rocks shortly after crossing into New Mexico. This once again evoked the fear of death in Butta. He shot to attention fists clenched and wide-eyed looking as if he wanted to fight the Grim Reaper himself. At that point I was simply too tired to laugh, but told him we were now just two hours from hitting Albuquerque. This news excited him, but since his cancer treatments had zapped his ability to drive in the darkness, at that point he was nothing more than a 6'4" 260-pound cheerleader.

The clock on the GPS read 3:43 AM, and by all calculations we would be pulling into our destination for the next two days just a touch before 6:00 AM. I was scheduled to meet veteran brawler Isaac Valllie-Flagg at the Jackson/Winkeljohn facility at 8:30, so this meant there would be some decisions that needed to be made.

Two days of driving through treacherous weather and rough road had me feeling like Keith Richards looks, and I was positive my outward appearance was borderline haggard, as the folks in the Midwest are so prone to saying. By the time we pulled into my senior editor's front drive in downtown Albuquerque, the satin cloth sky had begun to give way to a more gentle shade of blue. No matter how thankful I was that we had safely arrived in one piece, the looming static and energy of what could be a career-defining project added to the adrenaline frenzy that was once again pounding away at my insides.

Upon entering the house I hit the shower for a quick refresher in the hopes that it would clear my head and level off the wild-fire of emotion and anticipation that was consuming me. After a quick look in the mirror post-shower to confirm the notion I looked like twice reheated shit, I threw on a flannel shirt and my gray dickeys then crashed down on the living room couch.

"Please, please, please make sure I'm up and moving by eight o'clock!" I yammered for all to hear, and their collective grumblings assured me this would be the case. Just when sleep finally came to call, a fully revitalized Butta and an overly excited senior editor's conversation snatched such long awaited peace away from me again.

The apologies came flying in fast and furious when I rolled over to face them, but I had decided in that moment I would use their voices as the soothing tones to bring me down from the upper deck to the playing field. I had never been someone who could walk into a dark room and simply crash out, because the silence and darkness does something strange to my mind. It opens up an already long-running dialogue into some internal chorus, as if the squawking of my inner thoughts suddenly feel as if they have to fill the wide open canvas to capacity.

Maybe this is a dilemma all writers suffer through. Or maybe sleep deprivation has severely damaged me on a biochemical and mental level.

Soon enough the clock on my phone would hit the time to kick off the alarm, and I rose from the couch wobbly and with the feeling as if someone had jammed a large blade into the upper portion of my left buttocks. An unfortunate car accident back in 2012 had rendered me with shifted hips and what several doctors diagnosed as sciatica. So spending forty hours behind the wheel of a car had done that affliction no favors. I would later learn the root core of the situation was far more grim, but in that moment the only thing on my mind was showing up to meet Ike at the gym.

As I made my way out the door, Butta and my editor asked if they should accompany me, and I bid them to stay home and get some rest. I did so for several reasons. For starters, this was my project and I wanted to make sure all the proper introductions were made and the tone of the experiment was immediately set as a smooth one. The facility run by world renown fighting gurus Greg Jackson and Mike Winkeljohn is regarded as the best mixed martial arts collective in the entire world, and with this being my first visit, getting off on the right foot was imperative.

With that in mind, the second reason for wanting to go solo kicked in. Up to that point I had spent two years working for a major MMA news site and had become one of their main featured writers. Prior to my arrival back in the summer of 2012, this site was seen as a nonsensical wasteland for click-bait articles and slideshows that mocked and criticized fighters all across the professional spectrum—many of which just happened to be part of the Albuquerque-based team. The site was one of the first, but certainly not the last, to use the model of throwing outlandish and easily digested content to the masses who would in turn click away until their fingers were sore.

That said, a lot had changed in that regard in the 16 months I had been there before finding myself in the parking lot of Jackson/Winkeljohn. The focus had shifted to creative and quality written content that was produced by myself and a hand-picked team of veteran scribes from the MMA sphere. Where slideshows once dominated the front page layout, now deep and relevant stories were found in abundance up and down the MMA section of the site.

And while progress had been made in that regard, I knew there would still be fighters within the walls of Jackson/Winkeljohn who would look beyond any work I'd done previously and catch fire at the mere mention of where I worked. This sentiment was immediately confirmed when Vallie-Flagg walked up to greet me as he said, "Everyone is excited you are here, but let's keep who you work for out of the conversation, okay?"

I was quick to oblige as we passed through the doors of the most prominent MMA gym in the world.

"Man, you look like shit Finley," he laughed as we walked up to the front desk where Ricky (the gym manager and all around utility man) was sitting flipping through yesterday's mail. Vallie-Flagg walked over to get his attention and after putting a firm flat palm on the desk directly in front of Ricky said, "Hey this is Duane Finley and he's here on his road trip project. He's going to do a few interviews with some of us fighters today and tomorrow."

"Does Greg know about this?" Ricky asked not looking up to acknowledge my presence.

"Yeah," Vallie-Flagg replied. "He's worked with Duane before and said it's cool for him to be here."

I waited for several lingering moments to shake Ricky's hand, but once it became clear his attention would not be something I would be receiving, I followed Vallie-Flagg out into the gym space where scores of fighters were spread across the mats working on their wrestling. Once we were drew closer to the action, Ike bid me farewell and jumped into the fray with the rest of his teammates grinding away in their morning session.

After taking a quick look around I spotted gym staple and women's MMA pioneer Julie Kedzie standing off to the side of the mat talking to one of the younger female fighters. I had watched "Jules" step into the cage on numerous occasions, and the handful of personal interactions we'd had prior to that day in the gym had always been pleasant, if not hilarious.

In addition to being as scrappy as they come in the female ranks, Kedzie is an intellectual with an extremely sharp sense of humor that mixes highbrow and self-depreciating in effortless fashion. Once she recognized my presence, the recently retired Strikeforce and UFC veteran made her way over for a quick embrace and to welcome me to the gym she'd called home for as long as she could remember.

"I heard you were coming and I think the project you are doing is awesome," she emoted, flashing a mega-watt smile that instantly made me feel both warm and welcome. "There are a lot of characters in this gym and I'm sure you are going to get some great stuff. We normally don't let media in here to poke around, but you always do good honest work so Greg and the guys were totally up for it."

"That really means a lot," I replied as I watched light heavyweight phenom Jon Jones lock up with a fighter I had never seen before but would learn a short time later was up-and-coming prospect Phil Hawes.

"Otherwise we'd just kick your ass," Kedzie laughed as the strength of her nonchalant nudge knocked me off balance to where several recovery steps were needed.

She walked over and grabbed a chair for me to sit on and together we watched as wrestling coach Israel "Izzy" Martinez ran his wrestling practice with authority. On one side of the gym, middleweight veteran Tim Kennedy was grappling with *The Ultimate Fighter* alum Kyle Noke, and a short distance away perennial flyweight contender John Dodson was moving at a frenetic pace against his longtime training partner and UFC hopeful Nick Urso.

Vallie-Flagg and Clay Guida were going at it like rapid dogs behind me, and attempting to take in all of the intense action was a bit overwhelming. In short time I would be interviewing the majority of the fighters putting in work before me, but just watching the intricacies of each and every one of their movements drew me in further. It was just a hair past 9:00 AM and Dodson was the only man on the mat with a fight coming up directly, but the men and women who filled the room that day were working with such intensity one would think they all had title fights quickly approaching.

As I would find out later in my journey for this project, their intensity is what truly sets the squad at Jackson/Winkeljohn apart from the rest of the gyms around the sport. It would be easy for the bigger names and the even larger egos some of them carry to demand special treatment, but luxuries of that nature are nowhere to be found under Jackson's watch, and that isn't an element that will be changing in any regard in the future.

With the question of what brings men and women to a career in fighting as the primary thesis to this project, sitting down to pick Greg Jackson's brain was a must. Anyone who has followed MMA with any type of regularity over the past decade knows Jackson's mind for strategy and game planning is second to none in the fight business. He's groomed a collection of future champions within the walls of that very gym, and played a crucial role in the success of many others, including pound-for-pound great and the man widely regarded as the best welterweight of all-time Georges St-Pierre.

We walked back to his office and wasted no time jumping into conversation about the reason for my project and the deeper aspects of the fight game. It was an interview I'd wanted to do for some time and it absolutely lived up to my expectations.

Chapter 3

The Berque

Just as things were wrapping up inside the office, Winkeljohn protégé and elite-level striking coach in his own right Brandon Gibson, popped in to say hello. Having known "Six Gun" from our many conversations shared on various stops of the touring MMA circus, Gibson was quick to throw a big hug my way and join the list of those who were openly excited I had made the trip. Where other media members are quick to focus on the here and now of upcoming fights, getting caught up in the headline hook game, writers like myself are far more concerned with telling a deeper and more in-depth version of a story than what is commonly seen in the sport.

"A few of us are going to a different gym across town to put in some work and do a photo shoot for an upcoming Roots of Fight campaign. You are more than welcome to come along and check that out," Gibson suggested.

I agreed to meet back up with him at the main gym in an hour or two, citing a need to run back to where I was staying to grab my computer and the rest of my gear.

"Have you eaten yet?" he inquired with a smirk on his face. "If not you have to let me take you to one of the best spots you are going to find out here. It's in a bad part of town but those are the best places for food in Albuquerque."

Jackson in turn made a joke or two that hinged on my ability to fight, and I brushed it off by informing the room that my record in Waffle House parking lot brawls throughout the Midwestern circuit was a substantial one. After a few laughs we agreed on the time, and I caromed back to pick up my two traveling partners and the backpack filled with my gear that I had absentmindedly left next to the living room couch I had attempted to crash out on hours earlier.

While we would eat lunch and my first ever introduction to green chili was made that afternoon, the highlight of our time at the South Valley gym came when Gibson agreed to let Butta step in for a mitt session. Of the entire collective in the tiny gym decorated from wall to wall with portraits of local hero and boxing icon Johnny Tapia, no one knew about Butta's battle with cancer. No one knew how hard this man was forced to dig down to turn back a disease that had stripped his larger-than-life frame below 200 pounds, but suddenly there he was firing off combinations with one of the most highly touted striking coaches in the game.

The mitts cracked and Gibson floated about the cage calling out punch combos that Butta delivered with vigor. I watched as Gibson's feet slid in and out of range like a well-oiled prize fighter as he pushed my hefty companion to dig deeper into himself to find the rhythm and power Gibson was demanding of him. I listened to Gibson's voice. It was at the same time soothing and motivating. He made a man who 16 months earlier was on the brink of death move and crack like a seasoned machine.

It was a beautiful thing to witness, but told me all I needed to know about Gibson's effectiveness in the coaching realm. While Butta was just another big body in the grand scheme of things, the former kickboxer turned coach spends the majority of his time with the most talented and dangerous fighters throwing strikes with the worst of intentions in his direction.

Watching the focus and light in Gibson's eyes was only half of the tell in that moment, as the cadence of his voice registered profoundly in the chaos that is physical poetry at work. After Butta's spent frame slipped through the ropes, Urso and retired UFC light heavyweight Keith Jardine's wife Jody Esquibel, who was preparing for an upcoming bout under the Bellator banner, went back to work.

All the while the action was moving at a rapid pace inside the ring, photographer Will Fox was moving in smooth lines ringside to capture still frames that would be used for an upcoming Roots of Fight apparel release. The fighters swapped out one sweat-soaked tee for another in between rounds, but the intensity of the session showed the intention of all involved was focused on work to stay sharp rather than work to produce sharp shots.

"It's definitely a busy world down here," Gibson laughed as a white towel zapped the beads of sweat from his brow. "Most places would pull in an entire lighting crew or actors in some fabricated set up, but everything in Albuquerque is about hard work. Jody and Nick are both preparing for fights, and why not use this time to get in some actual work? That's just the mentality we have here and that's the way it's always been.

"This place was settled by hard men and it's hard men who still serve as the lifeblood to this place," he added. "It's still the Wild, Wild West here in a lot of ways."

As the crew rolled out of the dusty little gym, the alarm on my phone alerted me to the next stop on my agenda for the day. I was slated to head over with Vallie-Flagg to the Elevate facility where he was to do a private striking session with Coach Winkeljohn. The gym is also where many of the Jackson/Winkeljohn fighters do their strength and conditioning workouts, therefore it was no surprise to see a host of them in various forms of distress when we walked through the doors.

Perennial lightweight contender and no-nonsense knockout artist Donald Cerrone's legs were fastened to a squat rack as he worked through a variety of body-weight and dumbbell chest exercises, and up-and-coming bantamweight and Mexican sensation Erik "Goyito" Perez was pushing a weighted sled up and down the AstroTurf runway while his intervals were being clocked by one of the Team Elevate trainers.

It was a wonder to watch the determination pop from Perez and the splashes of sweat fly from his jet black hair because just a handful of hours earlier the same animal-esque output was being displayed during Martinez's wrestling session.

"That kid is a workhorse," Vallie-Flagg said as he wrapped his hands on the sidelines. "He never misses a single practice, and then there are days like today where he'll come up here to be a body during my session with Wink."

By body he meant Perez would be reducing himself to nothing more than an object for Vallie-Flagg to work his combinations upon, which is an incredibly selfless act for an athlete in a sport where looking out for number one is typically commonplace. Furthermore, with Vallie-Flagg's heart-driven and gritty fighting style, wrestling and defending the takedown is an issue that has plagued him throughout his entire career. By working with Perez, the Mexico-born bantamweight would be able to fire off takedown attempts as the Michigan native worked to smooth out his combinations under Winkeljohn's guidance.

It wasn't long before the two teammates were deep into their exchanges when I noticed a sweat-covered Cerrone milling his way over to where I was standing. Since "Cowboy" has competed at a frequency unmatched by any of his peers over the past several years, fans are no doubt familiar with his rangy frame and the tattoos that adorn each of his shin bones. What television screens may not pick up is the fact that his legs resemble that of a race horse, striated with lean flexible muscle that allow him to fire off his whip-cracking leg and head kicks with precision and power.

Cerrone also has a well-known disdain for anything media related—a fact I had personally discovered on multiple occasions in my time covering his fights. Depending on which mood you caught him in, surly and not-quite as surly, Cerrone was never one to not let you know there were a million things he'd rather be doing than a damn pre-fight interview.

In knowing these things I made sure to give him ample room and to stay out of his workout space, but that didn't stop him from continuing to float closer and closer to where I was standing. I would look up to see him giving a look my way—one that would only break when he would reach up and use the collar of his tank to wipe the sweat from his eyes. In that moment I wasn't quite sure whether or not I stepped somewhere I shouldn't have, but I absolutely knew being on the wrong side of Cerrone wasn't a place I wanted to be…ever.

After shifting down a few spaces and clearly out of the Colorado native's workspace, I was jolted to hear his gruff voice launched in my direction.

"Better be careful what you say around this guy," Cerrone said as he slammed down a pair of dumbbells to the matted floor. "He'll turn right around and write up a bunch of bullshit that's not true just to make you look bad."

Initially it was the shock of the hostility he blasted in my direction that spun me, but after analyzing the words that came out of his mouth I was downright baffled. In the five years I had been working in mixed martial arts, the only avenue I had ever traveled was that of writing profiles and feature pieces of fighters. These consisted of interviews either by phone or in person, then working the fighter's quotes into structured narratives. Never once in those articles were personal opinions plugged in, and I was supremely confident my fingers had never attacked the keyboard to smear Cerrone's name or take anything said on the record out of context.

I was admittedly cautious in my reply, but turned back to him and asked, "I think you have my confused with someone else. I only do interview pieces."

He didn't even take a moment to consider that could be the case.

"Nah, I'm sure it's you who wrote that bullshit about me. I remember your face. I'll look it up when I get home and I'll find it. I'm positive it was you."

By now the hard-charging lightweight knockout artist had completely abandoned his workout to put his focus squarely upon my presence. His arms were folded, head cocked back slightly to the right, and his eyes were glinting the same way that made Clint Eastwood famous. His body language wasn't postured to be intimidating, but that's only because it didn't need to be. I had personally witnessed Cerrone drop many a capable and dangerous fighter numerous times with power shots he slid through a split-second window of opportunity.

This exchange wasn't about physically beating me about the ribs and face, as it was proving a point that perhaps I was somewhere I didn't belong. Fighters have long been guarded about opening their sanctuaries to media types, and Cerrone had decided he was going to be the one to slap the "Not Welcome" sticker up on the door.

The feeling that I had to hold ground stung my chest, but that sensation was countered by a healthy fear of what the man standing before me could transform into if he felt disrespected, imagined or otherwise. Therefore I kept my hands up in a position that is universally understood as confused, and kept eye contact while I attempted to state my case.

"Sorry Cowboy, but it wasn't me," I replied. "I've written your past six UFC.com features and have done every one of your interviews for that site since coming over from the WEC. The only thing I can think where you may have been misquoted by me was during the interview we did for Fight! Magazine while you were in Indianapolis where I asked you what was more dangerous: dating or bull riding?"

Those words cracked a slight smile to the left side of his mouth, and his head rocked to the other side of his shoulders as if he were contemplating this entire snafu could be a case of mistaken identity. It was also in this moment Vallie-Flagg took notice of the situation and made his way over to play peacekeeper. He arrived, with enough sweat coating him to have soaked through a gray hooded sweatshirt, and the pink 16 oz. gloves he had been using were doing very little to take the moisture from his face every time he tried to swipe it away.

"We all cool here?" Vallie-Flagg asked in panted breath.

"I think your boy wrote some bad shit about me once and I'm trying to figure it out," Cerrone clipped back with a voice that was half-joking but with eyes that were still burning holes through my white and black checkered flannel shirt.

"That's not Duane's style," Vallie-Flagg returned. "He's only ever written positive stories and he's done some great work on a bunch of the guys on our team like me, Cub, and Dodson."

What Ike said was the truth. I had written numerous in-depth stories for both Cub Swanson and John Dodson throughout their respective rises through the UFC ranks. Cerrone then immediately switched subjects and began busting Ike's balls about a variety of things that were just out of ear shot. I could hear them both laughing as Cerrone put his left hand on Ike's shoulder, and was grateful the situation had been defused for the time being.

When Vallie-Flagg hustled back over to Perez and Winkeljohn to finish up his session, I made my way over to a stretching table where I pulled up a spot on the turf and watched the remainder of the practice. For a fighter who had made his name on a his ability to engage in wild brawls and walk through the proverbial fire, the 1-2-knee combinations he was cracking with Winkeljohn that afternoon showed a different side of the seasoned veteran's offensive arsenal than I'd ever seen before.

Coach Wink and Ike were just wrapping up when I noticed Cerrone making his way out the door. Never being one to leave negative feelings lingering, I jumped to my feet and hustled after him in an attempt to catch the "Fight of the Night" bonus machine before he disappeared into the haze of the day.

"Hey Cowboy, wait up!" I shouted as I scurried to make ground. My voice stopped him in the doorway and the wear of a taxing workout suddenly slipped behind the steely gaze of a rock-solid poker face.

"Yeah?" he questioned in a tone that drifted between annoyed and tired or both.

"Were you just fucking with me back there?" I asked. "I mean...were you serious about what you said or were you just busting my balls?"

"I like to kid around a lot but I never joke when it comes to shit like that," he blasted. "I can't recall the article or even the fight that it was about, but I'm positive you wrote some negative shit about me and I'm going to figure it out."

No sooner did the statement leave his lips that he was gone out the doors and back into his own world. Confusion reigned supreme in my head, and the tallied lack of sleep only amplified the strangeness of the situation. By that time Vallie-Flagg had caught up to me in the door way, as he too worked his way out of the facility, and when I put the question of whether or not Cerrone was messing with me on his brain, all Ike could do is shrug his shoulders.

"Dude I highly doubt he was serious," Ike said as he peeled off several layers of shirts all soaked through with sweat. "He has a different kind of sense of humor. We are all used to it because that's just Cowboy, but I'm sure he was just trying to rattle you or get a rise out of you."

"I don't know about that," I sighed. "He seemed pretty certain that I wrote some negative shit about him and that bothers me because that's just not my style."

"I wouldn't worry about it," he volleyed back.

"And why is that?" I snapped in irritation that raised Ike's eyebrows in surprise.

"Because if he really had a problem with you he either would have kicked your ass right there on the spot or tossed you out of the gym. Cowboy isn't the mess around type, brother."

His words crafted such a specific image that in that moment I immediately convinced myself Cerrone was just messing with me. Several weeks later during a media day at the gym in between road trip stops, he would physically nudge me out of his way, which Vallie-Flagg would later interpret as a surefire sign that it was all a joke.

I would receive actual confirmation of this from the man himself just north of a year later after his victory over Myles Jury at UFC 182 in Las Vegas. Despite not getting the fight he wanted from his opponent, Cerrone was happy to get out of Sin City with another victory—his sixth consecutive win at the time—and another paycheck.

I caught up to him backstage after the press conference and finally was able to ask the question that had been buzzing around in my brain for the past 12 months.

"Hey Cowboy were you really pissed off at me that day back in Albuquerque?"

Once again he cracked an exhausted but good-natured grin, cocked his head back to the side, and threw a quick pat to my shoulder.

"Shit man…I was just fucking with you. We're cool," he replied.

And that was that. Tracking down that confirmation was a long road though. There would be plenty of twists and turns before making peace with the future 155-pound title challenger, and some of them came before Butta and I ever made it out of Albuquerque on the inaugural leg of the road trip project. "The Land of Enchantment" is a rugged yet beautiful place indeed, where the only things that flourish work with a survivalist need to do so. There are no luxuries to be found in a place like Albuquerque, and the ones that are acquired are consistently guarded by hard men.

We were halfway back to my editor's house in Vallie-Flagg's car when a notification came across the top of my phone. Fortunately for me I just happened to be looking down at my screen, because the hole in Ike's exhaust turned the narrow neighborhood streets into a carnival of whines and war cries coming from a jacked and weathered tail pipe.

My drooping and tired eyes lit up when I read the name on the text. Carlos Condit had just confirmed we were getting together for dinner. Four months earlier I had interviewed "The Natural Born Killer" for a long form piece in my "Fighting Life" series, and the hours we spent talking didn't even scratch the surface of the bigger story sitting behind the eyes of the former WEC and UFC interim welterweight champion.

A man who holds that much calculated and controlled aggression behind a calm and warm exterior absolutely has a story to tell, and it was one of the biggest driving forces behind this cross-country endeavor to take a few steps closer to understanding the enigma that is one of the most brutal finishers to ever compete in the 170-pound weight class in the history of MMA.

According to the notification sitting on my phone screen, I was only two hours away from getting that opportunity, but the only thing I could think about was hitting that couch for a few winks. I floated back into the living room and instructed Butta to make sure I was back among the living by seven o'clock, and the big man kicked back into a reclining chair and assured me that would be handled accordingly.

Good ole' Butta....dependable as the morning sun and as loyal as God ever created them.

Chapter 4

Natural Born Killer

Being from the sheltered minimalism of a no stoplight town in Illinois, my sense of culture was at special bus ride to school levels. With the location of my dinner with Carlos being Vietnamese cuisine, there was plenty of room for error and awkwardness. Yet, being born with a natural gift for small talk and having already gotten along swimmingly with Carlos on my own turf, I entered the Basil Leaf simply excited to pick up where our conversation left off following his blistering TKO finish of Martin Kampmann in their rematch at Canseco Field House.

Upon clearing the doorway I immediately saw Carlos stand up from the waiting area, and noticed he was accompanied by his wife Seager and their three-year-old son Owen. The sport of MMA is filled with gnarly-eared bruisers and smashed-nosed hardasses who couldn't buy their way into a handsome contest, so when a fighter of Condit's regard also had the model good looks to boot; it came as no surprise to see how beautiful his family was.

Not joking in the slightest…the Condits are tailor-made for magazine ads or television. On Carlos's side, it's sort of a running joke in the sport he's been busting heads in for more than a decade, because it's never straight forward acceptable to call another man good looking. On the other hand, when clustered with fellow leading man types like UFC middleweight Luke Rockhold and Brazilian wild man Erick Silva, even the manliest and least secure in their sexuality could agree that, "Hey…so what if I think that dude is a looker."

The same phenomenon exists in sports all across the world. Hell, Joe Namath wasn't even a six by classic handsomeness standards but men and women alike once dug Broadway Joe.

Due to the hostess beckoning our group to follow her to our seats, the introductions were cut a bit short, but Owen was determined to get a proper introduction of his own. Being away from my own children for several days and seeing that bright-eyed little man immediately made me home sick, and even more so when he shook my hand like a miniature gentleman. For some reason just the gesture alone busted me up into a laugh, which apparently made young Owen believe I was laughing as his expense because he fired off a crisp straight right hand to my pills, and I doubled over with a sharp pain in my nether region.

Carlos and Seager immediately jumped over to apologize for the ninja strike their son had delivered, but the hilarity of how accurately the kid threw that shot while holding eye contact up top was proof positive the apple had not fallen far from the tree.

"Shit man sorry about that," Condit said with a slight bit of laughter in his voice.

"No worries at all," I returned as I resumed full upright position. "Should be proud of him for the technique because he turned his fist over exactly at the point of impact."

The humor of the incident carried up to the time we were seated, and before the waitress could bring our drink orders, the table had fallen into full conversation. Carlos asked about the trip and driving through the polar vortex, and Seager wanted to know where the rest of the trek would take me. Even with that touch of MMA at the front end of our conversation, it was no time at all before the subject of fighting vanished from the table entirely. Anytime a reporter and an athlete can sit down to talk and the sport they are both involved in disappears from the conversation is a wondrous thing. It was a warm feeling being in the company of great people while enjoying an incredible dinner.

With the Basil Leaf being a regular stop on their dining out circuit, the Condits knew precisely what to order. When my ignorance of Vietnamese food was lumped into that equation, they also knew what dish would suit a rookie such as myself, especially one who preferred to stay away from anything terribly spicy.

"How are you with heat and spice on your food?" she asked with a look in her eye that told me I was probably going to have to suffer a little bit regardless.

It was the mother in her coming out, and I recognized this because that look frequently appeared on my own wife's face all throughout the Gerber pureed peas stage of our children's development.

"He's not too big on anything too spicy," Carlos interjected, and he told the waitress to bring me a rice bowl of some kind.

The reality of what he said about my seasoning preference was absolutely spot on and sparked my mind to recall the exact genesis of what made me fascinated with finding out more about Carlos Condit. It was during his press tour through Indianapolis to promote his main event tilt at Fight Night 27 when I got the chance to sit down with him for our first face-to-face interview. We'd spoken over the telephone numerous times for a wide range of articles about upcoming fights and whatnot, but his physical presence in my home city provided the chance to get some face time with one of the best fighters in the game.

Condit was the only fighter who made the trip to do local radio and television spots, and one of the UFC PR reps had reached out the week before their arrival to ask if I wanted to get some one-on-one interview time while he was in town. Naturally, I jumped at the opportunity, and when I was informed that our meeting was going to take place at the world famous St. Elmo's Steakhouse in downtown Indy, it had all the makings for a pretty solid Tuesday night by any and all measurable standards.

The dinner and interview we knocked out that night sitting in the aged but still highly envied trappings of the historic restaurant was top notch and produced what is widely regarded as one of the best features of my journalistic career, but it wasn't the conversation or the brilliantly prepared steak that made me want to know as much as I could about the man sitting across the table from me.

In fact, it was something far simpler than asking about his childhood (which I did, and turns out it was an affluent one, as his father served as the assistant to New Mexico's Governor Bill Richards) or his favorite knockout (which I learned came at the expense of a loose-lipped Dan Hardy in a stone-silent O2 arena). No, the true moment that told me all I needed to know about Condit's inner-intensity came when the waiter brought three shrimp cocktail orders to the table.

In addition to having steak cuts that are consistently voted among the best in the country, St. Elmo's is also famous for its shrimp cocktail sauce. Where most cocktail sauce is at the very least tangy, theirs is loaded with horseradish that makes it next to impossible not to set the roof of your mouth ablaze. Per protocol, the waiter explained the story behind the sauce and then provided two options to each of us sitting at the table. There was the mild sauce, which by my standards was still lit matchstick hot, or the spicy version that could certainly ruin a $100 meal if not consumed properly.

While the rep and I took the easy way out, there wasn't the slightest bit of hesitation in Condit's choice to go for the bold option, and that is when I saw what I had been waiting to find out about Carlos Condit. It wasn't that he even particularly cared for shrimp cocktail, but more so that he's so naturally game to mix it up…to batter, fight and do whatever is necessary to prevail in his refusal to allow anyone or anything to get the better of him. Challenges that provided a test were immediately appealing.

Later on that evening in Indianapolis, we would delve deeper into how this tendency connected to his fighting approach, and I was honestly taken back by the candid and precise nature in which Condit broke down the complexities of the subject matter.

"Fear has a lot to do with it," he said as he adjusted his posture upright. "I know a lot of other fighters say they aren't scared before a fight and call it nervous energy or some other bullshit, but for me it's definitely fear of what I'm about to walk into. I know I've trained, am capable, and have done everything in my power to prepare for the fight, but knowing the man I'm about to step into that cage with is going to do everything he can to hurt me forces a reaction that can't be explained any other way than primal."

Intensity was the topic at hand, and in that moment his eyes were locked and fierce.

"It evokes an instinct that goes all the way back to the days when what waited for you beyond the safety of your cave or dwelling could and probably would kill you. Man has evolved over the course of thousands of years, but it is still against our nature to openly and willingly walk into a fight that very well could be to the death."

As he spoke, visions of the snarl and apex predator gaze that had become his signature mask during his walk to the Octagon shot through my mind on an endless rapid-fire loop.

"I'm going out there to be locked in a cage with someone who wants to hurt me, and there is no way I'm going to let that happen," Condit continued. "I have to go out there and fucking end him before he gets the chance to do the same to me. It's a kill or be killed mentality and you better believe when those stakes are on the line I'm playing for keeps."

Suddenly the flickering images of his walk-out were replaced by highlight reel finishes that were delivered in a variety of fashions—each more violent than the next.

"It's fear that keeps me sharp," he added in conclusion. "And when I can feel that in the pit of my stomach before it's time to make the walk to the cage I know I'm ready."

While that particular conversation had taken place months prior, once intensity of that caliber is noticed, it's something that will forever remain visible. Even watching as Carlos sat at the table sharing his food with his wife and child and totally at peace in the comfort of one of his favorite restaurants, the manner in which he spoke and the natural ease about him further revealed what he controlled beneath the surface.

It wasn't blind rage or even violence for that matter. It was a readiness. An understanding that he could go to places most men can't in their psyches when put in the position to defend himself.

The conversation had started to drift toward conspiracy theories when suddenly the feeling of having a firecracker go off inside of my mouth kicked off full alert panic. My eyes immediately welled up with crocodile tears that streamed down my cheeks as if someone had squeezed a bottle of hand lotion a bit too hard, and once again Seager's motherly instinct led her to pounce on the source of my discomfort.

Not wanting to weep in front of a child who had already proven his Alpha Male status over me an hour earlier, I did my best to fight the good fight, and after a swab of bread and guzzling water that was only going to make matters worse, I slowly but surely began to get a grip on the situation.

Upon examining my rice bowl, Carlos discovered the culprit to be a few tiny slivers of a red pepper. In the frantic and blurry moments in the aftermath of the four-alarm blaze and for the exaggerated sake of good storytelling, I believe he said it was a "ghost pepper," but the reality of what had stricken me at the Basil Leaf was most likely nothing more than your standard run-of-the-mill red pepper in the Southwest.

As I dried my eyes with the napkin from my lap I could see Carlos shaking his head and shrugging to his son in a moment of hilarity that did not require words or an explanation. Shortly after my mishaps the meal and our time at the dinner table had come to an end, and I was grateful for the time the Condits had committed to making a memorable appearance on the road trip project.

Just when I thought my time with Carlos had come to an end, he made a last-minute decision to stay out and hang a bit longer. My travel companion Butta and a few of the fighters from Jackson/Winkeljohn's had decided to hit a local sports bar for a few cold beers, and Carlos decided to join us in the festivities. First he would need to run his wife and child home before heading back out to meet up and provided clear directions for me to get to where I needed to go.

Getting to spend a bit more conversation time with Condit was already a definite plus, and the thought of an ice cold beer to ease the singe on my tongue was that indescribable euphoria that can only be found in rare turns of good fortune and high-range octave changes in Mariah Carey songs.

Brandon Gibson was the first person I saw when I walked through the doors of the establishment, and he pointed over to the right side of the room where a large table was lined with fighters cutting up and having laughs at one another's expense.

"How was dinner, brother?" Gibson asked as he walked to the bar with me. "Did you guys get some good food? Did you get some good interview time with Carlos?"

I kept the details of the pepper shenanigans to a minimum, because after seeing Gibson reach near-stroke levels of laughter earlier in the day as I struggled to handle the heat of green chili, the full story of how I nearly perished due to the accidental inclusion of a shred of pepper that registered far lower on the volcano scale (an unofficial scale of measurement created by me) would send him into endless hysterics.

As for the interview or conversation with Condit, I assured him things went well.

"He's actually on his way here," I shared as I directed the barkeep to the Miller Lite tap and his face lit up with immediate surprise.

"Carlos is coming out tonight?" Gibson laughed in a manner best described as shock. "That's awesome because he never usually comes out much anymore. He has kids and a family so it's totally understandable, but pretty cool he's going to hang out for a bit."

I wholeheartedly agreed with the notion and walked over toward the buzzing table, using tremendous care not to spill a drop of the beer I was holding and could already taste. Upon reaching the table I noticed Butta's eyes had the shine of a man several glasses into a good night, and the laughter blasting from the group came from John Dodson or "Little John" as his teammates affectionately referred to him. The heavy-handed Ultimate Fighter winner was in the middle of a story and from the smiles that were plastered across the faces of Kyle Noke and Erik Perez, "The Magician" was obviously holding court in strong fashion.

It wasn't long before Carlos arrived to the scene, and Gibson's prior sentiment immediately proved true by the expressions and cheers that rang out like a stadium wave all the way down the table. The decibel level of the group greeting produced a laugh out of Condit in turn, and he pulled up a seat between Gibson and I at the head of the over-sized table.

We spent the next two hours discussing the finer points of our mutual love of low-budget horror movies and supernatural phenomenon that was known to linger in different regions around the country. In between talking about specters and aliens the conversation would occasionally turn toward politics and it became clear that Condit was as equally versatile in the art of conversation as he was in the art of separating another man from his consciousness by use of force.

While the phenomenon we were discussing pertained to yetis and black-eyed kids (Google that one at your own risk), I was also informed of a phenomenon that was known to occur in Albuquerque at various frequencies. Where in most cases normal every day people and casual bar patrons would avoid creating conflict with professional fighters, in the "'Berque" it had become somewhat of a badge of honor over the years to start friction with fighters in public places.

Something that absurd was difficult to believe initially, but each and every one of the Team Jackson fighters sitting at the table nodded their heads in agreement and shared stories of their own run ins that immediately validated the next story that would come from the table. And as tales of shit-talking grocery shoppers or rowdy gas station attendants continued to roll in, I started to notice a roughshod line beginning to form around the corner from our table. Not wanting to stir the rest of the fighters into a frenzy, I only alerted Carlos and Brandon, and after a quick look over in the direction of the small crowd that had lined up on the other side of the half wall that divided our table from the rest of the barroom, they both returned to the conversation at hand.

Gibson was in the middle of telling a story about his high school days hanging with Diego Sanchez when a stocky man wearing a Raiders jersey walked over to where Carlos was sitting at the table. My immediate thought was that some heavy shit was about to go down, but once the man started talking my inner-turmoil was quickly put to rest.

The only thing the stranger wanted to do was shake Carlos' hand and tell him that he'd been a fan since the days when Condit fought in the little blue cage of the WEC. From the shakiness of the man's voice he was obviously a huge fan of Condit's work, and after getting one more handshake slipped away back toward the bar top. Once that man vanished another appeared wanting to do the same thing, and then another, and another, and it continued this way for the better part of the next hour.

People were lining up to share a quick story and or inform him they had a mutual friend, but every one of the men who came to introduce themselves to Carlos and shake his hand came with the utmost respect. And that respect was absolutely returned in kind from Carlos. I found myself sitting just a few feet away from the situation, and I immediately thought of the opening scene from The Godfather as people came to pay their respects to Don Vito Corleone on the day of his daughter's wedding.

All in all it was a pretty awesome sight to witness and more than likely was the reason Carlos's nights out with his teammates had grown few and far between.

The line of admirers would eventually thin out to just a handful of stragglers, and after looking at my phone and realizing my scheduled appointments in Phoenix were requesting to be bumped up a day, the juncture to depart for the evening had arrived. The cancer had left poor

Butta's resolve for alcohol the equivalent of a thin plastic poncho in a gale-force hurricane, and Gibson was kind enough to assist me in getting the big man up and moving toward the car.

Once he was tucked away in the passenger seat I exchanged farewells with Condit and Gibson and assured them both Albuquerque would become a frequent stop on my future journeys. As I drove away that night and back to the make-shift crash pad to hopefully steal a few hours of sleep before heading out for Phoenix, I took a few moments to appreciate all that had happened since our arrival to the sleepy and sometimes hectic metropolis planted out in the heart of the Southwest.

The entire reason for this adventure was to discover the reason fighters were drawn to such a life and in many ways the city of Albuquerque was a reflection of that struggle. In other parts of the country fighters flock to cities like Las Vegas and Miami because of the amenities that come with living and training in a place where luxury can be found around every corner, but down in the low down and dusty streets of Albuquerque, U.S.A. every inch is earned by fighting.

Whether that battle comes in physical form or the mental toughness it takes to keep a dream alive while so little of the reward is visible, it takes a special breed of person to call that city home. And even though that visit was my first, as I watched the orange street lamps of I-25 blur together into a stream of tinged fluorescence, I knew it certainly would not be my last.

Chapter 5

Little Orange Pills

The next morning we awoke with Phoenix on our brain and slightly less pep in our collective steps. The sluggish conversation and slow movements could have easily been chalked up to the morning after effect of having a few beers, especially on Butta's side of things, but I knew the feeling swirling from the top of my head to my feet was the wear and tear of the long drive west.

In most cases being in a car is little more than guiding a steering wheel that will remain straight if the wheels are properly aligned, and there is no extensive effort involved. Even the stress that comes through long trip journeys can be reduced with well-timed stop-offs and switching drivers at regular intervals. Not only had nothing of that sort happened thus far in the project, but battling the elements of the massive winter storm that shut down travel in a large portion of the Midwest and Northeast took a unique toll difficult to explain.

The lack of sleep and stinging pain in my lower back wasn't making anything any easier, but I hadn't come through a stark white Hell to lay around and gripe. That said, I knew a few issues were starting to pop up and I hoped to keep them in check until I returned home to Indianapolis.

Nevertheless, while Butta was in the shower I took the opportunity to borrow a few more of the little round orange pills, and immediately felt lesser for doing so.

Self-justification is a monstrous thing though, because in my mind the thought of the workload at hand and the amount of driving ahead trumped any guilt that came with stimulating my system in a way that it wasn't meant to be stimulated. It's easy for the mind to get twisted up when the rubber meets the road of ambition and execution, but too much remained undone to spend time arguing with myself.

It only took a handful of minutes before the head rush hit, and when a wave of that nature comes about it is necessary to take a moment or two to get a handle on things. Once those sensations passed through, a weary and tattered mind suddenly snapped into a determined one with razor-sharp focus.

Modern medicine can be a monstrous thing.

Butta emerged from Tim Scully's spare bedroom ready to go, and that is when my editor informed us he would in fact be joining the expedition from that point forward.

"Looks like it's a go, boys!" Scully shouted as he clapped his hands together in a single motion of enthusiasm.

The breakdown on Scully was that he was technically my editor, but the relationship was more about guidance than it ever was about editing by its definition. Scully had been with the site before it was one of the biggest things in sports media, and MMA was his baby
By the time I found myself in his living room, he was se\

removed from actually writing on the website, but was locked into the current surge he'd constructed by bringing in a different type of writer than he had in the past.

On the person-to-person level Scully was one of those free-thinking cats whose ideas were a bit scattered. Granted, there were many themes he was consistent with like clean eating, universal energy, and sobriety, but the day-to-day flow of things seemed to jumble him at times, which is something a free-wheeling seeker such as myself could jazz with.

He'd made mention of the possibility of tagging along the previous afternoon, but wasn't sure if he was going to be able to clear his schedule enough to spend the next four days skipping around the Southwest in a vehicle. There were other things involved as well, but relationships of others and the internal workings and spider webs of such things have never been a thing I'd ever been foolish enough to dabble in.

The addition of Scully to the situation came with a short list of pros and cons. The biggest positives came with having someone to split the drive time up with, and even more so since he'd offered to make his Toyota Four-Runner the primary vehicle. The only downside of this deal would be leaving my car at his place in Albuquerque, which meant we would have to circle back into New Mexico before setting sail back east.

The other element to factor was the compatibility of the people involved. I'd known Butta for several years and we'd taken plenty of weekend trips during our time in various roles in the fight business, but the big man and Scully were complete strangers until 24 hours ago. Butta is as easy going as they come, but every man has certain annoyances and the possibility of a third person in the vehicle and their travel needs had the potential to create friction.

In my lifetime I'd seen a fully packed Ford Escort filled with my cousins on my mother's side of the family erupt into a full-blown battle royal at 60 mph over the sound of gum being popped and snapped repeatedly from the passenger's seat. I'm not talking shouts and threats being launched over the headrest from the back seat, I'm talking about punches in bunches, and flying from every person trapped in the compact car including my Aunt Nina who was driving.

I wasn't expecting Butta to get fed up to the point where he would put a beat down on Scully, but hailing from the hard-knock streets of Gary, Indiana made my navigator somewhat of a wild card.

It also needed to be taken into consideration that Scully was my boss, and what several days and several thousand miles would do to that relationship. I'd been working for him for more than a year, and our ability to communicate through the tangled wires of work and the occasional misunderstanding turned the corporately-owned entity into a tolerable place to be employed.

A lot of that comfort for me at the site was largely due to Scully. He not only believed in my capabilities enough to bring me on at a nice salary, but furthered that belief by increasing it substantially when he believed I was being courted by another major news site in the MMA world. As it turned out, my going to Cincinnati to see my beloved Chicago Cubs trounce the Reds had everything to do with catching up with a friend who just happened to be the managing editor at a rival site, and nothing to do with jumping ship.

Scully caught wind of me being at the game with this person due to a few posts on Twitter, and started shooting inquiries via text in my direction. Shortly after a few came through, my phone died due to snapping pictures of the players during batting practice, and it sat dead in my pocket for two hours while we enjoyed the ball game on what was a beautiful summer night on the banks of the Ohio River.

When I reached the car and began my trip home, my phone powered back up and a slot machine worthy carnival of sound rang out as a slew of texts hit in rapid-fire succession. Much to my amusement the sender of those texts was none other than Scully, with each message containing a number that increased with every individual installment. Stuck between humor and amazement, I collected myself to return the final message with the words, "You have a deal my friend," and just like that my monthly salary nearly doubled.

Had things worked out differently and I wasn't the crazed tourist-level picture taker I am, then I probably would have jumped on the first offer he sent my way. But the universe had other plans, and I left Cincinnati that night riding high on a Cub's win and my market value having increased without having to negotiate.

Standing in his living room and looking at the excitement plastered across his face, it was impossible to say no, and a quick nod in his direction sent him off to grab his bags. Butta stood silent shaking his head with a slight smile that spoke volumes and rubbed the top of his head as if to mat his hair down the way he always did when he was uncertain about things.

Six hours of highway sat between our crew and Phoenix, and since my energy levels were through the roof due to my poor life choices, I slid behind the wheel of Scully's SUV as the rest of my companions piled in accordingly. As we drifted out of Albuquerque, the sun-singed blend of red and gray across the rocky and barren terrain provided a peace of mind that was borderline tranquil. After spending the majority of my life in the lush greens of the Midwest, the drastic change in scenery had me feeling as if I was experiencing something truly special.

And I was. By all accounts I was doing just that, and with the first city on our four-thousand mile quest checked off the list, there was a surge in confidence and determination that I was actually going to pull this off. Every time Scully would bark out another mention in his signature enthusiastic tones from the site's MMA Twitter account that pertained to the road trip, that surge would return, and this happened with increased frequency throughout the drive to Phoenix.

The road trip project was becoming the hot conversation of the moment inside the insulated bubble that is the MMA universe—at least that was true from a fan standpoint. As for my peers in the media sphere, many of those types acted as if it wasn't happening, and when those weird shifts occur I always know I'm doing something right.

Not everyone in the media took that stance, as several friends and a scattered group of acquaintances urged their readers and Twitter followers to tune into what was happening on the road. Raw Combat author and New York staple Jim Genia even penned an article on MMA Frenzy telling fight fans why they should care about my journey:

It may come as a surprise to many MMA fans, but there's a whole side of the sport that exists beyond the confines of the cage. It is an aspect never seen on any pay-per-view broadcast, a world that encompasses more than just the fights, fighter walkouts and the sanitized faux-drama of countdown shows. And Bleacher Report scribe Duane Finley is hopping into his car and driving cross-country to tell it.

Having followed the local MMA scene for over a decade, and examining nearly every aspect of it with a microscope, I'm excited at the prospect of Finley seeing and reporting on the stuff that happens "off camera". Whether it's about gym visits, nights "out with the boys", or even just the minor successes and failures that occur every day, the potential stories Finley will be able to tell are both limitless and compelling.

Should you follow along as Finley goes on his journey?

Absolutely. You should pay close attention, if for no other reason than to gain insight into what goes on unseen in mixed martial arts.

It's a big world out there, and MMA journalism as we know it has thus far only scratched the surface.

It started to feel as if the MMA community as a whole had taken notice of the mission I had engaged on, and at no point was this more obvious than during a quick stop in Gallup, New Mexico to grab a bite to eat. Kevin Stewart, an old friend from my childhood, had relocated from Illinois to New Mexico 15 years earlier, and when he heard I would be coming that way, insisted we meet up for old time's sake. "Stew" picked Gallup because it was an easy place to connect, and the four of us milled into an expansive and desolate sports bar that seemed to mimic the entire look and feel of the town it was located in.

The initial part of the conversation was the natural order of bringing things up to speed (wife, kids, work, etc.) before it turned to the road trip. Kevin shared that he had been following along with the journey, and being a fight fan, started talking about upcoming UFC cards and particular matchups that were on the docket. The time flew by, and when it was time to hit the road again, I stood up and gave my old friend a strong embrace and we shared a quick laugh about the time I fell thirty feet out of a tree, snapping both wrists in compound fractures, and my seventy-year-old grandmother had to wipe my ass for a month.

Back when that happened Kevin caught a lot of blame because he was sitting on a branch ten feet below me and had dared me to go out on the limb that eventually snapped and sent me crashing to the earth. My ten-year-old mind blamed him, therefore my family (which was his extended family), did the same, but the truth of the matter is no one forced me out on that branch. I did it because the feeling of danger and anxiety fueled me to make the decision.

One I absolutely regretted because there is nothing more humbling that having an old woman taking strong swipes at your backside.

Just as I bid Kevin farewell, the man who had waited on our table jogged over to catch me before I made my way out the door. He pardoned himself for the strangeness of the moment, but wanted me to know he too had been following along on the road trip journey through the website's mobile app. He also wanted me to know his name was Ritchie and asked for a shout out on Twitter and the live blog that was running on the site during the trip.

Now Ritchie Pate is getting mentioned in a book, so I guess it was a win all around for him.

Once the wheels began to spin toward Phoenix, I checked in with John Crouch to make sure my stop at the MMA Lab was still a go. I'd spoken with John a handful of times for various articles, but I was really looking forward to getting some face time with one of the best minds in the sport. Alongside former UFC lightweight champion and team leader Benson Henderson, the duo had quickly built one of the best collectives in MMA, and the eagerness I felt to get a firsthand look at the machine in motion was enough to take the labor of driving off my mind.

There is also something invigorating about crossing over into a new state. Every individual handles distance driving in their own way. Some create games for their companions to play along with, while others use mental trickery to block out time. The column I'd be categorized in would be that of an endurance driver, as long stretches of asphalt and reflectors typically do not dent my armor. I'm steel behind the wheel, but that doesn't mean I don't have a few psychological gymnastic routines of my own to make the passage of time and miles more tolerable.

Perhaps the most prominent marker in my mental commitment to the road is leaving one state behind to begin my journey through the next. Anyone who has ever trekked solid distance or logged absurd hours in the driver's seat can attest to the fact that there is a sense of victory that comes with knowing one more state can be checked off the list.

Getting through New Mexico was a breeze and Arizona figured to be more of the same. That was true in a literal sense because there is absolutely no change in scenery. The rocks are still blood red, and the flat land in between mesas cracked and scattered with the type of plant life that would be picked last if there were a junior high school dance for those sorts of things.

As we closed within striking distance of Phoenix, I began to think about the wealth of talent the city had produced and its long history and ties to MMA. Long before the MMA Lab popped up in Glendale, the Lally brothers were doing their thing at Arizona Combat Sports. The fighter fans love to hate, Jamie Varner, slugged his way to a WEC lightweight title, and Ultimate Fighter alums and former Arizona State standouts Ryan Bader and C.B. Dolloway got their start under their tutelage before breaking off to set up their own gym across town.

Regional promotion Rage in the Cage had logged two decade's worth of shows in and around the Phoenix area, and was putting asses in seats long before the UFC became the biggest game in town. Those elements are the type that spark my mind, but a one-day swing through the town where "Thunder" Dan Majerle used to rain three balls from the suburbs wasn't going to be enough time to scratch the surface on the wealth of potential stories that exist in the fight town buried in the long shadow Las Vegas casts.

The night air was crisp with a touch of warmth, the way September feels in Indiana, except it was January in Arizona. We pulled into a well-lit strip of nondescript businesses and warehouses. Toward the back of glowing strip, the MMA Lab logo called out. Our crew walked through the glass doors and the first thing I noticed was how aesthetically pleasing the environment was. I'd been in enough fight gyms to know what I was standing in was nice setup, and every step beyond the lobby further validated my first impression.

Since it was late in the day there were only a few bodies rolling on the vast mat space inside the Lab, but we stood and watched their exchanges until Crouch popped out of a back office and beckoned me to come his way. Once there, he greeted me with the only type of handshake that can come from a man with forearms the size he carries around, and his broad shoulders would be imposing if it weren't for the kindness in his eyes.

Nevertheless, there was a bit of a hitch in his step as we walked over toward his desk, and with this being our first time meeting in person, his temperament was difficult to read.

"I mean no disrespect," he offered as he sat down in his swivel chair, "but it's been a long day of classes and I'm going to sit down for our talk if that's cool."

Here I was standing in his gym, better yet his personal office, and he was asking if stepping around proper conversational etiquette would suffice considering he'd been on the mats coaching multiple classes that day. If that doesn't tell you the type of man John Crouch is then you need to make a few adjustments in your life.

"Oh by all means do whatever you need," I answered as I pulled up a chair to join him.

"Sorry you just missed Ben," he added. "He just finished leading the last class and then he got out of here for the night. And it's strange that you wouldn't catch him here tonight because he's honestly always in the gym. Some guys say they live in the gym, but Ben walks the walk. If he's not in here training he's coaching or teaching a class, and that's a rare thing for a fighter at his level. But that is the type of culture we have here and he definitely leads by example."

The culture Crouch pointed out at the Lab is certainly unique when compared to how other high-profile fight gyms operate. In most places fighters work according to their training camp schedules, and hit the occasional group session or pro class in between. Outside of the group practices, every bit of training is done with their personal preparation in mind as they weave through a mixed schedule filled with specific elements and the coaches that oversee those elements.

Fighting is an individual sport and singular focus is necessary in many regards, which makes the term "Fight Team" a very loose one. This is not the case at the MMA Lab as every individual, regardless of status or lack thereof, chips in to help the man standing beside them.

"We are a family here and we take that mentality very serious," Crouch explained. "We all help one another and that creates a unique bond between the athletes in our gym. There are no egos here and that is something you won't often see in other gyms around the sport. You've spent a lot of time in gyms, and I'm sure you'll see plenty of them on this trip your doing right now, but that's not something you are going to find here."

"So how does it work?" I asked as I leaned up in my chair.

"Our number one rule is you help the people who helped you. If your teammates made time to come in and spar or roll with you during your camp, then as soon as you are healed up and able you get back in here to do the same for them. Also…there is no rank or status here. We have fighters like Ben who have accomplished so much in the sport working with guys who are getting ready for their debut in a smaller promotion. Say Ben fights on a Saturday night, and if he's not too banged up, which thank goodness he usually isn't, then you can guarantee he'll be back in here on Monday helping the guys who pushed him during camp."

There was a directness in the way Crouch spoke that drove home his belief in the system they were running at the gym. Just the thought of a former champion and perennial contender like Henderson shrugging off the glory of a big win on the sport's biggest stage to lace up the gloves two days later to help a fighter who had yet to, and may never establish themselves on the larger MMA landscape, stamped a marker in my mind.

My brain couldn't imagine someone like Frank Mir or Anderson Silva diving right back into the mix after earning their paycheck, and the picture Crouch was painting absolutely hooked my interest and amplified my excitement to sit down with Henderson when the opportunity arose.

The more Crouch talked the more fascinated I became with him. Much like my conversation with Greg Jackson a day earlier, we drifted through topics with ease and he provided deep and poignant answers to each and every one of my inquiries. It takes a unique individual to become a leader of men, and this rings especially true when those men are fighters.

From the way Crouch spoke of the men and women on his roster, his care for them all showed through crystal clear. In a sport as rigorous and often times brutal as MMA can be, I found myself wanting to know more about a coach's perspective of when it's time for one of their fighters to walk away from competition. There is so much personal investment that goes into a fighter's career, and the emotion involved can't be duplicated in any other athletic endeavor.

That said, a coach watching a once agile and elusive player hobble up and down the court because time has done a number on his knees is a far stretch from a coach watching a fighter he's mentored and loves like a son being folded up after catching a stiff right hand on a chin that simply cannot hold up the way it once could.

I knew it was a touchy subject when I asked Jackson during my stop in Albuquerque, and from the caliber of bond Crouch has with his fighters already having been established in the conversation, I knew his approach to the matter would be a complex one. And I was correct in that assumption.

"Our team is unique in the sense that every person helps those who helped them," Crouch said. "It doesn't matter if you are a former champion like Benson or an amateur fighter working toward their pro debut; if someone put in their time to help you prepare then you give your time in return. That's the way we work here and it's created a strong bond between the members of this team. Seeing a guy like Benson fight on the biggest stage in the world on Saturday night, then to see him right back in the gym helping out on Monday, sets the type of example that cements a dynamic inside of a gym. There are no egos here, only hard work."

The weight of the subject was a good place to bring the interview to a close and I then steered the conversation back to general matters. Crouch was particularly interested in the road trip project as a whole and assured me it was something he knew fighters would appreciate. Coming from a man whose business it is to know and understand the mentality of fighters of all shapes and sizes, I took his words as a badge of honor.

"Making the effort to get out there, see what they go through and being interested to learn what their lives are like will mean a lot to everyone you stop and talk to," he added as we walked down the hallway toward the lobby. "I think it's a cool thing you're doing and we need more of this in the sport."

"Let's just hope I survive this drive," I joked in a self-depreciating manner that I hoped would hide the pride and flattery that was quickly rising to the surface.

Crouch returned the humor in a quick bit of banter and just like that I was back with Butta and Scully walking back to the Toyota with a different appreciation for the smaller details of a fighter's career. The entire relationship between a fighter and coach is built on trust, and that trust is constantly tested in a variety of ways throughout an athlete's career. Inside the cage the fighter has to trust their coach has prepared them properly, just as the coach has to trust they will fight according to the game plan, or listen if adjustments need to be made on the fly.

"I give all the credit in the world to my coaches," former lightweight champion and featherweight contender Frankie Edgar once told me. "They see everything that I need to do while the fight is happening. They call it out and I do it. I know it's me who is in there fighting, but following their instructions is what makes all the difference for me."

But what happens when that bond is brought under the stress of a coach telling a fighter it's time to stop doing what they love? While Crouch admitted it was a situation he didn't have much experience in just yet, listening to the way Jackson spoke about the process shed plenty of light on what can happen in the aftermath of such a frank discussion.

"I don't want to see my friends get hurt and that is what I tell them," Jackson said—his eyes wearing the weight of memory recall. "If that's something they are going to get angry about then that is what happens. I care and because I care that's why we are having this conversation, and I want to be able to have conversations with you years down the road when we are both old men.

"It's never an easy thing," he added. "But sometimes it's necessary."

We decided to grab a hotel for the night and I updated the live blog after dinner and a few cocktails to ease my mind. Since I was unable to catch up with Benson during the gym stop he suggested we meet up for breakfast the following morning, and a few quick texts later it was confirmed. Scully decided to call it an early night, while Butta and I hung for a bit and enjoyed some non-MMA related conversation.

With both him and I being huge fans of standup comedy, we would fall into spells where certain punch lines or bits would get stuck in our bullshit rotation. The routine of the moment came from an Ares Spears set where he talked about the different mentality his white friend had to his mother's approach to discipline.

We had listened to the bit numerous times on the trip out, and every time something came up one of us didn't agree with it wasn't long before the words, "You get out from around here with that foolishness," would be launched into the conversation. While there wouldn't be any notable foolishness that night, as sleep came to me with comfort and ease, the next two days would provide plenty of opportunity for Butta to sling that phrase, and in some cases do so with the comedic tones absent.

Chapter 6

The Laboratory

Working in a digital media requires multiple hats to be worn at all times. There was once a time where extended trips to acquire the information necessary to write a story was commonplace in journalism, but those days have long since faded in the current social media-driven news world. Every project has several more hovering in the periphery, and while more work is the only bit of security available in this realm, it can be a hectic and chaotic dance.

Two thirds of the road trip crew were up and working while Butta laid decked out across a tempurpedic double in a deep sleep. There was no need to poke the bear at such an early hour as Scully and I would shortly be off for a breakfast interview with Benson Henderson at a place of his choosing that happened to be two blocks down the road. Before we hit that stop I needed to put the finishing touches on a feature I'd written to go up on BR for the day, in addition to posting the latest updates to the rolling travel blog.

There was also a phone interview with former multi-weight UFC fighter Kenny Florian covering his analyst duties for Fox Sports 1, but that was going to take place in the Toyota to ensure my inability to converse quietly didn't disturb our still slumbering companion.

The former UFC 155-pound champion wanted to meet up at Muffin But, "the Best Café just off 19th Avenue". We pulled in a few moments before his arrival. As we walked up the sidewalk toward the front door of the establishment, Scully asked if it would be okay if he jumped into the conversation on this interview, a request I had no issue with at all.

"I don't want to mess up your process or your thing, but Benson seems to be a pretty interesting guy and there are a few things I'd like to ask him."

"That's absolutely cool with me," I responded as we caromed past the collection of two-seat tables just beyond the doorway. "You know how I do it, brother. It's just the natural flow of conversation. Feel free to jump in with anything at anytime."

While I never doubled back to ask him specifically, the reason I assumed my editor inquired was due to how Henderson had bristled with MMA media in the past. Despite proving himself as one of the top lightweight fighters on the planet and winning a collection of titles, Henderson seemed to operate with somewhat of a chip on his shoulder. This tendency seemed to intensify when dealing with media types, as a string of hard-fought yet razor-thin split decisions that worked out in his favor, were debated heavily among pundits in the MMA media sphere.

And even though I knew the criticism of his work to be a source for his displeasure with media in our sport, I also believed it wasn't the only one. Henderson had long been a fighter who always seemed to get left out of the bigger conversations when dealing with the best-of-the best lists writers love to put together and fans love even more to read. Even during his time as the WEC lightweight champion, the dialogue was always, "Yeah…Henderson is good, but he doesn't stand a chance against the top ten on the UFC's roster."

That conversation didn't change much after Henderson rolled to victory in his first three fights inside the Octagon following the WEC/UFC merger in late 2011—two of which came against perennial title contenders in Clay Guida and Jim Miller—and only shifted South after taking the title and then defending the strap in two classic tilts with iron-hearted New Jersey native Frankie Edgar.

People seemed to be focused on the manner in which Henderson acquired his wins rather than the fact he was defeating opponents those same people said he would get steamrolled by. I could sense this tension in every interview I watched him do, and even more so in my personal experiences working with him over the years.

That said, those vibes only served to make me that much more interested in digging in to what made Henderson tick, and his agreement to take time out of his life to sit down with me showed he was game to give me the chance—a notion further highlighted since he was stepping back into the Octagon just a few weeks later against Josh Thomson in the main event at UFC on Fox 10 in Chicago.

Added into the equation of his upcoming fight was that Henderson was also growing closer to his weight cut, and when a fighter endures the wear and tear of a long training camp and a strict diet over a six-week period, pleasant moods can be difficult to locate.

We decided to set up shop out on the sidewalk portion of the café, and no sooner did we sit down than Benson came strolling up with his dog in tow. He was quick to offer a firm handshake and greet us before asking if we had already ordered, which we had yet to do. The afore mentioned worries about his disposition quickly faded as pleasantries were exchanged before he took his seat at the table.

The first thing I noticed was how Henderson carries himself with a tremendous amount of self-assurance that comes off as gracious and polite without a touch of cockiness…and that in itself amazed me. His signature toothpick jutted off to the left side of his mouth as we got down to business, and while friendly and courteous throughout, it was definitely business he was there to do.

Over the course of the next hour we covered a myriad of topics that floated in and out of personal and professional aspects of his life. Throughout his career Henderson has been an open book about his clean-living lifestyle (has never touched alcohol, cigarettes or drugs) and his spirituality, regardless of public perception, as the first person he thanks in victory or defeat is his lord and savior Jesus Christ.

As Henderson shrugged off whether or not his religion rubbed people the wrong way, it was also clearly visible those critics didn't concern him. And while saying things don't bother them is something the majority of professional athletes are prone to throwing out in bulk, Henderson's tone and eye contact served to drive home the fact that the opinions of others when it came to his belief in God missed him entirely.

On the other hand, when the topic of not getting his due came to the table at about the same time his omelet and cup of tea arrived, the intensity of the conversation shifted noticeably. Yet, where I presumed it was the lack of credit for noteworthy accomplishments that pricked at his skin from time to time, Henderson's explanation of his overall mindset revealed key elements of the larger storm of motivation that swirled inside of him.

Rather than just being a fighter showing up to get a paycheck, here was a man who was pushing and demanding the very best from himself at the highest level of his profession. In order to do so Henderson needed to face the toughest challenges available and his track record was verifiable proof of the path and mission he was holding steadfast too.

As Henderson broke down his approach, the fog and mystery surrounding his adverseness to critics who never bothered to ask the bigger questions or work beyond the lay-up that came with pre-fight accessibility, disappeared into the clear blue Phoenix sky. In his mind he was putting in the effort to chase greatness, and while he would demand no mention or applause for his pursuits, he also wasn't go to sit back and let those who made no effort to understand or grasp his quest fire off shots without answering.

"I know what I demand of myself to do my job and it would be nice to see that come from the media side of the table," he said. "We are out there putting our butts on the line and some guy who has never taken the time to take a closer look jumps on his computer and pushes out some article of his opinion on how we did our jobs? That is what it is but I'd like to see some real effort put into what is being done on that side.

"I understand every fighter's goal isn't to be the best in the world, but that's certainly mine and that is what pushes me forward every single day. I'm not in this sport to be second best and that's why I've always been willing to step up and fight anyone they put across from me. Some fighters like to pick and choose hoping it will protect their legacy, but that's not who I am. I believe I'm the best fighter on the planet and I'm willing to prove I believe what I say. That's a hard thing to see criticized when you know the person writing it never made the slightest effort to understand it."

While Henderson's words and the passion in his voice lit up my senses and his words hit with immediacy, it would take some time for me to draw the parallels between his drive and my own. I would eventually come to realize that it wasn't only inspiration I found at that table, but the feelings and emotions beyond my grasp in that moment, was watching a man brave enough to acknowledge it was greatness he was chasing.

It took me driving coast to coast to finally realize that's what I was indeed doing myself, but it was an awakening that waited ten months beyond that morning with Benson.

By the time my editor and I made it back to the hotel, life had begun to flow once more through Butta's large frame. Just a step back inside the room and it was obvious a bit of solid sleep had done wonders, but he was admittedly saddened he missed out on a solid breakfast. With checkout time quickly approaching, there was little time for small talk. and I assured him he'd get a chance to get something in his stomach before setting out toward our next destination, which was still up for grabs.

When putting together my initial plan and layout of the trip, I had envisioned making the jump over to Los Angeles and putting in several stops in and around the "City of Angels." Thanks to the polar vortex and a day lost slugging through an ice storm of Biblical proportion, there wasn't going to be enough time to bring everything in my mind to life. The other option available would be heading north to Las Vegas where I knew I could lock down a handful of quality interviews.

Which route we chose didn't really matter to me at that point. The culmination of short term bouts with sleep and increasing sharpness in my lower back were starting to make discomfort the fourth member of our road trip crew. I shot a few texts out to fighters in L.A. and Vegas alike, and told my companions the direction we traveled would come down to who responded first.

A few moments later a text came through from heavyweight knockout artist Roy Nelson followed up by a positive reply from Joseph Benavidez. Scully was also confident he could get some time for us at Xtreme Couture, and if everything shook out right, Randy himself. That collective provided enough weight for the decision to be made, and we were rolling toward Sin City within the hour. Figuring I would have to take the wheel again, I provided myself with some secret assistance and a Red Bull energy drink on deck as a backer just in case.

Sitting at a gas pump I decided to go ahead and get into the go-go juice, as I pumped myself up in various fashions for the three-hour drive. It was right about the time when my hands started to shake from the rush of substance, that one of my cohorts offered to take the wheel for the drive into Vegas. I was initially thrilled to have someone else take the wheel, but as we pulled out of the station and hit the road the reality that I had far too much energy pulsing through my body set in.

The move was simply a poor play on my behalf all around. The change of drivers provided the perfect scenario for me to steal a few precious winks on the road, but there I was buzzing like I was plugged directly into a generator. In those situations it's important to keep the running internal dialogue in stride with what actually does come out of your mouth, and that battle became a grand struggle en route to the fight capital of the world.

The only saving grace came in being able to stretch out my legs a bit, which took the pressure off the stabbing pain that was now moving down the left side of my body. I wasn't sure how much more of the pain I could take before I started to verbalize it, but being stuck in a car for long clips is stressful enough without someone bitching and moaning about things beyond anyone's control.

Due to the vast openness and lack of police presence in the desert, you can push the pedal down a bit further, and we were coming up over the Hoover Dam in what felt like record time. The abundance of flickering lights in Vegas already make it beautiful at night, but coming in on Route 93 and seeing the city spill out like a vibrant wildfire from mountain to mountain is truly something to behold.

Sitting up between the seats and taking in the view was also the point I realized I was far enough from home and so deep into the trip at hand I no longer thought about the connective distance between myself and my family. Up until then I felt as if I had been leaving a trail of breadcrumbs just in case something terrible and ominous reared its head, but speeding headlong into the neon sea crossed the line where I'd officially come too far to turn back.

It was the make-or-break moment coming up hot, and what more appropriate battleground than Las Vegas?

Chapter 7

Fear, Loathing, and Sleep Deprived in Las Vegas

The gambling Mecca of the U.S. is a city that moves at the speed of track lighting and is a revolving door where human morality lessens at every spin. It is a place where otherwise civilized individuals go to let inhibitions and savings account balances hit the floor, and the concrete construct of time lets its hair down to join the rest of the 24-hour party people slipping and sloshing about the strip.

If Las Vegas had a physical embodiment and that body had a voice, it would be Ke$sha plain and simple.

Fortunately our stop in the desert fun town built on east coast mafia money was going to be a short one, and there was no time wasted as dinner plans with Joseph Benavidez and my former co-worker and close friend Megan Olivi jumped things off. It had been a good stretch since I'd last seen the tiny brunette wonder that is Ms. Olivi, but the beauty of forging lasting relationships is that you can immediately pick up where last you left off.

One thing I've always loved about Megan is the good vibes she always puts off and the same rings true for her longtime boyfriend and flyweight powerhouse Benavidez. They are a remarkable fit in so many ways, and seeing them together made me miss Renee even more than I did an hour before when I psychologically manipulated myself to put the blur of the road trip experience in front of the sting of missing those I love the most.

Also joining our posse was another brother in arms, Jeremy Botter. who was also providing us a place to crash for our brief stint in Vegas. Botter, Olivi and I had all been a part of the Heavy MMA team that made waves during its brief existence, and had remained friends even after that ship shattered to pieces on the rocky shores of MMA Island. The place we met for dinner wasn't what anyone would call high end, but neither was it of the greasy spoon variety.

Ironically enough we all ordered pizza, but not the type you reach in and grab a slice of as each of us had our own gourmet interpretation of pizza sitting before us. With everyone being acquainted, it didn't take long before multiple conversations criss-crossed the table, and I took the opportunity to catch up with the latest and greatest going on in Benavidez's world.

In a strange turn of similarity, the Team Alpha Male staple, just like Henderson who I'd sat with earlier in the day, was coming off a rough outing in perhaps the biggest fight of his career. In Henderson's case he was the champion going into his bout with Anthony Pettis at UFC 164, where Benavidez was on the challenger's side of his tilt with Demetrious Johnson at UFC on Fox 9 a month prior to our conversation.

Yet, while the difference of chasing and defending the belt was a major difference between their situations, both were facing men who have become the primary nemesis in their respective careers. Pettis had twice defeated Henderson inside the cage, and several weeks before we talked shop at a scenic Las Vegas strip mall, Benavidez had his title hopes stifled by "Mighty Mouse" for the second time in quicker fashion than the first go around.

Even though both came through the fire of tough results and disappointment, just like Henderson, the man sitting beside me at the table had a deeper sense of perspective in his eyes. There was no doubt the sting of the loss still lingered because it would be impossible for a man as competitive as Benavidez to simply write off a flawed performance, but it was interesting to hear him talk about making necessary adjustments that had nothing to do with the physical side of the fight itself.

I had interviewed plenty of fighters fresh off losses who want to lock the conversation into their awareness of the mistake made and how it wouldn't happen again under any circumstance. Fighting is a individual sport and losing said fight is a tough thing to wear and I get that, but hearing competitors trying to convince you they now know better never comes off as anything but desperate. The only thing that sounds more desperate is an excuse as to why they lost: injury or personal issues beyond the cage. It's an easy band-aid for wounded pride.

What Benavidez was describing was something far different and made a lot of sense in the larger trajectory of his career. Having interviewed him throughout his rise through both the bantamweight and flyweight ranks, I've known for years how much the dream of becoming a UFC champion has motivated the Las Cruces native. It has driven him to amazing showings inside the Octagon and a winning percentage the large majority of fighters would give up a kidney for, yet he had been unable to transition all of that success into a world title.

The manner in which things had played out created complex situations for Benavidez most fighters never face.

A pair of losses to Dominick Cruz kept the WEC bantamweight title out of his hands, and put him in a position where getting another championship opportunity would be a long shot while "The Dominator" held the crown. It was a reality Benavidez was well aware of, and the news of the UFC creating a 125-pound weight class was his ticket out of title contention limbo.

So motivated and inspired was Benavidez, that the mental pull of becoming champion morphed into an obsession in his life. It was no longer something he wanted to become; he needed it because somehow that 12 pounds of gold validated all the work he'd done under the bright lights. At least that was what he'd built inside of his mind, and it led to a tremendous amount of pressure being created for a man who was already as self-driven as they come.

In the aftermath of his loss to Johnson in their rematch, there was a sense of change about him I found refreshing. As we conversed throughout the meal he was loose and quick to laughter and to offer up humor of his own. Anyone who knows Joseph knows him to be quick witted and clever, and he registers an amount of laid back cool that is rarely found in the fight world. In all of the things that make him interesting, it's the depth he had always been willing to show and share since I first met him several years prior.

While other topics floated around the table, it was showing that depth once again that provided another piece to the puzzle I was building on the road. Just as Henderson had explained his drive toward something unseen, Benavidez explained how his previous approach had taken him so far off course.

"I had just built it up to be this huge thing," he said in regard to becoming a champion. "I talked about it at home, in the gym, and pushed myself so hard toward it that it became something I had to have. There was nothing that was going to stop me, and I refused to think about what would happen to me mentally if that goal wasn't accomplished. And when that last fight with D.J. turned out like it did, I very easily could have become lost. But that's not what happened.

"You know what I realized? I realized that all the great things that existed in my life before that fight were still there. It wasn't life or death, man. My girl still loved me. My family and friends were still there to love and support me. The only thing that was different is that I lost a fight rather than having my hand raised. And I found a tremendous amount of peace in that. Don't get me wrong…I'm in this sport to win. I go out there each and every time looking to give my very best, but there are going to be times when things don't work out your way. Knowing that my foundation and all the happiness I'm surrounded by every day in this great life I have is still going to be there has allowed me to take all that pressure off my shoulders and enjoy what I have."

Listening to him put all of that honesty and sincerity on the table was another solid gold notch in my search for answers. There was no awesome sound bite that was going to feed into a headline that would generate 300,000 clicks and be tossed around social media for fans to devour and debate. Instead, what I captured on my recorder was a man who had found something in himself and his life would be better for it. The frenzied atmosphere of the fight game makes it easy to forget the human element in the sport, but capturing that elusive thing and sharing it with those who want to know more had become my mission in life and the engine behind my career.

It is what brought me to the other side of the country, and Benavidez's words provided that much more assurance there was so much to be found in the life of those who are willing to bleed for their craft. That's a great and wondrous thing to find and a fantastic note to end a conversation upon.

We shifted gears after the interview had concluded and drifted away from talking about the fight game, because no one wants to talk about work more than is required. Joseph and Megan were going to call it an early night, and my pack of misfits echoed their sentiment. After bidding "Benalivi" farewell we hit a nearby liquor store to grab a few cold beers to sit back and chill at Botter's abode, but it's almost shameful to reveal not a single bottle was cracked because a hectic twist to an already insane schedule was now a triumphant possibility.

While sitting at dinner I received a text from my great friend and fellow scribe Chuck Mindenhall asking about the trip and my whereabouts in this grand country of ours. Chuck had become a big part of my life in recent years, as his guidance and advice helped me navigate the landmine-filled landscape of the MMA media world. It's an uncommon thing in that realm for an established and seasoned guy like Chuck, who at the time was writing for ESPN, to reach back and help an up-and-comer like myself, but he did it and never asked for a single thing in return.

Having been setup in Indianapolis with my family for the past decade, I had become a die-hard Peyton Manning fan, and when my then beloved Colts sent one of the greatest quarterbacks of all time down river to Denver, my loyalty followed "The Sheriff" to the Rocky Mountains. As it turned out, Chuck was also a Broncos fan and had one spare ticket to their upcoming playoff game against the San Diego Chargers. He messaged me to offer up that seat if I could make it to Denver and suggested it would be a great way to celebrate this incredible journey I was on. Since there was only one ticket available. Butta and Scully would have to sit this one out, but catching the game at a sports bar near the stadium would still be a pretty cool experience, and I was happy they both agreed with me.

Although that ticket was waiting for me in Denver, there was still the business to handle at Xtreme Couture the following day, and that was going to turn the hustle and bustle up to insane levels. In my mind calling the audible to Denver was going to be the reward for a gamble taken and executed, and I couldn't think of a better way to put the cap on the project than by hoisting an over-sized and over-priced pilsner with a man who had been a major influence on my decision to make the trip in the first place.

If there was one man who understood the humming lure of my call into the wild it was Chuck, and knowing I was going to see him became a beacon of light as I sat on Botter's couch trying to get my brain to switch off.

Chapter 8

The Natural

If there were a national scent the way we in America have national birds, anthems and such it would be bacon. It's a smell identified by gluttons, fitness freaks, and hipsters alike as universally amazing, and the aroma of sizzling strips on a hot plate brought me to life in a way that could only be topped if replicated in the company of a woman. That's how passionate I am about bacon, and I owe that deep seeded love to my late grandmother.

Many of the early days of my childhood were spent in her care, and she worked the stove the way a Chitlin Circuit musician worked the skins. Grease for sweat was the only major difference in that comparison, as her full-blooded Native American heritage and lack of appreciation for those she performed balanced out the rest. In her kitchen groove the woman was pure piss and vinegar and had the accuracy of a cruise missile with her swatting ability. If you came close with a question about nonsense, you were getting dealt with, and that fate was one well established to each and every grandchild by the time they were three.

In the shadows of the kitchen beyond the burners where the dining area sat, she held court like a Sicilian Don. A problem solver of firm resolve who found the poncho-like flower print dress more comfortable than the finer materials in the fashion world. As the great Jehovah as my witness, she would sit at her chair dolling out advice and justice in fell swoops as she chain smoked cigarettes and de-canned Pabst Blue Ribbons from sun up to sun down.

Long before Adrian Peterson brought "the switch" to national attention, my kinfolk and I shared a healthy fear of the cherry tree that lingered like the gallows in my grandfather's garden.

Funny how just something as the smell of bacon can spark so much fear and nostalgia. In one sharp turn I was snapped out of my morning mind wandering by the site of a disheveled Botter in his chonies with kitchen utensil in hand. I was instantly reminded of the lack of comforts found on the road, but as Conor McGregor's coach Jon Kavanaugh would later instill in me, "You are where you are. All you have to do is breathe."

It wasn't long before the rest of the crew sprung to life, and I took a moment to appreciate how this crazed long-scoped mission had now turned into a four-piece band of misfits. Just a few days back I was snapping off the door handles of my Nissan in the frozen tundra that was Missouri, and now here we were sharing delicious meats and fine morning conversation. It wasn't home by any means, but the camaraderie was a warm feeling.

Where the previous stops on the trip had come through my connections, going to Xtreme Couture was a monster of Scully's creation and that was clear in his eagerness to get moving. I certainly had enough relationships at the facility to make a comfortable stop, but my editor was working with newly placed head coach Robert Follis and had pep in his step to get on site and into the meat of such things.

We weren't certain how long the stay would last, but with a date in Denver a day away, we knew time was not something we had much to spare.

Upon arriving at the gym the first thing that struck me was how different it felt than the last time I had walked through the doors at XC. The sound of mitts being popped and feet shuffling across canvas were present as they would be in any gym, but the energy that once pulsed through the place just a few years prior when Randy Couture, Gray Maynard, and Martin Kampmann were notching big wins felt absent in that space. It was as like revisiting the party house of a time before responsibility had come into your life and the tangible energy generated from good times had evaporated.

While that was my general take on the situation, I wasn't alone in my assessment, and that is where Follis's presence came in. The veteran grappling guru had been summoned to bring the team feel back to XC, and it was a charge he was excited to take up. Vegas was already a funnel chute of nomads and drifters by its very nature, but it takes a special type of animal to call it home as a fighter.

"Most fighters can't handle living here," Vegas staple Roy Nelson once told me. "They get caught up in the night life of partying and hitting the clubs and it isn't long before they wash out. Your life can't be about those things if you're trying to make it here. And I'm not even talking about being a successful fighter in that sense. I'm talking about being a sane, functional person."

The stigma of setting up shop in Vegas was something Follis was well aware of, but he was determined to change the revolving door system that had taken over the gym in recent years. With the presence of several other high-profile facilities scattered around the metro area, fighters in Vegas began drifting from place to place to find bodies. Whether that work came at XC or Syndicate didn't seem to matter as much as just finding experienced fighters to practice with.

The newly instated coach already had the Hawaiian contingent led by Ray Sefo and his protégé Brad Tavares to build off of, and bringing in MMA power couple Miesha Tate and Bryan Caraway was the first of many strong moves he looked to make. Tate's rise to popularity over the past two years was nothing short of impressive and trumped only by her rival Ronda Rousey. Bringing in Miesha to train full-time at XC would bring eyes, and Follis knew that would bring other fighters back to the gym that once dominated the Vegas scene.

Midway through my conversation with Follis on a half set of bleachers that mark the dividing point of the gym, the attention turned to the arrival of the gym's namesake Randy Couture. The hardened exterior of his army jacket, distressed denim jeans, and scuffed motorcycle boots was offset by the scarf draped around his neck, but the combination looked authentic in a way most money doesn't.

Turning in his fight gloves for a ticket to Hollywood had been a good move for "The Natural", and his sun-kissed skin in the midst of a Vegas winter was a sign things were rolling good for the living legend. After walking away from a sport he helped build, Randy's presence on the fight scene had been thin at best, and when he walked up to join our conversation I found myself trying to figure out the angle of the situation.

He had no movie to promote, and there had been zero talk of any other article other than the work I was doing on the road trip. The chance that Randy had taken time out of his day to come up to talk to me about the deeper themes of a life committed to combat sports seemed like a stretch, and I was shocked to discover that was the exact reason for his appearance that afternoon.

It took a few seconds to put everything into focus, and the ease of his body language quickly eliminated the gap between my ability to find the beat and the out of my element feel that struck in the presence of a man who was a big part of my initial attraction to MMA. From the comfort of my living room I'd watched this man accomplish great things, and even in the moments he came up short against fellow titans, the same awe was resonated.

There were other factors at play as well. Perhaps more so than any fighter in the short history of the sport, Randy had battled diligently to maintain his independence. And while the lawsuits and contract disputes didn't work out in his favor when the gavel struck, he was still a man who had fought for and obtained his value in the gold rush of a post-TUF UFC.

Hell…here was a man that was standing toe-to-toe with the best a younger generation had to offer well into his late 40's, and when he could no longer play the game at the level he once could, rode off into the sunset with his legendary status intact. There was so much I wanted to ask him, but at the same time I had to make sure to keep my Chris Farley "hey, remember the time" moments in check.

As our conversation kicked off we moved from the metal bench seats of the bleachers over to the draping of the boxing ring that sat in the opening section of the gym. Randy alternated from resting against the ropes at his back to leaning in with hands clasped to address the heavier topics as they came across the bow.

Every time he would draw closer my eyes would fixate on the cauliflower ear that stuck out prominently like the badge of honor it was beneath the camouflage hat on his head.

"My passion for individual combat started at an early age and it obviously started with wrestling," Couture said. "I initially started wrestling as a way to get my dad's attention because he was a bit of a deadbeat and was never around. I heard stories from my mom that he was a wrestler so that's what I gravitated toward. It's one of the oldest individual combative sports in human history and I wanted to be great at it.

"I seemed to have a knack for it and everything you put into it is what you get out of it. Fighting is an extension of that for me. There was a purity in it that I loved. Granted, as things grew and I lost my autonomy and privacy and there were a million people pulling me in a million different directions that was tough to deal with, but even then fighting and training camp became my respite. I could push all the other stuff away and put my focus on what I loved to do which was fighting and training.

"There is not a more honest test than having a flesh and blood fight lined up at the end of a ten week camp," he added. "Going into fight week after all the hard work is done, the next challenge is the time where you sit and wait for the fight to arrive. Early in my career I didn't want to do the media or any of those things, but later on I realized how well it all helped pass the time and I embraced it. Being willing to do the interviews and radio tours where other fighters shied away from it really served to help me in a lot of areas. Doing those things went a long ways toward building my fan base, and that is something I really would like to see up and coming fighters get a better grip on."

Losing track of time is a natural side effect of being in Vegas, and by the time we exited XC the cold desert sun was already fixing to set. A quick look over at Butta and Scully mirrored my own condition as the drain had taken hold on us all. We needed to eat. We needed to sleep. We needed to get on the road to Denver. We knew all three things needed to be ticked off the list, but there wasn't a firm decider among us.

In those lingering moments of uncertainty, we somehow saw it best to head to the strip to find food, and it's a decision that makes zero sense in hindsight. The strip is a bungled mess of traffic and obstruction, but like a litter of slow-minded puppies, we were drawn to the lights that called out from just a few miles away. At least it seemed as if we were that close, but the illusion of distance is just another magical bend in the villainous construct of the city of vice.

It was a Florida in June conversation at dinner as the talk between us was labored and slow. On the night before, talk of Denver was filled with electricity and excitement, but sitting at a Mexican establishment in the sea of consumerism that is the Miracle Mile Shops, it felt more like a punishment. My run of two-hour sleep sessions and diet of uppers and energy drinks had taken a serious toll, and from the looks on the faces of my fellow travelers, their internal gas lights were also flashing.

There was simply no way we were going to be able to make the Denver run without first catching a few winks, therefore we returned to Botter's apartment to do so. I nestled up on the same couch I'd managed to crash the night prior and set my phone alarm to wake me up in three hours. We had eleven hours of road time waiting for us beyond the walls of that apartment, and leaving at midnight would give us the necessary window to arrive just before opening kickoff.

Chapter 9

Hell on Wheels

The unspoken rule in late-night driving is that the person sitting in the passenger seat has to keep the man behind the wheel company. This is primarily a safety feature, as working the buddy system ensures the entire collective doesn't meet a fiery death as the result of a slumbering driver. We were already well into the vast nothingness of Northern Utah, and a severe emotional distress had firmly taken hold.

Butta's lack of vision in the dark void of night made it difficult for him to keep his eyes open, and I watched as his head bobbed and rocked two feet to my right. The sound of Scully sawing logs in the backseat only amplified my own longing for sleep, but I knew I was still several hours away from that becoming an option I could explore. With my friends decked out around me, the fear of failure of the worst variety made me anxious.

I tried to take another pill but my body was already far past the point where it would have any effect. That meant I was in for some tough miles to trek and I found myself physically shaking my head at frequent intervals to combat the double vision that had vexed me. In those moments I thought of my family and doing whatever it took to make it back to them safely, and in doing so, the entire road trip project paled in comparison to the more important things in my life. I was becoming a madman trapped lonesome behind the wheel of a four-door prison, but the only thing my manic mind could produce was the will to drive onward.

Scully had filled the tank before leaving Las Vegas so there wasn't even the cold-jolt wake up of a gas station pit stop available to me. I wish I could say there was some deeper meaning to life or mission found in those twisted and desperate moments, but it was nothing more than dumb luck that allowed me to make it through until the sun finally popped up near the Colorado state line.

With dawn upon us, I whipped the Toyota over to the shoulder of the road and informed the crew someone else had to drive. I simply couldn't do another mile, and was relieved when Scully and Butta agreed to take their turns as I hit the backseat. I wasn't even thinking about the game or the project anymore, as I was finally able to close my eyes without the fear of meeting a grim fate.

We were well into the Rocky Mountains by the time I returned to life and the Colorado sun was shining brightly. Despite my venture into madness, we had managed to make good time coming through Utah and the GPS showed we were going to make the game with a little time to spare. Once fully revived and realizing we were going to hit our window, the energy returned to the vehicle in the form of humor and a free-flowing conversation.

Butta was cracking on Scully for the multitude of bathroom stops he'd made during my nap, and I found amazement that we were still on track in spite of his small bladder. The vibe was rock n' roll as we approached Vail, and being less than two hours away from our destination allowed the anticipation of seeing Peyton Manning sling the pigskin and playoff football to return.

With time on our side we pulled off in Vail to grab a few refreshments, and for Scully to hit the bathroom once more. Getting out of the backseat produced a cat-like stretch from my janky frame and doing so lessened the hitch in my step by the time we entered the general store. The mood was good between our group for the time being, but the young woman behind the counter did her best to swerve that sensation by telling us the odds of making it to Denver in time for the game were slim. This made no sense as we still had three hours of cushion before kickoff, but she was adamant that a winter storm was fixing to blow through that would shut down the pass and make exiting the mountains impossible.

The sun was shining high in the clear blue of the Colorado day, and Butta and I shrugged off the information. We had already come through the heart of a polar vortex, and the thought of anything winter-related stopping us now seemed absurd.

"Get out from around here with that foolishness," Butta jested as we walked back to the Toyota. We shared a solid laugh at the expense of the junior meteorologist behind the cash register. A few moments later Scully finally emerged from the depths of the store and we were back on the road.

Vail was 45 minutes in our rear view when ole Scully began to complain from the backseat about having to go the restroom again.

"You aren't serious, are you?" I asked in confusion.

"I'm dead serious, man," he replied with a bit of distress in his voice. "I am cursed with a small bladder and I really have to go."

"Why you keep drinking so much water?" Butta chimed in half-jokingly. "You know we are on a timeline here, and you've been stopping like crazy."

"I know, I know, I know, but I can't help that I have to go. It'll be a quick stop, just make sure you pull over at the next place you can."

"We are in the mountains, brother," I blasted as I looked back at him in the mirror. "I'll definitely stop, but I'm not sure there are gas stations every 10 miles out here."

Fortunately for Scully there was a roadside bathroom sitting just a few miles up the road, and I steered the vehicle around the twists and turns in the bend until we arrived at the location, which was nothing more than two tin-sided outhouses beneath the exit ramp overhead. The sun was still a prominent fixture in the sky as we watched our friend skitter out of the Toyota and make haste to the rust covered shack.

Butta decided he would take the opportunity to use the bathroom as well to just to make absolutely certain there wouldn't be further need to stop, and he returned to the Toyota a few minutes later with a grin plastered from ear to ear.

"What's so funny?"

"Dude…your man is in there lighting that thing up," he gasped as he fought through the laughter.

"Yeah? I thought he said he had to pee."

"Well if his peeing sounds like a machine gun or firecrackers ripping off inside that tin box then I guess that's what he's doing," and the humor remained at grade school levels until the door to the shack swung open and a relieved Scully returned anew.

He could hear the laughter from outside the vehicle and immediately inquired as to why upon re-entry. Butta assured him it was nothing to do with him just an inside joke between us, but the long-standing editor was no dummy and knew his digestive pyrotechnics were the source of the hysterics.

"I don't know what's going on with my stomach," he said in a moment of straightforward confession. "All this driving and lack of sleep is tearing me up."

I couldn't argue with his reasoning at all, and didn't want to upset him by pushing the jokes too far, so I quickly changed the subject as I pulled back onto the road, or at least I made an attempt. As the vehicle came back up around the bend, I noticed there was no way to get back onto the road traveling in the direction we had just came off of, and instead it was leading us back toward Vail. Anger, anxiety, and confusion popped to the surface as I scanned the road ahead for some way to turn us around.

"I'm sure there is another exit up here close," Scully barked from the backseat, but my memory couldn't recall having passed another turn off in miles.

The tension grew thick as precious distance already trekked was backtracked and minutes ticked off the clock on the dash. It became more so when the sun that had hung prominently overhead for the past few hours, started to fade back into the gray that was engulfing it as the storm the teenage girl previously forecast was suddenly coming to life.

We had to go back 20 minutes before turning around and by that time a light snow had started to fall. I pushed the gas pedal down as far as the slowing traffic around us would allow and watched the tiny blue dot that marked our location on the GPS inch closer to our destination. Just as we blew by the previous bathroom stop, the wind around us kicked up fierce and it forced my grip on the wheel to tighten. We were in for something awful and the environment surrounding us was shifting with force.

The shoulder of the road turned into a snake of semis lined nose to ass as trucks began pulling aside to chain their tires for snow that was starting to pour into the pass. This was the worst of signs for my football playoff hopes and that dread reigned supreme when our tires were brought to a halt due to a dead-locked traffic as the result of the pass being closed.

The car was silent and the only sound to be heard came from the gusting wind whipping in waves off the windows. We were trapped, and there was no other solution than to sit tight and wait for it all to blow over.

Being a man who prides himself on character, I had always assumed it was beyond me to be pushed into a tantrum, but an explosion of torrid bitching and a stream of expletives longer than the line of helpless semi trucks that sat shouldered between Vail and Denver came pouring out of my mouth. It wasn't the bathroom stop, or missing the football game that forced the blow out, but the sum of all the moving parts slamming together in a crash of twisted metal and emotion. It was just too much to handle.

The silence eventually broke when I turned on the radio to tune into the game and had to listen as the Broncos worked toward a victory. I'm sure it would have been exhilarating from the seat next to Chuck to cheer on the orange and blue. Less than an hour after the Broncos had officially moved into the next round of the playoffs, the travel ban in the mountain pass lifted and we were once again free to get our wheels rolling.

The collective dejection inside the Toyota kept us moving out of the Rockies and right around Denver on our way back to Albuquerque. Colorado's capital city sits pretty much due north of where my Nissan was sitting, and we wanted to put the entire mishap behind us, even if that meant notching nearly 24 hours behind the wheel in a single shot. Scully took the helm as I once again retired to the backseat, because Indianapolis was still going to be a very long way once we returned to Albuquerque.

Somewhere in transit, Butta suggested the idea that we head out as soon as we get back and I immediately pushed back against the idea. I knew I was going to have to take the lion's share of the driving responsibilities and there was no way that could be done without getting a solid bit of sleep. I just didn't have the power to push through any longer, and those limits would be hit again and again on the drive back to the Hoosier state.

I simply couldn't believe I'd miss that damn football game, and it was a thought that refused to skip out of my mind.

There wasn't too much said once we returned to Scully's house, as he immediately rushed off to spend the night with his girl who was excited to have him back. Butta and I went into his house to crash for a few hours in hopes of building up enough steam to make the entire run back in a single clip. Ambitious as all hell for sure…but our respective buffers had worn so thin that lingering out in the void of the west any longer was only going to create friction.

We took turns at the wheel for long clips as we burned up the day with wheels turning eastward, but our progress slowed considerably once the sun slipped below the horizon. Butta did his honest to goodness best to fight through his condition and give me the breaks I obviously needed, but it was impossible for him to hold ground in the driver's seat for extended lengths of time after nightfall.

Nevertheless we switched out as often as we needed to, and when we hit junctures where neither could drive, we'd hit a truck stop or hotel parking lot to sleep until one of us became able. The other major factor at play was the frigid cold outside the car. Having to leave the Altima running and the heat flowing while we nodded off, we quickly zapped our fuel supply. That meant even more stopping and the two-hundred mile stretch before hitting St. Louis again was absolutely the worst of the entire experience.

In the blur that was the road home, there was also a brief argument in regards to the musical selection Butta had chosen. In times of pure exhaustion and potential death, a mix CD of classic soul-music, cuts from The Chi Lites and Billie Holiday, was a poor choice, and I didn't care how much my companion argued for his case. Tempo dictates a lot of things and he simply couldn't grasp why his selection wasn't conducive with what we were attempting to accomplish.

Once the morning sun cracked and we were coming into Indiana, that strange phenomenon of rejuvenation occurred. We had home base in our sights, and Butta took the wheel like a man possessed. We talked about the food we would eat and how it would feel to finally sleep in our own beds again. We talked about seeing our children and hugging the women we felt we had neglected by being unavailable for so much of the trip due to the obligations of the project.

He was 20 minutes gone from the vehicle when my mind finally came to grips with having pulled off such a crazy expedition. A few moments later I was pulling into my own driveway, and the faces of my two beautiful children were plastered lovingly to the upstairs window. Their daddy was finally home, back from whatever it was he was chasing, and their hugs made me forget about the cold and awfulness that was my entire world just twelve hours before.

I gave my wife a kiss and a long embrace, then went upstairs to hit the shower. The entire family was not only over the moon that I was home, but wanted to hear about the places I had been. Renee did her best to keep them up to date by following the live blog on Bleacher Report and showing them the pictures I'd sent her via text, but they wanted to hear their dad tell stories in the way they'd come to love listening to them.

They waited for me to get out of the shower then all came into the bedroom to snuggle up to me. They started to ask all the questions they had been saving up for days. I could hear the excitement in their voices just before everything faded to black.

Renee covered me up with a blanket and assured the children I'd have plenty of time to tell them all about the trip once I got some rest, but daddy had come a very long way just to make it home, and they needed to let me be. Thinking about how the disappointment must've hung on their faces twists me up still, and that sensation is only relieved by the fact their father was running something down on his trek out west.

He was chasing a dream, and them coming to know the same ambition runs through them is something that makes the ends…both tattered and clean…meet at a place where everything becomes worthwhile.

Chapter 10

Home Sweet Home

Travel across time zones has a way of disorienting the senses like few things can. Jetlag is obviously the most commonly shared experience due to the popularity of air travel, but similar effects creep on after extended car rides as well. I'd been home three days and was still out of sorts enough for my wife of more than a decade to ask if I was okay at regular intervals.

Time and time again I'd nod to both comfort her and stop the line of questioning, but I wasn't completely sure if that was the absolute truth. The pain in my back was still very much there, and the short-wicked irritation that comes from removing stimulants of all types from the body was within reach in every direction I turned.

The biggest cause for Renee's concern was my admission to substituting uppers for sleep during the trip. While she understood my reasoning in the parts that were of genuine origin like fear of death and pushing through when no one else could drive, her sky blue eyes folded sharply when I explained the thought process that opened that door in the first place back in Albuquerque.

She did her best to balance things out and keep her thoughts level, but my sordid history in dark places made that particular light switch easy to flip. Back before the responsibility of kids and careers came into our lives, I fell into a few old habits that had existed since my early years of adulthood. Allowing those demons to catch up to me nearly destroyed our relationship, but Renee has always been as ride or die as women are made in the modern age, and she refused to let me self-destruct.

She believed in the man she knew I could be, and that belief was the thing that got me through the early days of recovery, when love and support are needed the most. And even though trying times were nine years behind us, it never really fades away entirely for those who watched you go through it. She was stern and direct as we sorted out the issue and sincere in her belief that that mess was left behind in the Southwest.

On the professional side of things, the road trip appeared to be a success and a sense of validation arrived because of it. A project of that nature had never been attempted before on the larger platforms in MMA media, and the reception from the overall community was a positive one. Even though the first run was an experiment for the most part, the grander vision was to make my way across the entire country in three total installments. Surviving the initial 4,000 miles, and creating content that generated the type of positive feedback it had received during the five-day excursion, created anticipation for the second wave to begin even though there wasn't any sort of time line set.

After a few days of rest I returned to my normal grind of interviews and features for my home site, and it wasn't long before everything fell back into the usual groove. The ins and outs of being a husband and father filled the majority of my day and the spaces between were filled with

MMA. That had been the order of things for the past few years, with many more to come if my plans shook out to my intentions.

It was great to be back home, but I wouldn't be there for long, as the UFC's return to Chicago would pull me away for a few days at the end of the month. It's never easy, especially on children, to settle back in only to jump back out just as quickly, but I assured them daddy wouldn't be traveling at all in February, and the concession was made and accepted.

Nevertheless, we still had two weeks in change before I would have to hit I-65 North en route to the city by the lake, and I planned to make each of those days count with my little ones. Being the big softie that I am, my children were already well versed in how to work the things they wanted out of me. This was true in the days before I started to travel for work, but amplified exponentially after I began skipping around to place to place for my career.

My wife had always deemed me a sucker in that sense. She knew the kids would angle for things they wanted as soon as I returned home, just as she knew those things would show up at the house before long. I was admittedly defenseless to their charms and had been since their little blue eyes locked onto mine for the first time in each of their lives. There was just nothing that could be done about it, and despite her resistance to the issue, nothing I wanted to do about it either.

One of the best and worst parts of doing freelance works is the irregularity in which invoices get paid. The money never seems to come in a timely fashion or when you need it the most. By the time it does show up in the mailbox or appear in your bank account, it's usually after you've forgotten about it, therefore the check feels more like a bonus rather than something earned.

Several magazine articles I'd written in recent months magically all hit at once following my return home from the road, making my children believe a second Christmas had arrived. The influx of cash flow also allowed us to get our six-year-old Atticus a new pair of wrestling shoes since he'd already burned through the starter pair our family friends the Moreys had given us. The timing of it all was perfect because "Savage" (as he was known throughout the MMA world) had a tournament on deck shortly after I returned home.

His new kicks would come in handy as he won all three of his matches on that icy Saturday afternoon, and watching him roll around on the mats at Hamilton Southeastern High School made me think of the gym activity I'd seen so much of during the trip. It made me eager to get back after it, and sitting on the corner of the mats with Atticus, I decided the second section of the project would cover gyms up and down the west coast.

Yet, no matter how badly I wished to keep the momentum of the series rolling strong, there was no way I was going to break the promise I'd made to my wife and kids about not traveling for a month. We are a tight family unit, and having one piece missing for a lengthy amount of time creates a weird imbalance that has never existed when we are all together.

A solid stretch of normalcy was exactly what our family needed, and I very much looked forward to passing the gray days of winter in front of the fireplace with them, which was the vision I see in my mind when missing my family on the road. No matter the season or trip, the four of us tangled up snuggling in front of the television with a warm fire at our feet was the vision evoked during those moments of homesickness just before drifting off to sleep. It's a thought that can turn any situation to a happy one, and I planned to add a few more fireside installments before setting out west once more.

Chapter 11

The Rolling Stones In My Gut

As much as I love my children, the moment the youngest one gets on his bus and zooms off to school for the day, serenity sweeps throughout my household. Renee and I usually alternated duties as I took care of breakfast and the early morning shift for our 11-year-old daughter Zoe, then she would get up with little man an hour later and take care of getting his day started. Afterwards we would return to bed for a bit unless a scheduled interview or deadline kept me from crawling back under the covers. Renee knew of no such obstacles and being a natural sleeper was an unstoppable force getting back to the bedroom to resume her slumber.

After my few days of necessary sleep recovery where she covered both shifts, I took over for a promised three-week run of morning duties. My natural energy had returned and on this particular day, I was planning on going to the gym to hit the sauna in hopes of softening up my back. The heat typically served to loosen things up, and despite the fact I was going to be covered in sweat in short order, I decided to take a hot shower before to warm up after my morning kitchen flow in an ice-cold kitchen.

There are few places of sanctuary more precious to me than in the shower because it is there I'm truly left alone. I leave my phone downstairs so there are no notifications to disturb me, and no children barge in to ask me a series of pointless questions. I'm alone with my thoughts and steam, and that morning was no different.

I was in a state of peace and gratitude as the water bounced off my shoulder blades, and just as I turned around, I suddenly lurched forward as my stomach ejected the contents from breakfast. I was stunned and shocked as the jolt shot through my abdomen, and I wretched once more before I knew what was happening. I immediately attempted to place the reason for the vomiting, but no source could be found.

I wasn't sick with the flu, and scrambled eggs had never been an issue before. Aside from the puking I felt absolutely fine, and when a third wave didn't hit I became even more baffled.

"People just don't randomly throw up," I muttered to myself as I looked down at the mess in the shower before crouching down to clean up what parts couldn't be washed down the drain. Still shocked by what had transpired, I grabbed a towel to dry off, pausing from time to time to see if another knot in my stomach or side would arise.

It didn't, so I shrugged the incident off for the moment and slipped on my gym clothes. Several minutes had gone by since the strangeness in the shower and I made my way back downstairs thinking it was all some freak occurrence. By the time I reached the kitchen I had fully convinced myself this was the case until three more painful rips left me slumped over the sink panting for air.

Something was most certainly wrong, and I frantically attempted to put some fluids back into my body since what had come out in the most recent expulsions was water. I attempted to rehydrate myself, but the puking continued to hit in one painful burst after the next. I was in full alarm panic mode when the urge to urinate came to call, and said panic went through the proverbial roof once the color my urine registered in my mind.

It was a color I'd never seen come out of my body, and I crawled up the stairs in agonizing pain trying to get my wife's attention so she could take me to the hospital. In one push of energy and adrenaline I burst into the bedroom and began to shout for her assistance.

"Wake up Renee! Wake up! I need to go to the hospital!"

Not only did my cries not register with her, but the peaceful expression on her face never shifted in the slightest. I knew waking her up was going to be a chore, and there was no time for such things. I snatched up the car keys and a plastic bag from Target and made a frenzied and vomit-filled drive to the hospital up the road. Due to the relative newness of the facility, the emergency room was empty and they addressed my condition with immediacy.

A nurse relieved me of the bag of refuse I held in my right hand as another nurse put me onto a gurney and wheeled me back to one of the rooms. The same nurse who took the Target bag handed me a bucket that I instantly utilized. I had no clue what was happening to me and wondered if I'd caught some rare disease during my time wandering out in strange lands.

They immediately hooked me up to some government fluids and gave me something to ease the nausea before rushing me off to get a CT scan of my midsection. The nurse apologized that nothing could be administered for the pain just yet until they checked off a few possibilities as to why this was happening, and the invisible knife continued to slice downward toward my groin area as I nodded and grunted that I understood.

A male nurse held my legs and stretched me out long enough for the machine to do the scan, then I was taken back to the room as the same man watched over me. A few minutes later, another came in armed with some news and a needle as they conversed next to the rolling desk computer that was set up in the corner of the room.

Walking over to me she said, "You're definitely a stoner," before plugging the needle into the I.V. ports hanging out of my arm.

Shocked, appalled and twisted up I replied, "I don't even smoke lady," which forced a hearty laugh out of her and her male counterpart.

"No, no, no," she chuckled. "I didn't mean stoner as in weed. I meant you definitely have kidney stones."

And there were the words every man never wants to hear in his lifetime.

While I had no experience with the tiny jagged deposits personally, plenty of my friends had done battle with the microscopic terrors in previous years. Men are always told kidney stones are the closest thing anything with a penis will ever experience comparable to child birth, and having watched two children emerge from my loving wife and the pain those monsters caused her; there was no part of this affliction I wanted anything to do with.

Laying helpless in the hospital bed, it was clear I had no choice in the matter, and I suddenly believed in a higher spiritual force once the morphine she plugged into the line went to work. The pain let up enough for me to regain a regular breathing pattern and all the anxiety went with it. But that's the beautiful thing about morphine…everything melts away in the immediate aftermath of its arrival.

She was explaining the situation when my phone began to rattle across the plastic chair beside me, and I looked at a number from Brazil with blurry eyes. It slowly registered that I was scheduled to speak with Gegard Mousasi that morning, but was certainly in no condition to do so at the moment. Funny enough, I had my digital recorder in my left pocket because it's always with me anywhere I go. You just never know when the opportunity for an epic interview is going to arise, but nothing was going to make me answer that phone in that moment.

In hindsight, my condition probably would have made for a pretty interesting interview in his lead up to his tilt with Dan Henderson, but I didn't figure my employer would appreciate me doing the interview in the hot-mitten grips of a morphine swing.

When the doctor came knocking she did so with a print out that showed the villainous stones live and in living color. She used a pen to point out three minor specks in what were apparently my kidneys, and said those were of no major concern.

"You'll probably pass those without even feeling them," the good doctor assured.

On the other hand, there were two much larger dark globs on the scan as well and the change of tone in her voice told me there was a bad moon arisin' for me in that hospital room. It wasn't the sound of fear coming out of her mouth as much as it was compassion for what I was fixing to go through.

"These two are not going to be pleasant," she said with a slight cringe in her face. "We will give you some medicine to help, but you are going to have to suffer a bit to get these out of you."

There wasn't a photo taken of my expression in that moment, but I would imagine it the same as the freeze frame taken on the final dive of The Shocker at Six Flags Great America. Pure terror. They were gracious with another few CC's of morphine before starting the process of cutting me loose, and since I was under the influence of some heavy voodoo, I had to call for a ride to come and pick me up.

Six calls to Renee went unanswered but this didn't surprise me. This was the same woman who slept through the chaos and panic that came with the attacks on September 11th, only to wake up mid-afternoon and wonder what everyone was going crazy about. I knew there was no waking her and called my good friend James Morey to come and get me. The Morey family were close friends and since he worked from home I figured he would be my best shot.

James was there in no time and I was back on my couch with a strainer in hand and a bottle of assistance ready to do battle within the hour. I fired off a text and an email to apologize for missing the interview with Mousasi and was relieved when I received correspondence it could be made up at the same time the following day. I agreed to those terms, but secretly hoped I would still be alive to take the call.

In the entirety of my life there had been plenty of things that rattled me or gave cause for concern, but urinating had never been one of them. Almost like breathing, it's one of those things a person needs to do and is never given an afterthought, but when you are waiting for what your mind has built into a jagged spiked boulder to come out of a place so sensitive…it's difficult to not have fear crop up.

A few days later it was all over.

Although the actual passing of the stone was uneventful and nowhere near as terrible as I had imagined, I was still left feeling busted up. The doctor would later tell me the worst of the affliction happens when said stone makes the journey from the kidney down through the urethra, but I'll spare further details because too much time has already been spent talking about things that involve my dick.

Beyond the immediacy of the medical issue the stones brought, the other floating issue around the household was with the medicine required to keep the pain levels in check. Renee had just come to grips with the use of helpers on the road trip, and here was the very thing that caused so many problems so long ago sitting right on the countertop. Aside from the obvious, the most pressing issue back in darker times was my lack of accountability, and eggshells were everywhere now that those mineral deposits came to call.

When a relationship has survived addiction in the past, the dialogue may go unspoken but never actually stops. Her blue eyes reflected her hesitation of all things medicine related, but her love and compassion for me wasn't going to remove them from the equation. She wanted the same thing she's always wanted, and that was for me to be okay. I've always loved her for that.

I was finally back on my feet when it came time to head to Chicago to cover the UFC on Fox event, and I still wasn't feeling incredible. The dead tones of a Midwestern winter were setting in with the annual case of the doldrums somewhere to follow in the gray distance. Past years had taught me the best way to deal with any type of seasonal dip was to simply keep moving, but negative degree wind chills and ice storms usually have a say or two in that process.

Nevertheless I jumped back behind the wheel and made my way the three hours north to Chicago. After the road trip, I'd made special pacts with imaginary protectors. If my survival was allowed, I wouldn't drive for such and such amount of time, but just like authorities beating confessions out of suspects under extreme duress, those pacts would never hold up in a court of law.

The time in the Windy City clicked by quickly by normal standards, but it was all worthwhile when I locked down an interview I had been chasing for the better part of four years. Outside of the major entities in the sport, and of course national television outlets, getting sit down face time with UFC President Dana White is next to impossible, and I found this out through my attempts to make it happen.

I wanted to speak with Dana for my "Fighting Life" series and had worked every avenue and connection I knew in the business to make that happen. I'd come close several times, but had never been able to execute the conversation. And just when I started to feel as if my time would have been better spent in further recovery on the couch rather than freezing my toes off up North, a text came through that turned my entire perspective around.

White was launching a new show on the Discovery Channel and was doing a private screening for select media at a nearby cinema. If I were able to get down there for that event, then getting a foothold on the interview I really wanted would become possible. I shot Scully a quick message outlining the situation, and he was all for me chasing it down the way he always had been.

I received a message from him several moments later informing me that if I wanted to send the quotes over from the screener, he would have one of our senior writers put that story together so I could focus more on the one-on-one I was a step away from obtaining. It was great to know I had backup standing at the ready, but was quite certain I could knockout both stories without a problem. It was also in these messages he suggested BR's big brother CNN may be interested in running the stories on their main page, which was always a huge incentive for the writers on the roster.

Later that night I hit the screening and was able to speak with Dana for a few moments after the closing credits rolled. He assured me that I'd get some time after the media day for UFC on Fox, and I closed out my night jotting up the story about his new show and dusted off the questions I'd been carrying around in my mind for the past four years, just in case that particular moment materialized.

Sure enough I was able to pull up a chair with Dana the next afternoon and as we were speaking I was throwing a huge checkmark on my career bucket list. Where the majority of the interviews he does are focused on immediate issues and journalists seeking comment on the ins-and-outs of things that were currently rolling across headlines; my approach was vastly different.

Long before I came to work in MMA I was a fight fan and had watched the UFC's rise from a struggling promotion to a global powerhouse. There were other competing promotions in Zuffa's early days, but as we sat in the bowels of the United Center that winter afternoon, anything close to competition had been laid to waste during the UFC's rise. Sitting two feet away from me was the man who was at the forefront of it all, and I wanted to know what his experience had been like.

The story of the UFC's turn from near bankruptcy to becoming the premier promotion in MMA around the world had been told time and time over, but I wanted to know how White felt through it all, as rival companies fell away and Zuffa set their sights on a global push. From the opening moments of our conversation, I could tell he was excited to be jumping out of the normal routes and there was a happiness that shone through and enthusiasm in his voice as he recalled what it was like to see his company grow into what it had become in that moment.

White has a unique charisma about him that is often lost in the "angriest man in the room" role he often falls into during media interactions. I'm not saying he doesn't jump into that seat willingly when he feels opposed, real or imagined, but watching him relax for the 30 minutes we spoke, I could see other elements beyond the tough exterior.

There wasn't a video camera or production team surrounding us, just two men talking about MMA for a bit, and his ability to get down to that level of comfort surprised me. Rather than a rolling train of expletives and frustration, the UFC President openly laughed and shook his head from time to time throughout the interview as he replayed moments that were undoubtedly memorable to him, but had become blurred bus window scenery over the past decade.

At one point his sincerity came front and center when talking about the efforts the people who work behind the scenes put in to make the UFC a success. White held a thousand-yard stare into the distance just over my shoulder for a few brief moments before he snapped back into the eye contact he holds with a George St-Pierre level of dominance.

It truly was a remarkable talent that he maintained throughout the entire conversation. Where the large majority of his interviews were based around the current hot-button topics of the moment, I decided to take my questions in a different route. I not only focused on his personal journey, but the men and women who have worked tirelessly to make the UFC the global force it's become as well.

"This thing is growing so fast and it isn't going to be slowing down anytime soon," White explained. "If you go back to 2007, I knew every fucking employee in our company by name and knew every fighter personally. When we started this thing fighters were at my house for the holidays and shit like that, but now I walk around and I don't know half the people who are working for us. That's crazy to me, but that's the reality of where things are because we've grown so big so quickly.

"Everywhere I go all over the world people come up to me and tell me their lifelong dream is to work for the UFC and have no idea how thankless this job is. We hire badasses who know what they have to do and go in and get the job done. They do one great job and then it's on to the next. There isn't time for a pat on the back or 'Hey nice job' because we are moving at 100 mph; moving from event to event to event at a crazy pace.

"In all honesty the only time anyone probably hears anything is when they fuck shit up, and that's not the type of attention you want," he added. "But I know the people we have working for us are the best of the best because the results speak for themselves. Our company continues to grow and we are consistently making great hires who come in and knock it out of the park for us. It takes a lot of great people doing a lot of great things to accomplish what we've accomplished, and I don't think that is something too many people understand."

I walked out of the interview feeling like I'd launched a shot over the left field wall at Wrigley, and when I started receiving texts from UFC PR members who spoke with White following our conversation, I knew the bomb I'd launched into the stands was going to make SportsCenter's Top 10 that night. Apparently White was impressed on a personal level at how that interview had played out, and knowing I'd turned a long-sought after conversation with a man who has been interviewed tens of thousands of times into a memorable one was an excellent payoff for me personally.

The interview would run a few days later, but due to one of the senior writers becoming angered he wasn't granted that time with Dana White, my inclusion in the space reserved for lead writers on the site was revoked. Of course I would be told a fellow writer's scorn wasn't the reason, and the eventual removal of the secluded blog space was rapidly approaching, but I knew the score, just as I knew the blog space would still continue.

Nearly two years later, said space is still intact, and the writer whose name isn't worth mentioning is still scorning away behind the scenes. Not that I have a care for that because I can't comprehend why anyone would allow that level of negativity into their lives, but such is the way of things in the world of digital sports media. That's a lesson I would learn the hard way.

Chapter 12

Real Talk

February came and went and I kept my promises to my children that dad would be home for the entire month. The weather outside prevented any grand family adventures, but spending that precious time without distraction strengthens bonds and gives children and parent alike that sense of calm in knowing that everything in their little worlds are being navigated smoothly. It provides them the warm sense of safety and comfort in knowing their father is truly plugged in and there for anything they may need.

Time passed lovingly and easy, but it was measured nonetheless. The second installment of the road trip was quickly approaching on the horizon. Since the first run had been a success, the next trip was going bigger and would include many more stops along the way. On the fighter's side of things, those who read along with my initial go or spoke to their peers who had been featured were more than up for me rolling through their gyms.

I knew that would be the case if I did things the right way, and the amount of invitations I received while setting up the schedule had things shaping up to be a good bit of adventure. The opening leg of the project provided many crucial lessons—tips as to what worked and didn't in relation to the audience—and I had a similar feeling as I imagined those drivers who got out to walk across the bricks leading up to the wild run at the Indianapolis Motor Speedway held.

The decision was already made to go west, but I was happy to know I wouldn't be making the stretch from Indy to Albuquerque again behind the wheel. Flying out to the brush and gray rocks of New Mexico would take a large chunk of stress off of the start of the project, and hopefully keep me from burning out as quickly this time around. Since Butta was heading down with Matt Mitrione to train at Blackzilians, he wasn't going to make the trip, and this made flying out to start in the "Berque" that much more appealing.

I was less than a week away from launching out when the pain in my kidneys returned. Initially I feared it was another stone, but when the stabbing and shooting sensations never arrived, I was relieved but anxious because of what I had on deck. The last thing I wanted was to get two thousand miles away from home and have my body break down into some unknown mess that I couldn't get help for. So I decided to schedule an appointment with my primary care physician.

Or at least attempted to go that route, but since I couldn't get in for a few more weeks, I decided to head back to the ER where they had treated my previous situation. Once there I was shocked to find out what the earlier scan had revealed in addition to the kidney stones. From the doctor's best guess, somewhere over the past year, some sort of spinal infection had set in and ate away at the gel-like tissue in the discs between the lower vertebrae.

The day of my son's birthday in 2012, I had been the recipient of a side-impact collision due to two other vehicles smashing into one another in an intersection just outside of my subdivision. The Ford Explorer that was initially hit then caromed off and belted into the driver's side of my car that was sitting still at the stoplight. Fortunately I wasn't badly injured, but the impact knocked my hips slightly out of place. I did physical therapy and whatnot, but I'd be lying if I said it was a process I had taken seriously, because my body wasn't hurting.

That was a mistake in hindsight as the scrambled heap of that day worked itself out into serious situation in my lower back. Epidurals plugged into my spine would be needed, nerves burned off and countless hours spent in traction, but that would all come in the future. There was no time to get anything fixed beyond the tic-tac box sound of rattling pills in a bottle that assured any amount of driving or sitting in a car wouldn't stop sleep from coming to call.

All of that tangled mess got pushed to the backseat with the force of a third grader shoving a classmate out of the swing line once the road trip resumed, and I landed back in Albuquerque with just enough time to catch a quick shower and hit the couch. In the two months that had passed, Scully moved to the opposite side of town and had brand new digs for me to flop at for a night before we shoved off west.

He had to run a few errands before we jumped up to Jackson's for a media day situation, and when I came out of the bathroom my head was swirling from the flight and the lack of sleep from the previous night filled with anticipation. I had to be at the airport by 4:00 AM and my wife had kicked me out of bed twice because of my squirming. All I could think about were the endless white stripes of the highway and the thin Albuquerque air as I tried to close my eyes and curb my composure toward sleep.

I sat down on Scully's couch and cracked open the backdoor that led to his back patio. The cool breeze of March in the desert was soothing. Besides a nice steady rainfall on a gray day, a long cool breeze was the stuff dreams were made of in my mind. I laid back and closed my eyes, but sleep would never arrive in that window. And that was okay by me.

We swung up to Jackson's where the who's who of MMA media was gathered for the event. With a collection of big names from the team stable all drawing close to scheduled bouts, the UFC thought it best to assemble the fighters involved for the media to interview at the gym. I thought it was a convenient move for all parties involved, but judging from the negativity flooding down my Twitter feed, I could tell that sentiment was not shared across the board in the insulated MMA bubble.

And that, sadly enough, was truly par for the course.

The painful truth about operating in the MMA media world is that jealousy and envy are everywhere. Those who have made it to a place where they can earn a decent living typically refuse to step back and help those hungry upstarts who are looking to do the same. There is also a lot of glad-handing and smiles when individuals cross paths, but the niceties disintegrate once said parties have gone their separate ways.

Drama and things of that nature have just never been my way, and I always kept a mental tally when I heard flip-flopping of this nature transpire. As for the media day in Albuquerque, the outliers in MMA media complained about who was there, and many suggested those who were had been hand-picked by the UFC because they would write favorable stories. I laughed at this notion because there was no doubt in my mind any single one of those pulpit thumping journo types would have been on the first flight to New Mexico had their news outlet offered to send them on the trip.

My arrival to Albuquerque for the road trip happened to line up with that specific date, and was the sole reason I was even in attendance. There was a swarm of fighters bouncing from space to space as media members put them in front of cameras for their respective outlets one after the next, and in situations like that there just isn't much freedom or space to get down to the real talk I was looking for.

Instead, I simply kicked around toward the back of the gym and caught a few quotes for stories I would need to write when their individual fight weeks approached. In that regard I was able to get a ton of necessary material, but not much in the way of this bigger thing I was chasing. I sat back and watched as my peers shuffled and stumbled to get time with a veteran like Diego Sanchez or wait 30 minutes until Jon Jones could make time for a five minute spot, and it was gratitude I found in those moments because I never allowed myself to be pigeonholed into those constructs.

Had I done plenty of pre-fight interviews in the past? Will I do plenty more before I'm gone? Sure thing…but my body of work afforded an air of non-requirement to which I was grateful for.

Later that afternoon I joined Vallie-Flagg and Gibson for lunch downtown, and it was there Ike took notice to my ongoing situation. He first asked about the kidney stones because he'd seen a post on social media about that, but it was the sound of my voice that tipped him that I was on a medical schedule.

"You alright with all that?" he asked as he leaned back in his chair in a manner that was at the same time sincere and non-threatening.

It took a moment for me to realize exactly what he was chipping away at, but once I located the cause for his inquiry, I felt a sense of relief. Throughout the time I'd known Ike we had gotten to know one another on a personal level, and our talks revealed that we both had our bouts with darker times in the past. Perhaps it was a common thread, perhaps it wasn't, but people who have walked those roads to find brighter days are never too far away from where the shadows initially fell that pulled them under.

"Yeah, brother," I replied. "This back thing is just out of control and life doesn't slow down because my body isn't keeping up to speed."

"Oh, you don't think I know that?" he laughed rubbing his beard then folding his hands on the table in front of him. "It's easy to get focused on this bigger thing and lose track of yourself in the process. It happens much quicker when that bigger thing involves getting punched in the face 100 times before getting your hand raised like you see in your dreams. I'm just checking in."

Over his shoulder I could see Gibson walking back from the food counter with a tray full of fixings, so I decided to quell the conversation for now. I nodded to Ike to assure him that everything was copacetic on my side of the table, and a few minutes later we were back to busting jokes about the crazy sport we all loved and lived in. I sat there looking at them both, Gibson with his solid hair game and good natured presence, Ike with his wild eyes and contagious laugh and knew these two men would be my friends for years to come.

I knew this because there was a wealth of humanity in both, and I've never been wrong in my life when tracking down other good people.

The desert sun would eventually submit to the spacious and brilliant stars of the Southwestern sky, and I accompanied Ike and a few other Jackson's fighters to a watering hole/sports bar to chill out for a bit. Flyweight powerhouse John Dodson was once again holding court, and I found myself wondering why his natural charisma never seemed to translate or connect with fight fans.

While no one would ever doubt Dodson's athletic gifts or ability to salt fools inside the Octagon at will, most fans seemed to bristle at his smile and antics in and out of the cage. That night I watched him crack jokes and talk shop with the rest of his cohorts, and found myself wishing—for his sake—those people who tune in and criticize every ounce of anything with the letters UFC attached to it could get a look at the man I was talking to right now.

Things remained on the chill level until a few locals toward the back of the bar in the pool room got word there were a few UFC fighters hanging out in the next room. These grumblings arrived courtesy of the cocktail waitress who mentioned to Ike there were a few dudes in the back talking shit. Dodson rolled his eyes at the thought but no sooner did his eyes return back to the menu he was looking at did they sharpen. His body language didn't shift from relaxed even a smidge, but I could see he was ready to go if all hell broke loose.

Fortunately for the drunkards in the back room, nothing jumped off, and before long Ike was driving me back to Scully's house where a decent night of sleep was waiting for me. The drive back was filled with gym stories that included an unwashed bag of shorts and an unfortunate digestive issue while training.

"You can't stop when you're trying to fight off being swept," he laughed as he leaned over the center counsel just slightly, as if to drive home the visual.

"I think there are some things worth stopping for and that's one of them."

"Well I couldn't," he returned. "Dude couldn't hear me because his gi was covering my face."

His small car filled with laughter at the thought of poor Vallie-Flagg, whose ground game had always been a weakness, suffering a fate no person over the age of four should suffer, all because he was too focused on the work at hand. In some ways that was his determination showing through. In others it was his lunch.

Jokes and stories of varying morality were exchanged throughout the drive, but we also homed in a more grim issue between us. Although Ike and I had only known one another for the better part of a year, our respective battles with darker demons had been a common bond. We had both enjoyed lengthy periods of sobriety before crushing relapses, and it takes someone having gone through that misery and shame to truly reach another.

There is simply no bullshit that will float among those in recovery because shading the truth is an art form addicts are well versed in. Even though one may have left whatever vice had plagued them long in the dust of the past, the sting of disappointing steps taken to secure said vice never completely fades away. Therefore when Ike asked the one question the majority of people in my inner circle had always failed to ask me, I knew a straight shot would be the only possible route to travel.

"I know you have a lot going on, but how are you really doing?" he pushed as we cut through the deadness that becomes Albuquerque after dark.

"I'm fine on the level," I replied attempting not to sound like it was a stock return. "That said, this back situation is actually pretty terrifying."

Having dealt with back and neck issues of his own, Ike nodded to show agreement, but I knew I needed to keep peeling away in order to make the conversation as real as intended.

"It almost feels like some strange karma shit coming back around," I continued. "There I was way back when messing around with something that caused me a tremendous amount of problems only to have it rear back around almost a decade later as something I need just to move my legs in the morning. It's like jumping into a pool that nearly drowned you once and trying to convince yourself you can swim this time, you know?"

"I know exactly what you mean," Ike said with a sigh as the car pulled to a stop at a red light. "The biggest thing is just being accountable, man. We get into these grooves and patterns where for some reason we just stop talking because we either don't want to hear what anyone else has to say or we think we can handle it."

From the look on his face I could tell he was doing his best not to sound so 12 Step-ish, but the point he was making still resonated.

"As long as you have someone to talk to and you utilize that then half the battle is already won," he finished as he pressed the gas pedal down and the tiny shit box roared off down the boulevard. "There is going to be a lot of driving and stress on this road trip, and I just want you to know you can call me at anytime, brother."

I thanked him for his commitment and friendship and found comfort in knowing such a topic most would never come close to understanding would be something I could bring to him if things ever sunk to reaching that point. And in those moments the constructs of a job pale in comparison to the real life matter at hand. Two minutes ago we were joking about him shitting his pants during a jiu-jitsu practice and moments later he's throwing out the life preserver just in case it was ever needed.

It would be, and his guidance and insight would be crucial deep into the year when desolation and confusion blanketed my snow covered and frozen shell, but on that night on the somber and silent streets of "The Land of Enchantment," it was just nice to hear.

Chapter 13

Kingsbu Ayahuasca

The second stop of the second leg brought us once again to Phoenix, but this time Gilbert and Power MMA was the destination. I was immediately struck by the beauty and appeal of the suburb, as palm trees lined the medians before fading into one open-air mall after the next. It was as if someone decided to take all the pretty parts of Las Vegas and pressure washed the filth off before opening the gates for people to settle in.

Scully and I pulled into the parking lot where recently retired UFC veteran turned head coach at Power, Aaron Simpson, was waiting to greet us. I had worked with Simpson plenty during his time competing inside the Octagon and had managed to build up a solid rapport with the former Arizona State wrestling standout. Anyone who had ever worked under Coach Simpson had a granite grip on his full throttle sense of humor, and the "A-Train" wasted no time cutting a few jokes at our expense.

Poor Scully seemed a bit taken back at first, but as his eyes floated past mine and saw my shrugging reaction as we walked inside the facility, he quickly returned to a level demeanor.

With this visit being my first to Power MMA, I was admittedly taken back by how massive the facility was. Simpson provided a walking tour of the gym and all of the additional amenities it offered, which included a huge strength and conditioning area and a basketball court that was built at co-owner and multi-time NBA champion Mike Miller's request. All in all it was easily the most state-of-the-art MMA gym my eyes had ever stumbled upon, and I didn't even bother trying to hide the fact that I was flat out impressed.

We walked toward the center of the gym to where light heavyweight Ryan Bader was cracking mitts with his boxing coach inside the cage. Since earning his entry into the UFC by winning The Ultimate Fighter, Bader has long established himself as a walking powerhouse, but the magnitude of his physical size is something that can only be appreciated in person. Bader launched 1-2 combinations with vigor, and the entire cage shook as he sat down on the right hands that echoed through the expanse.

Where at one time the former standout football player and wrestler at ASU was deemed as a grappler with a bomb of an overhand right, the way he shuffled his feet and bobbed his head in and out with smoothness showed the prototype that once existed was long gone. After blasting through a few more transitions, he made his way over to the chain links and coughed, "Good to see you, Finley. I'll catch up to you once I'm through here."

While I appreciated the acknowledgment, there was nothing I or Scully wanted to do to interrupt the weaponry that was being unleashed in that session.

Simpson told us to follow him back to his office, and I noticed former MFC champion Ryan Jimmo working on the mats at the far corner of the gym. The Canadian striker was in the midst of rolling through a few progressions of his own, and I made a mental note to ask him to show me his signature "Robot" dance. I mean…that's what the road trip project was all about; the deeper questions and the ever-elusive answers.

We had just kicked back at Simpson's when C.B. Dollaway made his way through the front doors. While "The Doberman" always seemed to catch a tough break from the passionate UFC fan base due to his arrogance and attitude during his time on TUF, I never much fed into anything in that regard with Dollaway. Much like Bader, the Ohio native hit the reality-based fighting program fresh out of college and with very little responsibility in his life. The years that filled the stint up to that afternoon in Gilbert were all about growth for Dollaway.

In addition to a mixture of solid wins, tough losses and lengthy stretches of serious injury, Dollaway had also started a family and became a business owner. I had interviewed him many times throughout the twists and turns he experienced navigating the UFC, and was looking forward to sitting down with him on his home turf. In all honesty that was one of the most appealing aspects of this stop on the trip, and after some quick conversation he assured me that we'd get that time in once his workout was done.

Scully slipped off to go watch some boxing rounds in the far corner of the gym right about the time Bader made his way over to where I was standing, and exchanged some banter with Simpson as he peeled the last of the wraps off his hands. Their manner of ribbing showed the depth of the bond between them. No matter how sharp the barb launched, a laugh immediately followed as they scrolled through years of material in split-second fashion looking to land the right shot.

The more I sat back and analyzed the situation the more unique the setup at Power MMA became to me. Both Bader and Dollaway had wrestled for Simpson during their time on the mats in Tempe, and all three would eventually make the transition to MMA. Ryan and C.B. would arrive to the sport's biggest stage through The Ultimate Fighter vehicle, while Aaron would take the old fashioned way of building up a winning streak before entrance was allowed.

The trio ran together every step of the way and eventually broke out to establish their own gym/business in the Phoenix area. And while each of the three would experience roller coaster results rife with both success and defeat inside the cage, the brotherly bond between them never suffered. In fact, on that afternoon in Gilbert their respective relationships seemed downright fraternal in nature, as it became clear they all still very much enjoyed the fight game.

The biggest difference seemed to fall on the fact they were no longer 25-year-old kids fresh out of college and throwing caution to the wind. Each had settled down to start families in recent years, and the creation of Power MMA was a signal to building something bigger when their time smashing faces inside the cage had come to an end. Of the group, Bader seemed most in tune with the larger scope of his time remaining in the sport, which is a forecast only certain levels of experience can create.

The roller coaster track that comes with having a career in mixed martial arts far exceeds the twists, turns, loops, swoops, and dives attached to anything Six Flags has to offer. Prize fighting is a fickle thing where glory is fleeting and the fan base unforgiving. Where other professional athletes have the luxury of bouncing back from a rough outing the very next night on the court or the next Sunday afternoon on the gridiron, that is a luxury MMA doesn't offer.

If a fighter has an off night inside the cage, all the hard work invested in the lead up goes to waste and previous setbacks become amplified. One high-profile loss will wash out a large percentage of love and good will fans carried for you, and multiple defeats has the potential to turn the fighting faithful into a downright nasty mob.

Few fighters on the UFC roster were more aware of how quickly things can turn than Bader, and it was clear by watching his body language those mountain range shoulders had become accustomed to shrugging off the critics. That's not to say the TUF winner hadn't experienced his fair share of praise throughout his journey from powerhouse prospect to potential title contender, but several missteps in crucial tilts cast a long shadow of doubt in the MMA community in regard to his future championship potential.

That doubt can be a crippling thing if a fighter starts to buy into it and believe the talking heads of the sport, but standing in his presence it was crystal clear nothing of the sort was anchored in Bader. Later conversation between us would reveal just the opposite in fact, as he explained how he has always been able to find threads of positivity in the lowest of moments inside the Octagon.

As a lifelong athlete before strapping on the gloves, Bader came to the sport well versed on how crucial continuous development was for success on a consistent basis. Previous generations of MMA fighters were able to ride lengthy stints on one dominant skill, as some of the biggest names to ever grace the cage forged their legacies on big right hands and signature choke holds, but one-trick ponies had long since gone the way of the Dodo in the hurt business.

When Bader came to the UFC back in 2008, he did so equipped with little more than a strong wrestling game and a blistering right hand in his arsenal. Those tools, in addition to his shocking natural power, allowed Bader to overcome a batch of experienced veterans to find victory in his first five fights out of the gate following his run on The Ultimate Fighter.

The "if it ain't broke don't fix it mentality" can be found in abundance throughout MMA gyms, and his early success kept Bader and his team on the front edge of a tide that was rolling strong. Nevertheless, while his confidence and visibility continued to rise, Bader admits the thought of a hard lesson to be learned never floated too far from his mind. Being the realist he is, the Power MMA leader knew his limited skill set would eventually be faced by something far more complex and diverse, and he was absolutely right in that sense.

"There is a tendency in this sport to not make changes when things are going your way," he said as we sat down at a table in the lobby area of the gym. "Every fight was bigger than the one before it and I was winning them in dominant fashion so the push to switch things up just wasn't there as much as it should have been at that stage of my career. Make no mistake about it I was working my ass off inside the gym like I always have, but there were certain areas of my game that were being neglected.

"My first two losses in the UFC were a huge wakeup call for me," Bader continued as he hunched over with his hands folded on the tabletop. "I hate to lose at anything, but even more than that I despise the feeling that I wasn't prepared enough. I've competed in sports my entire life, and learned from a very young age to use adversity as a learning tool. I knew the work that needed to be done and I hit the gym full force to add the things to my game I needed to be an elite-level fighter. It also helped that I suddenly felt I had something to prove, and that chip on my shoulder, if you want to call it that, is still there to this day."

As Bader talked about the evolution of his game I interjected in clips with examples from his recent fights to highlight the points he was making. In his past losses to fighters like Jon Jones, Tito Ortiz, and Lyoto Machida, the former Arizona State University standout was flat-footed and gun shy, but those tendencies were nowhere to be found in his most recent stretch of action.

Where Bader was once a wrestler with a bomb of a right hand, recent opposition had found a much different animal with them inside the cage on fight night, and far too much for them to handle once things went live. The stiffness and uncertainty that once plagued him was gone and replaced by slick footwork and a game plan in constant forward motion at all times.

Even in his loss to Glover Teixeira, the light heavyweight smashing machine had looked crisp until he was caught with a big shot, and the way his hand rubbed his chin while he recalled the fight was a sure sign it was something that still didn't sit well with him.

"I'd love to get that fight again," Bader said with his teeth in a slight grit. "I had him hurt, lost my composure and rushed in. I paid the price for that mistake and it's one I wouldn't make a second time, but like I said, there is a lesson to be found in everything."

He would bounce back in his next fight and absolutely destroy journeyman Anthony Perosh in a brutal and bloody affair down under in Brisbane, Australia. The contest was as lopsided as they come in the 205-pound ranks, and the win once again put Bader on the climb back up the divisional hierarchy. Despite pulverizing Perosh and taking little to no damage from the veteran himself, Bader would smash his hand up over the course of the three-round tilt, and be forced to the sidelines for surgery and recovery.

As he explained the process to re-connect the bones in his hand, Bader reached his massive paw across the table to show the markings of where the recently removed titanium rod once protruded from his wrist. Despite the serious nature of what he was describing I couldn't help but to bust up at the sheer size of his fist, as I pictured what that thing would look like if it were flying in the direction of my face with horrible intentions.

"Jesus man," I laughed as I put my hands up in defense.

"Right?" he returned with a chuckle as he held up his fist for self-examination, as if he too were wondering what that brick looked like from the perspective of the unfortunate souls whose nights had been ruined by it. "It feels good though. I just started hitting full force with it again and haven't had any problems at all."

Knowing a fighter's hands are the keys to their success, I assured him I understood the weight of the situation, and replayed the thunder sound of the mitts he was cracking earlier as further proof his haymaker was intact.

"Even with my hand off limits, I was still in the gym though," he continued. "I'm at this place mentally where I'm so tuned in and focused on my career. I wasn't about to allow the rest of my game to slip because of the injury. I was back in here right away following my surgery and worked everything else but my hand. I'm going after that belt and feel now more than ever that it's my time. I'm coming into my prime, and it's going to take more than a robot hand to slow me down," he laughed.

Just as Bader held up his hand to take another look in the sun that shone through the glass entry doors, in walked the large, fresh from the surf, tank top and board shorts adorned Kyle Kingsbury. There wasn't a drop of conversation exchanged between any of us before both Bader and Kingsbury started laughing. Strange as an interaction like that would seem to most, I chalked it up to the natural reaction that comes when their paths cross, like two people who have a wealth of party memories and inside jokes between them.

Kingsbury's flip flops scuffled across the floor as he walked over to join us, and I instantly found myself fascinated by the strength of his base tan. Despite not having competed inside the Octagon since late 2012, the Arizona native still looked to be in tremendous shape, as it seemed it was taking all his tank top had to give in order to cling onto his broad shoulders. Bader turned in his direction with a visible eagerness to hear what Kingsbury had to say, and that anticipation was quickly validated as the American Kickboxing Academy product jumped into a story from his weekend back home.

Much like Bader, "Kingsbu" had come to the UFC through The Ultimate Fighter, but hadn't quite enjoyed the same level of success. As a former football player turned mixed martial artist, there was plenty Kingsbury needed to add in order to round out his game, and those holes had been exploited on numerous occasions. That said, what he may have lacked in versatility, he more than made up for in overall toughness as his rock-solid reputation for bringing the rock n' roll inside the cage was one earned in blood and broken bones.

A nasty orbital bone break and the lingering after effects were the reason for his extended absence from competition, and from the tone of his voice those elements weren't something he was willing to simply glaze over and hurry back to the cage.

"I'd be making love to my girl and my nose would just start bleeding out of nowhere," Kingsbury explained in a voice that was part shock part eternal jokester. "She has blood pouring down on her so she's freaking out and I'm freaking out because I have no clue what the hell was going on. Shit like that started to happen all the time following my orbital bone situation, and that's not okay. Something is wrong when you start randomly bleeding and gushing blood."

With the girl in question being the lovely Natasha Wicks, his story somehow managed to avoid seeming as gross as it should have seemed in the moment, and the tinges of humor he sprinkled in certainly helped to keep his recollection on the lighter side of tragedy. Bader shook his head in laughter as he stood up and walked back to gather up his equipment while Kingsbury pulled up next to me and started asking about the road trip. His interest in my wanderings came off as genuine as the vibrant fire of his free spirit was amplified by the crazy mop of hair he was rocking. The veteran slugger simply loved some good travel and wanted to know the details of where I'd been and planned to go.

We caromed over to the open mat space on the left hand side of the gym where Kingsbury decked out and slipped back into his mode while the conversation resumed. I expanded on a few of my future plans for the road trip material and that's when he started to explain a few of the strange trips he'd navigated in his two years away. During that time, the laid back chill yet chiseled from marble look remained a healthy contradiction, but there were other wires buried much deeper within him that needed to be sorted out.

In order to break through the shortcomings locked in his subconscious, Kingsbury sought out the ancient ritual of the Ayahuasca ceremony to guide him back to the more compete self. The indigenous tribes of South America had been cooking down the Ayahuasca plant for thousands of years to produce yage, which is a drink that when consumed will push the physical form into a deep slumber.

Once under the influence of the potion, the subject, or in this case Kingsbury, would begin to experience hallucinations at a rapid rate as he collected a wealth of self-improvement knowledge scattered about the warm smooth chaotic scene of the coma he was trapped within. Kingsbury described the overall transition the way women have been known to talk about the healing qualities of the female orgasm. And while nothing of a sexual nature was evoked during his time under the spell of the yage, Kingsbury absolutely returned to the realm of the living with a better understanding of his life, goals, and wishes in the aftermath.

"There is just so much madness leading in, and the sense of calm that arrives at the end is nearly impossible to describe," Kingsbury emoted. "Shit man I'm getting goose bumps all over my arms right now just talking to you about it, so when I say it was a life-altering experience,

I'm not exaggerating. You're a searcher too Finley, and I really think you should make time to take the ride. You won't regret it."

With my checkered past and my life being an open book about such things, I was quick to throw out a drug reference in a nonchalant tone, but he wasn't about to let me off the hook that easily. "Whatever your past experiences were with psycho-tropics, Ayahuasca has nothing to do with LSD or anything like that. The leaves are distributed during an actual ceremony and being in a controlled environment allows you to strip away the binding elements of your life and really ask yourself all the profound questions your busy life always allowed you to brush aside."

His eyes stayed lit like mega-watt beams as he continued to share stories from his experiences, and he locked those laser lamps onto mine a few times before I finally agreed to participate. The particular weekend at hand wouldn't allow for such things due to the frenzied schedules of every man pacing through Power MMA that afternoon, but Kingsbury assured me he'd keep close tabs on my journeys out into the proverbial ether with the solitary goal of being there to guide me through the haze.

Following his workout, Dollaway walked over to the mats to join the conversation just as Scully re-emerged from the back of the gym after watching several rounds of boxing. The mood was light when he walked up, but Bader saw a ripe moment to drop some humor into the conversation at Scully's expense.

As Bader and his crew kicked back on the wrestling mats, Scully stood before them wearing a button up flannel shirt and jeans, and wasted zero time showing them what he'd picked up from several rounds of observation outside of the squared circle. As Scully explained to Bader and Kingsbury the things he'd saw and supposedly picked up, the Albuquerque-based editor then moved to mimicking the motions with his hands.

I could see Bader's face hit a bright sheet of red as he fought back the force of a gut-twisted explosion of laughter begging to bust out. Even Kingsbury's California chill seemed thrown off by this skinny man without a lick of fight in his body suddenly trying to blister rapid-fire combinations before the gathering and seeking their approval. In that moment Scully appeared in my eyes as the guy at the party who is adamant he can hit the one great magic trick he knows, and begins to slide of the rails of denial when the crowd in attendance starts to shower him with doubt.

Not that Bader, Kingsbury and eventually Dollaway were openly discouraging Scully from attempting to rip off 1-2-3 flurries, but with the editor getting through them with the coordination and grace of two drunk sloths fucking, it was impossible not to find the disaster unfolding as humorous. With Scully being none the wiser and refusing to catch on that he had willingly volunteered to be the butt of the joke, it wasn't long before all parties in attendance eventually gave up the ghost as a jarring roar of laughs connected into one loud roar.

It was as if Danger from Million Dollar Baby put on a flannel shirt and went for broke in his moment to shine.

A few moments later Scully excused himself to grab a drink of water, and after that performance no one doubted he needed it. He walked away seeming at least somewhat keen to the amount of embarrassment he'd just brought himself, although he'd never come close to mentioning it again throughout the remaining portions of the project.

With a break in the action, Dollaway and I slipped a few feet over from the rest of the group and settled into the questions and answers I'd come to Gilbert seeking. The first thing I noticed about C.B. was how the white tee shirt that clung to him now soaked with sweat was somehow just a shade darker than the color of his skin.

"Man, it has to be hell out here in the desert with that complexion," I exclaimed.

The comment popped a quick nod and laugh from Dollaway and he replied, "You have no idea man. I've been out here for a long time and SPF is my best friend."

As he finished packing away his training gear I mentally prepped a few questions to ask him for the video piece we were going to do later on. Everything in that regard would be focused on his return from injury and his upcoming fight against Cezar Ferreira in his comeback bout, but the time we were about to spend was going to head in a different direction.

The way I saw it Dollaway had always been an underrated talent in the UFC ranks. I'm sure his personality during The Ultimate Fighter and how he seemed to rub fans the wrong way had a lot to do with that, but as a fighter he'd always been solid. In addition to adding some slick jiu-jitsu to his wrestling chops very early on (see his Peruvian necktie on Jesse Taylor or his guillotine rodeo on Joe Doerksen), Dollaway had a scrappy nature to him. He was as game as they come inside the cage, and if his body held up, he was going to be dangerous.

But his body and several major injuries were the biggest obstacles Dollaway had faced in recent years. When he stepped in healthy, C.B. looked great en route to picking up gritty wins, but jumping into the Octagon despite nagging ailments produced the opposite results. Back-to-back losses against Mark Munoz and Jared Hamman dropped his stock severely, and a lackluster showing against Jason "Mayhem" Miller shoved him into irrelevancy despite picking up the victory.

Proof of his status came when the UFC booked the Michigan native to go down to Brazil and serve as the sacrificial lamb to highly touted knockout artist Daniel Sarafian at UFC on FX 7 a year earlier. Sarafian had a ton of hype surrounding him coming off the inaugural installment of The Ultimate Fighter: Brazil and appeared poised to be a star in the making. Adding Dollaway's name to his resume would progress the UFC's apparent plans along nicely, except C.B. had something else in mind.

Following the bout with Miller, he took the rest of 2012 off to allow his body to fully recover. It was a decision that would serve him well as Dollaway came out looking like a fighter reborn against Sarafian. Where most figured the Brazilian's power would be enough to level Dollaway in the early going, not only was he able to weather several nasty shots in the opening round, but returned with a few of his own that dazed and surprised Sarafian.

The end result was an upset victory for Dollaway, and in the process he had sent a message that he was far from finished in the UFC.

"It felt like I was being set up to lose and that motivated the hell out of me," Dollaway recalled. "Here was this guy everyone seemed crazy about, and I was going down to his country to fight him in front of the crazy Brazilian fans. I know that rattles a lot of guys but I actually loved it. I know they weren't cheering for me, but I couldn't understand anything they were saying so it didn't bother me. All I could feel was the energy in the arena and I stepped in for that fight ready to go."

Over the next hour we discussed several more fights and his take on what did or didn't happen inside the Octagon. He held steadfast to his belief he had defeated Tim Boetsch in his previous fight, but wasn't willing to allow "shitty judging" to break his momentum. When we arrived at the topic of being underrated or overlooked, Dollaway cracked a slight smile and just sat shaking his head.

"Most guys would probably have a problem with that but I really don't," he explained. "The only thing I can do is go out there and fight and I fought for a long time when I wasn't at my best. That falls on me, but I'm a fighter so that's what I do, and a stubborn one at that, so I'm always going to think I'll be able to win no matter what hurts or how badly. Taking the time to let my body heal has made a huge difference and that's what is showing out there now. People can overlook me all they want, and I hope my opponents do the same. That's the biggest mistake they can make."

Two weeks following our conversation at Power MMA "Mutante" Ferreira would do precisely that and suffer a punishing first-round knockout for his troubles. Dollaway salted Cezar with the caliber of combination that would have made Scully proud, and I sometimes wonder if there wasn't a direct correlation between the "Flannel of Fury" and the "C.B. Sleeper."

Chapter 14

The Killer Cub of Palm Springs

We set our sights on Los Angeles after wrapping up business at Power MMA, but decided a spot of food would come in handy before another four hour drive. Due to the type of connection Facebook provides, some old friends had spotted my posts coming from Phoenix and messaged about catching up over lunch. Scully and I were in nothing remotely resembling a rush so I replied in mass to meet at a strip mall deli located down the street from the gym.

While we sat and waited for my friends to arrive, strange thoughts of Tijuana popped into my head. Throughout my life I'd heard crazy and wild tales of what happens just south of the California border, and that type of adventure suddenly became very appealing to me. The road trip was already an epic undertaking, but how much crazier would it be if we drifted down into Tijuana for the night.

That manner of thinking had gotten me in trouble time and time again. I simply couldn't help myself.

"Want to go to Tijuana?" I nonchalantly asked Scully as I took a drink of lemonade.

As soon as the words hit his ears I saw his eyes light up with a severity that can only be described as Vegas strip-like.

"Are you serious?"

"I'm not sure if I'm serious but I just realized that it's not all too far away."

"What would we do down there?" he asked as he laughed a confused laugh.

"Couldn't say for sure," I replied. "We would do what everybody else does when they go to Tijuana."

I'm sure the same visions of cheap tequila and the potential donkey show that were flashing through my mind had taken over his, and we sat there in anxious excitement waiting for the other to green light the journey.

"I think you need passports now and I don't have mine with me," Scully said.

"I don't think that matters," I laughed. "It's Tijuana for God's sake."

After a quick Google search it was not only confirmed that passports were absolutely necessary for the trip, but the city was also clearly listed on the "Do Not Visit" list as well. As soon as Scully related the news, a collective letdown swept through our booth, and I allowed the insane and unforgettable night to fade from my brain for a later date. Even though there would be no trip to Mexico on this journey, the thought of cantina sitting sipping warm beers and telling lies to strangers will never lose its appeal to me.

"Probably for the best," he said as he sat his phone back down on the table top.

"Hard to update the road trip blog from a Mexican jail," I returned as we both busted up with a hearty guff.

Lunch and the conversation with friends would come and go, and before long we were back behind the wheel en route to the "City of Angels." The plan was to swing through Orange County and visit Mark Munoz and Jake Ellenberger at Reign Training Center, but with the lateness of the day and the length of the drive, those sit downs would have to come in the morning. Therefore we planned to head into L.A. for the night, grab a hotel and try to get into some adventure in our free time. It wouldn't be Tijuana-level adventure, but shenanigans nonetheless.

The sun slid into the void that is the desert between Phoenix and Los Angeles, and the white lines on the asphalt started to blur and double a bit. I looked over to Scully to see if he had the zest to carry us the rest of the way into Los Angeles, but my companion's constant eye rubbing told me he would be none too happy to jump behind the wheel. Just as we came around Joshua Tree on Route 10, a gust of wind slammed into the right side of the vehicle that forced the steering wheel to jerk and violently shift into the other lane.

I was grateful to the Universal Gods in that moment we were alone on that stretch of highway, but at the same time reinvigorated by the jolt that only a near death experience can bring.

"What the fuck was that?" Scully asked with fear in his saucer-wide eyes.

"That was the goddamn wind man. Get a hold of yourself."

Funny how in moments of panic it's always the first reaction to blame someone else's proper reaction as one without cause or grounds for concern.

After another dozen or so miles of being battered by the wind and the sweeping clouds of dust that accompanied the gales slamming into us, we collectively decided that pulling off for the night would be a wise choice. Scully pointed out that Palm Springs was just a few more miles up the road, and while stopping in "The Springs" was appealing because it's a place I'd never been before, it was even more so because that is where featherweight knockout artist Cub Swanson called home.

Of all the fighters I had ever interviewed or worked with, "Killer Cub" was definitely on the top of my favorites list. Here was a guy who had been on Zuffa's featherweight roster longer than any other fighter under contract, but it wasn't until a string of victories in 2012 that he finally started to gain traction. His case was always strange to me because anyone who had ever watched Swanson fight could easily recognize his talent for beautifully timed violence, but when it came to Cub, skill was never the question.

It was putting the mental game or confidence in sync with his physical abilities, and his run of destruction to become a certified title contender in the 145-pound ranks was proof of that transformation in process.

The first time I sat down with Cub was in the lead up to his bout against Ross Pearson in Atlantic City, and I immediately noticed the chip he seemed to carry on his shoulder. Although most assume fighters are full of bravado and are looking to knock someone out and fuck said victim's girlfriends at all times, that is very rarely the case at the top level of

MMA. This is especially true with Swanson as the SoCal representative is naturally shy and beyond that trait sits a good natured personality.

He told me that day in Atlantic City he was going to knockout the heavy-handed Brit and that's exactly what he would do a few days later in highlight reel fashion. We would chat for an article after his brilliant KO and would continue to do interviews all the way up until I launched off on the road trip project, which was a special thing because Cub's relationship with the MMA media would take a hard turn over his run up the featherweight ranks.

Tired of being misquoted and having the things he said taken out of context in order to paint a catchy headline, Swanson had basically stopped doing interviews. And while a move of that nature can hurt a fighter in the self-promotional aspect, building his personal brand was something Cub was starting to excel at. It was right around my pit stop in Palm Springs that he launched his "Killer Cub" line with Virus Clothing, and it wasn't long before it became one of the most popular logos to be found in the sport.

Even though it was late as we pulled into Palm Springs, I still shot Cub a text to let him know I happened to blow into town and was a bit surprised when he answered back that he was down to come out and play tour guide. Scully jumped online and booked a room at the Hard Rock Hotel downtown, so Cub told us to check in and text him from wherever we pulled up to grab a bite to eat.

The first thing on my mind after dropping off our luggage at the hotel was grabbing a cold beer, and as Scully and I made our way toward the main boulevard in Palm Springs, we couldn't help but to notice how lively the city was on the late night tip. There were people moving about in every direction, and each storefront we walked past pumped music from outdoor speakers.

The town was alive and kicking with some voodoo energy and I dug every second of it.

We finally settled into a sidewalk bistro, and after a few text exchanges, Cub confirmed he'd be there shortly. By the time the waiter delivered my frothy glass of pilsner, Scully had already become fixated by whatever was moving up and down the walkway immediately to our left. And when I say fixated, I say so in a fashion that is equal parts amused and confused. The commonly used term is rubbernecking, as his head whipped around each and every time something female walked by.

And the amount of women strolling by us on the late night seemed entertaining at first, but eventually led us to question said amount.

"There are women everywhere," Scully laughed. "I mean it. Literally everywhere."

As he questioned why women of all shapes and sizes were scooting down the avenue in packs. After a few drinks of beer I started to pay closer attention to the packs of females who were wandering around the downtown area and it became clear many of them were holding hands and walking closer than most people do on a casual stroll.

I've never been the labeling type, but I brought it to Scully's attention that it was quite possible Palm Springs was some kind of haven for lesbians. He wasn't listening to much of anything I was saying as lack of sleep and the eclectic nature of the situation had him floating out into the ether.

His gaze was eventually broken with the scraping of chair legs on the concrete as Cub and his brother Aaron pulled up at our table. Cub's signature smile was plastered ear to ear as he made mention of the phenomenon that had up to that point baffled us.

"You guys sure picked an interesting weekend to come to Palm Springs," he said with a laugh as he kicked back in his chair.

"Is there some kind of female convention going on here?" I asked in full honesty.

"You could say that," he returned as he nudged his brother.

"What gives, man? Tell me the scoop."

"It's the Dinah Shore Festival here this weekend," Cub explained.

"I don't know who or what that is," I replied.

"It's a lesbian festival and they completely take over Palm Springs."

Suddenly it all made sense, and for the first time in my life, the fact that I had a penis made me feel like a Martian. It was a feeling that would return ten-fold just three days later as we somehow found ourselves back in Palm Springs for the third time on the trip, but sitting in that moment I was admittedly dumbfounded by my general lack of situational awareness.

Despite Scully's road weariness, he seemed to perk up in the presence of the Swanson brothers. Cub has a fascinating back story, and as my editor, he'd read plenty on the trials and tribulations Cub had overcome in his life. Being able to speak to him live and in living color seemed to put my counterpart in an elevated mood.

I finished my drink and we moved down the street to a place Cub liked to frequent, and two minutes later we were receiving the red carpet treatment because of the hometown hero. The bouncers escorted us to a private V.I.P. area in the outdoor section, then was kind enough to ask Cub if he wanted him to bring any girls by for our group.

"I know you're married so I know your answer but what about your friend?" Cub asked as he pointed in the direction of a star-struck Scully.

"I think he's cool with just hanging, but tell the big man I'll take a few beers."

Two minutes later a bucket of cold refreshments were delivered to our table and we jumped into conversation about the trip. When it came to the deeper conversation and elements about the fight game, Cub was a top-notch subject. Even with his relative shyness, the grittier elements of conflict and refined technique were topics he could work with ease. The scars on his face were earned and paid for with drive and passion, and I could always sense there was something much larger than victory or a payday he was chasing.

"There is something in adversity and how you deal with it that teaches you about yourself," he offered across the glass table top that encased a high-dollar fire pit. "I've been through a lot in life, and even more in the fight game, but there are gut-check moments where self-discovery happens. You can have all the tools in the world to be successful, but if you don't believe in yourself then it all falls apart. And it doesn't matter how many people tell you that you're capable or gifted, because once doubt sets in then you've already lost."

As I sat listening to him slice into the deeper realms of the fight psyche, I asked about some of the fights where he'd come up short. In my time working with fighters, I'd seen very few who didn't treat their losses like the plague, but Swanson wasn't of that variety. He talked in depth about his disappointing losses to Jose Aldo and Ricardo Lamas like the pivotal moments they were, and didn't shy away from what those setbacks did to him in the moment.

"I still, to this day, get jackassess on Twitter throwing the Aldo fight at me," he sighed as he sat rubbing the stubble on his chin. "That fight has never left my mind, and I use it every day as motivation. I mean look man, I'm chasing down this dude right now begging for the title shot the UFC has promised me, and the last time I was in there with him he ran right through me. How many people would want to fight someone again after their first fight ended the way that one did? Nobody, but here I am begging for it."

He continued to talk and I could tell he was dead serious about the pursuit of Aldo and what it meant for him in his mind, because the man who fell in under 10 seconds back in the little blue cage of the WEC was not the man sitting before me that night. The self-belief and confidence he spoke of minutes earlier had created a different kind of monster, and that monster was settling fools left and right inside the Octagon and doing so in poetically violent fashion.

"Beautiful destruction," he clarified when I made mention of his penchant for dismantling dangerous opposition with unorthodox techniques. "I call it beautiful destruction."

"You know I've heard rumors that George Roop's mouthpiece still hasn't landed and it's hovering in space over Lake Michigan right now."

The comment got a chuckle out of him, but in typical Cub fashion, he downplayed the moment. "Ah George is a good dude and I hated to make him look that bad, but I needed that win. I'm glad he was okay."

I was about to delve deeper into the finer points of hitting a man so hard his mouthpiece goes flying 20 feet away, but he swerved back into the earlier topic of triumphing over obstacles.

"Leaning into adversity isn't a natural reaction but it's absolutely necessary," he exclaimed. "Most people want to turtle up and duck and run when things start to go south in life, and you see it all the time in the fight game. People are different when things are going their way in there but become a completely different fighter when their opponent suddenly has the upper hand. You start to quit on yourself and that's the beginning of the end. I've faced adversity my entire life, and I've developed the ability to lean into it. The storm is coming, and it's how you react that is going to show you what you really have inside.

"There was a time when I didn't know what I had inside, but I came face to face with that. It wasn't easy, and it took some dark times to bring me to where I am now. I probably shouldn't even be alive right now to be honest with you, but I had the courage to dig deep and find my way through and that changed everything. Now I have a fulfilling life, and even when my days of fighting inside the cage are over, I'm still going to be able to pass that positivity onto others. That's what life is all about for me. Do I want a title and all the respect I believe I deserve? Sure I do, but there are other things far more important than money, fame, and recognition."

And just when our conversation was at its peak and ready to turn the corner, where I could touch the soul of who Cub Swanson was as both a man and fighter, the sound of ruckus kicked up from the other V.I.P. area directly across from us. What began with the crash of breaking glasses immediately turned into laughter as none other than comedian Andy Dick was standing on a chair and holding court for a group of friends.

Dick, a notorious loose cannon and lover of vices, was clearly several sheets into the proverbial wind and making passes and gestures at a man and woman standing on the opposite side of the velvet rope. We watched as Dick continued to get animated, and with every laugh he earned from the swarms of bystanders looking on, the more obnoxious he became. I'd often heard celebrities talk in interviews about feeling the need to be "on" all the time, but that wasn't something the cameo king had a problem with.

"That dude is here all the time," Cub laughed as Andy Dick grabbed the woman's breasts and asked her boyfriend if that was okay with him, which her companion abided.

In the TMZ "gotcha" instant video upload live streaming world we live in, I was surprised Dick was so eager to jump into a potential sexual harassment situation, but the powers of alcohol and most likely amphetamines are wild and mysterious.

The Andy Dick Show was drawing a massive crowd, so we decided to skip further down the avenue to a different bar Cub's brother preferred. As we walked and talked, there was a male and female drunkenly shuffling down the sidewalk toward us, and from their respective body languages it was clear there was a spat in process. The girl would randomly shout something back at him and the man would flip her the bird behind her back.

Our group found collective amusement in this, and as they approached, we scooted over to the side of the walkway to give them room to pass. Even though this was the case, the man made it a point to walk directly at Cub, and despite Swanson attempting to give him another foot or so to pass by without friction, the drunkard purposely swerved in to knock shoulders with Cub as he passed by.

"Watch where the fuck you're going," the imbecile shouted as he stopped and attempted to mean mug Cub in the middle of the sidewalk.

As the man stood there attempting to puff up his chest, Cub shot him a smile and held his ground. I immediately feared for the man's well being because his drunken stupor was about to evoke the Wrath of Kahn on his poor unknowing soul, and the look on Swanson's face amplified my fears. The easy laid back chill that had been present during our conversation back at the club was gone as his eyes sharpened and lit up.

I noticed Cub immediately put his hands in his pockets as a way to restrain himself, but if the man made a move Swanson was going to make sure his night ended quickly and brutally. Fortunately the poor bastard found some sense in those lingering moments and pulled an about face before resuming his sloppy slide down the party trail.

"Jesus," I sighed as my heart rate came back into a healthy range. "That dude has no idea how close he came to catching a world class beating right there."

"They never do," Cub laughed, and his comment told me that interactions of that nature were somewhat commonplace in Palm Springs.

His restraint impressed me though and would again less than an hour later at the next bar we attended. Besides having no less than fifty people come up to shake his hand and sing his praises, this particular watering hole seemed to be a much rowdier joint. There were a few meatheads sitting at the bar, while a handful of merrymakers floated about offering up goodwill and stories. No matter how chaotic the scene, it was made absolutely clear how much the people of Palm Springs loved Cub Swanson, and he was courteous and patient with each and every one of them.

While the frequent interactions permitted us from continuing our conversation, one pleasant side effect came from the constant interruptions. Since Cub doesn't drink, every time an adoring fan would buy him a beer or a shot, he would pass it off to me, which managed to get the job I was looking to get done accomplished with no bar tab. That's an excellent shake out any way you cut it, and we laughed every time the patron who purchased their hero a drink was unaware the dude next to him was the one actually putting down the booze.

The night was ticking to a close when the final bit of friction unfolded. The small barroom suddenly turned into a scene from Road House. Scully had just announced he was heading to the back of the bar to hit the restroom before we left, and no sooner did he disappear into a sea of bodies did the distinct sounds of a fistfight in progress erupt. I heard stools over turn and the smacking sound of a fist smashing into a face and my heart dropped to the floor thinking my buddy Scully had just been dusted by some testosterone filled drunk.

It was impossible to see who was involved in the fray but as the mass of bodies throwing wild punches and kicks started to amass and roll closer to us, I flipped the beer bottle I was holding around and prepared to smash. My heart was beating like a piston, and I tried my damnedest to maintain my composure when I looked over to Cub to see the featherweight contender completely relaxed on his barstool.

Here I was looking like I was about to walk the Green Mile, and Swanson's demeanor was as if he was relaxing at a Sandals Resort. The next few seconds were a blur as a body bounced out of the brawl and came crashing into me, but before I could make a move in retaliation, Cub had already sprung up to make sure nothing else came my way. The man looked up to see Cub standing at the edge of the ruckus and he suddenly found the humanity he'd lost seconds earlier.

Within a minute the fight was over and everything began to calm down. As it turned out, the man who caught the ass whipping was the bearded hipster who had been obnoxiously bumping his way down the bar talking to anything with tits since we arrived, and apparently he happened to throw a comment or three within earshot of some girl's better half. He caught what looked like a broken nose for his troubles, and before they could clean the blood off the floor, our group was three blocks away.

Nothing erases a finely crafted buzz quicker than the flickering lights of a police car, and I was shocked to find myself stone sober during the final bit of our walk back to the hotel. Before Swanson and his brother headed off for the night, he suggested we get in touch after the road trip to continue the conversation we'd started earlier, then offered to help with anything I needed while I was in his part of California.

I was grateful for the time he'd given us that night and even more so for how our connection had continued to build. Fighters are a guarded bunch, and the more Cub trusted me as a storyteller the more he would continue to open up during our discussions. With my particular search being one focused on the deeper elements of the fight game, having a seasoned and complex subject such as Swanson willing to dive into the different facets beyond the bright lights of competition was crucial.

I didn't realize I would see him two more times during that leg of the road trip, and his offered assistance would come in extremely handy further on down the road, as I would encounter a crew of hostile Dinah Shore goers and Coachella masses alike.

Chapter 15

Hills of Fire

"Still no response from anyone. Dammit!"

Those are the words I blasted in repetition as we drew closer to the Pacific Ocean metropolis on the fifth day of the excursion. More than 2,000 miles had already been logged on the odometer, and here we were heading into L.A. with our appointments hanging loose at best. Working with fighters can be a fickle thing because anything outside of training for them is disposable when it comes to keeping a schedule, and the lack of texts coming in from my targeted subjects in the city had started to dent up my typical cast-iron strong positive demeanor.

With a good night of rest under his belt, Scully was a man reborn behind the wheel and didn't seem nearly as bothered by the situation as I was, in fact, he seemed downright chipper. In my mind the thought of plowing through the traffic and bullshit that comes with Los Angeles would only be worth it if I could farm some excellent material out of the Orange County area, which would serve as a final reprieve before heading into the chasm of Los Angeles proper.

Not that I had anything personal against the city, but the vibes and frequencies that flow through that turbulent bubble had never been anything I'd ever found welcoming.

The O.C. on the other hand was like the rich uncle that lives in the suburbs where L.A. was concerned, and that area's role in the rise of MMA in general was crucial. One of the most famous fighters to ever work inside the cage was from Huntington Beach in Tito Ortiz, and a plethora of other names of varied success also called it home. While the former light heavyweight champion would have been a great get during our time in Orange County, the large headed beast of lore wasn't a particular focus of mine.

Instead I'd chosen to set my sights on working with Mark Munoz and Jake Ellenberger because of their relevance in the current scheme of things on the MMA landscape. Munoz, a former NCAA Div. I national champion wrestler from Oklahoma State, was a native Southern Californian and had been building a small empire at his Reign Training Facility in Lake Forrest. In addition to his own success in the ranks of the UFC middleweight division, Munoz had also created a home for a large list of fighters to set up shop and get their training in.

Between Reign and the Rafael Cordeiro led Kings MMA, the Orange County scene was pretty much on lock. I had visited both facilities on a previous run years earlier and was excited to see if the same energy I encountered on my inaugural visit still existed.

One element I knew would be absent was the frenetic presence of one Jason Miller. More commonly known as "Mayhem," the clown prince of the fight world was once a staple with Munoz and company at Reign, but that situation would eventually take a nasty turn that drew national attention. Granted, Miller was never one who struggled to draw the spotlight, but making headlines for crimes both alleged and confirmed was not the way anyone needed to get through life.

As we drove closer to Lake Forrest, I found myself feeling bad for Miller's current lot. The man I sat with back in 2011, as he prepared to make his long-awaited return to the UFC, was one filled with hope and an energy that was almost tangible. While his personal decision making abilities can be disputed, no one would ever argue that Mayhem wasn't quick on his feet, and the day I encountered him at Reign his ball busting skills were cranked up to eleven.

The only reason he agreed to grant my interview was due to the Johnny Cash shirt I was wearing when I popped into the gym, and even though that threw me off guard a bit, the ensuing interview was pure gold. We strolled over to an empty room adjacent to the front office at Reign, where just the two of us sat for an hour getting into some serious and straight forward conversation about his life and career in the fight business.

I was surprised by his candor but also somewhat fascinated by his ability to lighten the mood with a simple gesture or comment. Even though the only recording device in the room was the Sony digital I was holding in my hand, Miller would from time to time look up over my shoulder and adjust his hair as if we were shooting a video interview. Once he noticed me noticing this, it was something he locked into his arsenal. Anytime I dug a bit too deep about something he didn't feel like discussing, he would go back to it and occasionally shout an instruction at the imaginary producer that wasn't standing behind me.

Unfortunately for Miller and Munoz their relationship would sever due to

Mayhem's personal issues, and I knew from talking to the Reign contingent this was something that was sad but necessary. Where Miller once seemed to find peace and sanctuary with the group at Reign and plug into a rhythm that had long eluded him in life, eventually the pulling tides of chaos that had haunted him for years became too strong.

That was what I took from my conversations with those who were present at the time of his collapse, and I know seeing Miller fall apart was something that affected Munoz deeply. That was definitely something I wanted to get into deeper with Mark, but getting him on the phone continued to be a struggle as we pulled into a Starbucks a few blocks from the gym.

We decided to update the road trip blog on the site and grab a coffee while we waited for things to hopefully pan out. My nerves were starting to get the best of me. Up until that point my back issues really hadn't been a problem because the medicine and switching out time behind the wheel had managed to keep things at bay, but once my mental game started to slip a bit, so did my grip on the physical threshold of my situation.

While I continued to stare down at my phone, Scully suggested we stay the night in L.A. no matter the outcome. He had a friend who lived in the area and wanted to catch up to him in Hollywood. I may not have shown it at the time, but I was honestly quite relieved that at least something redeeming would happen in the city if my appointments failed to come to fruition.

We sat on leather couches and watched well-to-do housewives march in and out like primped ants with coffee in one hand and a smart phone in the other, and once we'd waited for an hour I decided to call it quits. It was a sad state of affairs, but enough for us to call it a day in Orange County and head into Hollywood. Of course, as things often play out in the MMA world, we were 20 minutes away from the hotel of our choosing when both Munoz and Ellenberger finally got back to me.

There wasn't enough energy in the car to turn around and go back, so I told both we could try to set something up for the next day. Scully had already made plans by then and I wasn't going to deny the man his fun, but I was mentally fried by the time we pulled into our lodgings for the night. The stress and friction of having the interviews fall through put me in a dark mood, and those feelings opened the doors for a massive bout of homesickness to set in.

My wife and kids are never too far from my mind at any given moment, but sitting in the hotel room that night as Scully headed out for an evening in Hollywood, I missed them severely. Furthermore I started to feel lost in the shuffle and entirely without traction in what I was attempting to accomplish on the road trip. Organization was never one of my strong suits, but I'd always managed to pull things together to craft the complete chaotic vision in my mind. I'd done this throughout my entire life, and the first installment of the project was rolling hot-shit proof I could do it under any circumstances.

But for some reason I felt alone and without purpose that night in Los Angeles. I feared the failed appointments of the day were going to lead to everything else in California falling through, and this led me to send out a massive series of texts to all the fighters I'd planned to talk to in San Francisco, San Jose, and Sacramento. The entire bulk of the California run rested in NorCal, and my asinine superstitions began to overwhelm me.

What if this was the beginning of an awful streak? What if none of these interviews materialized and the coming days were filled with one failure after the next? That feeling of doubt that Cub Swanson had so clearly explained the night prior was looking me dead in the eye, and I was allowing it to back me up across the cage. To make matters worse, the road trip blog was happening live for the entire MMA world to see in real time, and if I was to go up in flames, I would do so literally before the eyes of tens of thousands of people.

The only texts to come through my phone that night were from my wife and Scully making sure I was okay. Naturally I told both all was well, but as I sat on the windowsill of the hotel room looking out onto the hills of fire that is Hollywood at night, I was the furthest thing from okay. No one was responding to my messages and that brought dread, despair, and isolation crashing like one wave after the next through my mind.

Chapter 16

Indecision in the Desert

There is perhaps no place more solemn and desperate than a Hooters in the middle of the afternoon. Since there was yet to be any word from the fighters in the Bay Area, Scully and I were trying to buy some time and work out a game plan before making our next move. Rather than drive and waste gas and patience, we decided to stop off for lunch and Hooters was the only place we had come across driving North of the city.

I sat staring at my overcooked burger and wrestling with the thought of pulling the plug on the entire project. Scully had a more upbeat outlook on things and suggested we push through into Northern California regardless, because he was somehow certain the laundry list of fighters I'd set things up with would eventually come through. The thought of driving another 10 hours north only to come up empty handed again was simply too much for me to handle from a mental standpoint, so we decided to quit bitching and try to find a decent solution.

Much like the detour we'd pulled on the first leg of the adventure, I knew Las Vegas would be a solid last ditch resort. For God's sake it's the fight capital of the world, and if we were forced to head back east then we could hit Vegas again to find a few fighters. Scully wasn't necessarily hip to this idea, but he could tell from the shift in my mood that it was a crucial time to allow me to take the lead. That's not to say he didn't show contention and make a few solid points because he did, I just wasn't entirely open to hearing logic or reason in that moment.

In a strange turn, a text came in from an old friend I had grown up with in Illinois asking when I was going to be in Palm Springs again. He'd seen the pictures I'd posted on Facebook from our first stop in the Springs and him reaching out created a secondary option of sorts for Scully and I. Rather than make the full trek to Vegas and abandon the mission completely, we compromised to only backtrack three hours to Palm Springs and give things one more day to pan out up north.

Once this option hit the table, I shot Cub a message and he was quick to reply that he'd be around to shoot some video and play tour guide again if we came through. Scully had a great experience our first go around in Palm Springs, so that was what we agreed to do. There was no denying the change of direction and the hovering shadow of failure affected both of our temperaments, but it was the type of situation that arises when you constantly walk the jagged line of the notorious "Edge."

The evening was quickly approaching by the time we pulled back into Palm Springs, and Scully's zest for life itself was non-existent. His night out in Hollywood zapped him physically, and the strain of indecision sitting across from one another at a lonely desert Hooters was enough to do him in for the night. Just like I did the night before, he decided to recharge his batteries and stay in the hotel room while I jumped out into the sea of lesbians to meet up with Swanson and my old friend from back home.

Since Cub had a few other things going on that evening, he gave me a spot to connect with him later on so it was up to my friend "Little Scottie" to show me the ropes for the most part. Scottie and I had known one another since we were eight years old, but had drifted apart the way people do when marriage, kids, and careers come into play. He'd been living in Palm Springs for a handful of years and working as a bartender, so he knew all the spots to hit where the Dinah Shore Festival wouldn't be the primary source of entertainment.

This idea worked well and good for most of the night, but when Scottie decided to hit one of his favorite haunts for last call, he was shocked to find it overrun with festival goers. There was really no other option than to stay and have a drink before calling it a wrap, so we embraced the situation and continued about our merry way. Eventually the drink forced me to hit the restroom and I was shocked to walk into the men's restroom and find it brimming with ladies from wall to wall.

It was like a scene out of the popular HBO prison drama "Oz" as the door closed behind me and I was surrounded on all sides by women. Knowing I just couldn't turn and walk out without causing some sort of scene and very much having to piss at a Defcon Level 5, I attempted to defuse the situation and find common ground.

"Excuse me ladies," I offered in the most polite fashion but not wanting to sound as if I were giving ground. The jungle mentality of prison is a factual phenomenon and the daggers this group of unhappy ladies were shooting me was impossible to avoid.

"What the fuck do you want?" one shouted at me as she flicked water from a running sink faucet toward my face.

It was an intimidation move plain and simple, but I kept my cool.

"I want what most people want when they come into a bathroom at a club…..cocaine."

My joke landed like a bowling ball in mud as the sweaty crowd wasn't of the comedy seeking type. Their eyebrows raised and a few arms crossed in the background as there were at least seven women ready to throw down standing between me and the urinal.

"I just really have to go to the bathroom and this is the only option I have."

I could see logic setting in on a few of their faces but the two platinum blondes with lobotomy eyes sitting on the sink tops with their skirts hiked up weren't buying my play for some reason.

"Well go ahead and piss then," a tall brunette with a unicorn imprint on her tank top commanded. "We'll let ya."

In that moment she forced my hand and I slowly made my way through the crowd to hit the urinal trough at the back of the room. In my mind I secretly hoped that once I pulled up in position to do my business they would go back to theirs but that just wasn't the case. They were going to watch me take a piss and there was nothing I could do about it.

And that brings me to an interesting and long-suffering phenomenon about urinating in public. While I've heard other women, mainly my wife, describe stage fright, it's something that absolutely happens to men in public situations. It does not matter how badly you have to piss or how urgent the situation is, your entire urinary system can shut down if it feels the pressured eyes of anticipation. This had happened to me numerous times at sporting events where droves of other men were waiting to release the beast, and it was absolutely happening in that Palm Springs bathroom as a crew of angry women surrounded me.

Fortunately I'd learned a trick somewhere along the line about holding my breath, but that wasn't a guaranteed solution. Sometimes it worked, sometimes it didn't, and I prayed to everything good and genuine in the universe it would come through for me in such a drastic situation. Therefore I lined up to the urinal, held my breath and closed my eyes.

After a few tense seconds the sacred waters began to flow and I stamped my enthusiasm with a triumphant fist pump.

"Pretty proud of yourself?" someone crowed from the gaggle behind me.

I offered no response in the moment, just finished up doing what I came there to do. Once all was said and done I put away my parts, zipped up my fly, and hit the unicorn wearing brunette with a high five as I made haste out the door. I'm pretty sure it took her a minute to realize that was the same hand I had used to take a piss, but by the time anything of that nature could set in I was already back at Scottie's side shouting that we needed to leave.

Here I was worried about having my road trip project become an epic failure just hours prior, and now my biggest concern was not getting my ass kicked by a gang of angry festival goers. We hustled through the parking lot and jumped into Scottie's car and peeled off into the night feeling as if we'd walked through the lion's den and lived to tell the tale.

He pulled up to the rundown shithole Scully found on Priceline, and we parted ways thinking it would be another twelve years before we saw one another again. I walked inside the room to crash out pulsing with pure adrenaline, as once again the hectic happenings of Palm Springs had stolen yet another solid buzz from me. I plopped down on the abused mattress, and the green neon glow from the hotel sign covered the entire room like a haze from some neo-noir cinematic venture.

While the light was a bit much to find sleep within, I found it somewhat appealing for some reason or another, and only partially pulled the blinds down as I crawled back into bed. Out of habit, I went to send my wife a good night text and realized that my phone had been on silent the entire night. I was elated to find a dozen or so unread text messages waiting with names like Gilbert Melendez, Gray Maynard, and Luke Rockhold at the top of the list.

The game was back on, and the fires of war were once again raging! I sat in the green glow of the room and thought about Jack Kerouac and Hunter S. Thompson. I looked around at the areas of the floor where something awful had happened in the name of fun or debauchery and suddenly found my footing in the bigger picture of the mission at hand. Those literary heroes of mine were constantly faced with uncertainty on their respective quests, but ultimately allowed the road to be their guide, because a story lurked just beyond every horizon. They only had to find the energy and motivation to drive and push a bit further each and every time, and that's precisely what I was going to do.

My shuffling around must have been loud enough to rouse Scully from the depths of his slumber, because he sat up with a ruffled look about him.

"We're back in the game, brother!" I shouted with enthusiasm.

"Fucking A!" he laughed before crashing back down to sleep.

"Fucking A is right."

Chapter 17

Ain't No Party Like a Donner Party

In all the parts of America my eyes have seen, there is something majestic about the scenery in Northern California. The redwood trees seem to touch the sky itself, and the fog that rolls through the bay twists and wraps around the trunks like a ghostly tribe whose assault on the day fades and blends into the swirling exhaust of the traffic coursing between cities.

Before jumping into the hustle and bustle of work waiting for me in San Francisco and San Jose, there was a stop that I was incredibly excited to make. With the longing for family having swelled up something fierce since the dreaded stop in Los Angeles, being in the comfort of friends was something I wanted at all cost, therefore we traveled out of our way to pull up shop with Gray Maynard and his family in Santa Cruz.

After years of living and training in Las Vegas, the former two-time lightweight title challenger needed a change of scenery and headed north to California. The sleepy harbor town of Santa Cruz had always been somewhere he and his girlfriend Jess had found calm and peaceful, so when his career hit turmoil in late 2011, that was where they headed.

In regards to the aforementioned turmoil, two hard-fought battles with rival Frankie Edgar had left "The Bully" sitting at a strange crossroads in his career. Where he was once an anchor on the team at Xtreme Couture, that particular collective began to dissolve as the major players involved began to head elsewhere for their training, and Randy Couture's presence fizzled away to nothing more than a name on the side of the building.

It was a tough situation for Maynard, because anyone who knows Gray personally understands how loyal he is. Almost to a fault, his close friends would tell me time and time again, and the chance to leave the bizarre drama that comes with living and fighting in Las Vegas behind was a welcomed change. Their decision was also bolstered by the arrival of the couple's first child as Gray and Jess wanted their daughter Estella to grow up in a different environment, and what better place than the shores of the Pacific Ocean and lush green scenery Santa Cruz provided?

I'd gotten to know Gray through my work in the fight business, but it was his second fight with Edgar—the one that became an instant classic and set the course for the future of a post B.J. Penn lightweight division —that really brought us closer. It's a strange thing working on the media side of things to make friends or acquaintances with the athletes you cover, but my niche existed in a far different area than most of my peers.

Where the other major players in the MMA media world made their careers off their respective opinions, mine was made telling fighter's stories, and the only way for me to be able to do so better than my competition was to get to know them personally. In most cases a working relationship was all there was, but things were different with Maynard. Following his five-round war with Edgar at UFC 125, I sat with him and his family in a hotel room as they tried to make sense of what had just transpired.

Gray came out of the gates like a man possessed in that fight and had Edgar on the brink of unconsciousness multiple times in the opening round. As the three-time All-American wrestler from Michigan State continued to deliver hammering shots, referee Yves Lavigne hovered just a step away seemingly ready to stop the fight at any second. But he wouldn't intervene, and Edgar somehow managed to survive a brutal beating in the opening frame.

Although the case could and would be made for the fight to have been stopped during Maynard's onslaught in the first, what Edgar dug deep to find in the second became the sparks that ignited an epic fight that will stand the test of time. The undersized fighter with an over-sized heart fired back strong in the second round and capitalized on the lack of energy Maynard had to offer, as he expended so much trying to finish off the gritty New Jersey native.

Going into the third round it was crystal clear a war was in progress, and the next 15 minutes would validate that notion as each man found their moments and attempted to swing the tide in their favor. While both would finish strong with their hands raised in potential victory at fight's end, when ring announcer Bruce Buffer announced the judges' decision as a majority draw, it was as if the air had been sucked right out of the arena.

Maynard stood with his mouth agape looking for an explanation, while Edgar hung his head and carried out his belt in a way he wasn't satisfied with. In what is perhaps the most bittersweet moment in the current generation of MMA, Maynard was forced to watch a belt he'd dreamed of acquiring and nearly snatched away, drift out of the Octagon that night in Vegas. He would never get as close to touching gold as he was that night, and it was a topic that came up during a late night conversation between us that night in Santa Cruz.

Maynard sat with a beer in his hand rocking back in forth on his chair calmly, facing up to the fact that his career had taken a downturn since his tussles with Edgar.

"I was so close man and that's still hard to shake," he said looking off in the distance. "It haunts me to be honest, and it's something that goes all the way back to college for me. As a kid I dreamed of winning a national title and came so close but was never able to accomplish that ultimate goal. Wrestling was my life and still is something that means so much to me. My dad and uncle were both great wrestlers and that's all I wanted to be. I wanted to be a champion and that fight with Edgar was my chance to put some old ghosts to rest and all it really did was create new ones."

As the night continued he would talk more about his trilogy with Edgar a bit, but was never willing to give it the credence of being anything great or memorable in the way that the epic boxing matches of yesteryear he was so infatuated with became to him. In a way I could understand how the end result would jade that perspective, but that didn't stop me from trying to make him realize their fights were two of the greatest to ever go down in the history of the 155-pound division.

"You have to at least see what those fights meant to people, yeah?" I asked leaning in to break his thousand-yard stare but Maynard just shrugged.

"Yeah I don't know about all that. I don't look back on them and think it was this crazy thing like Hagler vs. Hearns or anything, but maybe because it's something so close to me. I fucking hit that kid with everything I had and saw his eyes roll back and all of these emotions just exploded in me. My brain was jumping like finish, finish, finish, and I didn't hold anything back. I tried to pound his head in and everything was just moving so fast and crazy in there. Still can't believe he made it out of that round and probably never will."

The topic would eventually shift to his overall plans for the house and how fatherhood had changed his life. Watching little Stella bolt around the house earlier in the night warmed my heart, and I could tell the way Gray melted every time she looked up at him that he'd found something greater in his life beyond fighting. And that was another element of where the bond between him and I grew deeper. In the years we'd known one another he moved into the role of Godfather for my own son, and Gray's influence on Atticus was a major reason my son started wrestling.

Even though he was still in the junior stages of learning the sport, Gray would call and talk to Atticus from time to time about wrestling and text me before his tournaments to make sure I sent video of Atticus's matches afterwards. Gestures of that nature were a big part of the reason I became more passionate about a career in MMA storytelling, and sitting with him that night provided a different rawer perspective of that life.

Here was a person I cared dearly for and he truly seemed to be finding himself beyond being Gray Maynard the fighter. His body and mind were still in great shape, but a few crucial losses had pushed him out of the realm of title contention where he'd existed for the better part of five years. We'd talked long into the night, where the bayside fog crept around once more, and the lingering topic of ghosts was as fitting there as was it ever could be.

On the flipside, the backyard fire pit also served as a bit of symbolism. Maynard's drive carried him to great things, but sitting there burning the midnight oil in Santa Cruz, the fire seemed to represent the warmth he was surrounded by in this new chapter of his life. Eventually our collective old man status caught up to us, and we headed back in to catch some shut eye. Scully was tucked up like puppy on the living room couch, and Gray showed me to the spare bedroom toward the back of the house.

"None of the rooms have doors yet," he laughed pointing out the open frames lining the hallway.

"Is that some open floor plan you are going for here?" I asked trying to sound architecturally sound.

"No," he cracked. "I just haven't had time to put any of them in."

His joke mixed with a dozen or so beers sent us into hysterics, and I bid the father/fighter/builder farewell until the next morning where the lack of doors would actually keep the laughter rolling with the start of the day. I opened up my eyes to see Maynard's head and legs sticking out of the bathroom across the hall as he flipped through a magazine while sitting on the toilet.

"Doors, right?" he laughed as we were forced to communicate in the most awkwardly hilarious of moments. My stomach twisted so hard from the realization of what was happening that I simply flipped over and busted up.

While I admit that's not the normal way to start a day, it certainly set the tone for humor as the household came to life. After brewing a pot of coffee and offering up some fruit, Gray loaded up his truck and took us down to the boardwalk to get a breakfast burrito. We kicked around some loose conversation as we watched Stella ride her scooter up and down the boardwalk, only stopping from time to time to snatch a bite of her dad's eggs.

We would shove off a short time later, but getting a chance to spend some time with people I considered family warmed my heart and recharged my soul's battery enough to get through the rest of the road trip until I was back home with my own. Scully rocked the wheel as we left Santa Cruz in the rear view and made way for the bay where another highly touted lightweight fighter was waiting to meet up with us.

Gilbert Melendez was going to show us a few cool spots in San Fran, and it was coming at the perfect time. Where I'd felt lost in the void just two days prior, suddenly my love for the road had returned and I was ready to tear it up. The next two days would see our trip blow through four cities and put 600 miles under the wheels, and I was ready for whatever craziness came our way.

Chapter 18

Sitting on the Dock of the Bay in San Jose?

I've never been one to be attracted to anything for conventional reasons, and my pull toward San Francisco has certainly been anything but normal throughout my life. Although far from what would be considered a hippie, the cultural revolution of the 60's that sprung up at the intersection of Haight and Ashbury always held some interest with me, and the city's thriving diversity is something I had always found appealing.

That said, Full House and Ronnie Lott had just as much influence, and those were the things rolling through my head when we entered the San Francisco city limits. That and the time my wife made me drive us across the Golden Gate Bridge and turn around just to say we crossed the architectural marvel on a visit two years earlier. The famous landmark wouldn't come into play this time around though, as we were heading down by the waterfront to meet up with Gilbert Melendez at his El Nino Training Center.

While Melendez had spent the early years of his career bouncing around to several different gyms with his infamous Skrap Pack brethren in the Diaz boys and his mentor Jake Shields, he decided to put his focus on building a place of his own with his wife Keri who also knew how to throw them thangs, as the kids like to say nowadays. At one time the gym was literally their home as they dwelled in a living space above the mats, but the success of Gilbert's career had allowed them to branch out and find a more comfortable location several miles up the road.

Much like everything else in Melendez's life, the gym, the house, and the sharp white BMW SUV he pulled up in were all the products of hard work he'd invested during his time as a professional fighter. He put everything he had into becoming one of the best fighters in the world in his weight class, and it was a progression that required him to tap into an ingrained work ethic he always knew existed but wasn't always necessarily motivated to utilize.

Melendez had given plenty of interviews in the past where he talked about stumbling into MMA as something wild and crazy to do during his college years. And although he may have been aimless in those early days, a strong wrestling pedigree and what he refers to as the "Mexican warrior spirit" allowed him to find success at a frequent clip. Before long Melendez started racking up wins and collecting championships, but it was his time under the Strikeforce banner that served to define him.

While the modern scope of MMA creates an environment where the perceived and often times literal value of a fighter lives and dies according to their affiliation with the UFC, Melendez was the rare breed of fighter who commanded respect despite not competing inside the Octagon. Where other fighters in different organizations were laughed off when talk of facing top-ranked UFC competition would arise, Melendez wasn't a cat anyone was willing to sleep on, and that was for good reason.

Much like Maynard and Edgar's epic trilogy helped usher the UFC's lightweight division into a new era, "El Nino" and his rival Josh Thomson's classic slugfests were a major factor in Strikeforce remaining relevant as competition between the two promotions continued to slant. Melendez and "The Punk" took years off each other's lives in those wars, and with Gilbert taking two of the three fights, he carved out his place as one of the elite 155-pound fighters on the planet. If a slew of exciting fights weren't enough to keep the passionate MMA faithful wanting more, his outspoken nature and quest for respect made Melendez a fighter fans were eager to see crossover and mix it up with the shark tank of fighters under the UFC banner.

When Zuffa purchased the San Jose-based operation in late 2011, those fans were hyped to get their wish, and that's exactly what would be delivered when it was announced Melendez would face Benson Henderson in a clash of champions at UFC on Fox 7 in San Jose. It's a rare thing in combat sports to see that type of scenario unfold and an even rarer thing when the fight actually delivers the way Melendez vs. Henderson did.

Those two men dug in and slung leather with horrible intentions for the duration of the 25 minute tilt, and when Henderson emerged victorious via split-decision, it launched a portion of the fight community into an uproar. Some felt Melendez had been robbed, where others believed the right man exited the Octagon with the belt around his waist, but the one thing everyone agreed on was that they wanted to see 25 more minutes of El Nino and Benson scrapping it out.

I caught up to Melendez one night in Las Vegas shortly after his first loss in five years, and his overall outlook in that conversation was indicative of a man looking at a much bigger picture. Rather than pine over what could have been, the father or a beautiful daughter named Laylakay, was happy with how the transition to the UFC had brought certain financial turns he'd been working doggedly toward for years.

"Nothing against Scott Coker or Strikeforce because that's familia to me, but coming over to the UFC has certainly helped my overall brand," he said as we sat at casino bar in the MGM. "Not only am I getting the big fights I've always wanted, but those fights are allowing me to progress my life in the ways I've always envisioned. I have been able to start a business and put away money for my kid's future."

That particular sit down with Melendez in Las Vegas was just one of many we'd had since I took up a career in MMA in 2009, and strangely enough, he was actually the first fighter I ever interviewed when I started working for B.J. Penn's website. That factoid became somewhat of a running joke between us as our respective careers began to soar, and just like he did the first go around, Melendez always gave his time and sincere attention whenever I came to call.

My connection to Gilbert was similar in many ways to the relationship I had built with Gray. Both were two of the earliest subjects for my fighter features and both kept in touch because they appreciated the honest representation that translated in my articles. As a writer on the come up trying to make a name, those details meant the world to me, and it's something I don't believe I'll ever stop appreciating when it happens.

During the trip where Renee and I had made our voyage across the Golden Gate Bridge, Gil and Keri made sure to show a pair of first time visitors the city they called home. The four of us went to dinner and later met up with Shields to catch a Russell Peters set at a local comedy club that made for a great night on the town that had absolutely nothing to do with MMA. Getting a weekend away from fighting was an accomplishment unto itself, but spending time with people who also make a living in the fight business and not having fighting come up as a topic of conversation even once was damn near miraculous. But that's how things went down on my first visit to San Fran, and it's something Melendez himself would note as refreshing in later conversations.

We weren't at his gym but for a second when Gil told us to follow him down the street to a spot on the marina he and Keri liked to hit from time to time. Keri shot a wave from the passenger seat, and I was happy she would be joining us. As a man who has been married to the same woman for 13 years and has every intention of being with Renee until I'm no longer breathing, it was great to see a couple as strong as the Melendez's in the fight world.

The "ride or die" expression is often overused in the world of relationships, but the bond between them embodied that notion, just as I had always perceived my own marriage had. The interactions I'd seen from them showed two people who took a tremendous amount of pride in one another, and the spotlight Gilbert garnered didn't seem to affect them whatsoever.

Of course with Keri also being a fighter, I imagined their disagreements could get interesting, to which Gilbert would always cock his head back with a laugh and say, "Yeah bro…she definitely gets the remote when it goes up for grabs."

Our meeting that day at the marina came at an interesting time for

Melendez, as he was back on the title hunt after picking up his first victory under the UFC banner several months earlier against Diego Sanchez at UFC 166 in Houston. The lead up to the fight saw both men promise to represent the Mexican fighting spirit and that's exactly what unfolded when they got to handling their business down in Houston. Sanchez pushed forward the way Sanchez always had, and Melendez met him with bludgeoning shots at every turn.

The punishment Melendez doled out quickly amassed on Diego's face during the opening frame, but as the blood began to flow, it only drove the intensity of the fight into a higher realm of violence. Going into the final frame, Melendez could have cruised and eluded during the final five minutes to pick up the win, but that's not the way he's wired and the firefight continued...nearly at his own expense. In classic Diego fashion, "The Nightmare" baited Melendez into a wild exchange that saw the former Strikeforce champion hit the deck courtesy of a well-placed uppercut from Sanchez.

Nevertheless, while his body hit the canvas his mind was still in order, and Melendez was back on his feet slinging leather in short fashion. The end result was a unanimous decision victory and confirmation that Melendez deserved to jump right back into the lightweight title picture. And while he was in good spirits as we picked at a plate of calamari that sunny afternoon, he had a few other reasons to be happy as well.

A few weeks prior to my visit he took a bold stance and decided to test the free agent market, which was as bold a move as there is when the UFC is involved. The MMA juggernaut has a long history of not taking kindly to fighters pushing back, but Melendez has never been one to be dissuaded by confrontation. Coming off his electric performance against

Sanchez, he knew his stock was high, and decided the time was right to find his value in the open market. Naturally Bellator was quick to throw him an offer, and for a few days in the doldrums of February, it actually seemed as if Melendez may become the first highly relevant fighter to buck the UFC's prestige and take good money elsewhere. With his concrete status as one of the best lightweight fighters in the game, the UFC wasn't about to let him go, and they ultimately came to the table with an offer that locked the Skrap Pack leader down for another stretch of fights.

The deal was further sweetened by a guaranteed title shot against Anthony Pettis that would come following their coaching stints on the 20th domestic installment of The Ultimate Fighter. When asked about landing the bout with Pettis, Melendez was visibly stoked, but that joy didn't necessarily extend to having to serve as a coach on the reality-based fighting program. And while he wouldn't exactly cop to his lack of enthusiasm being a direct result of that particular season being the first to feature an all-female 115-pound cast, it wasn't a topic he would gloss over either.

"Getting another shot at the title is great, bro," he said with his signature laid back Cali chill in his voice. "Am I crazy eager to do TUF? Not really, but being on the show will put me out there and help build my brand, and that's what this whole thing is all about."

"What is your take on all the fighters this season being women?" I asked in an attempt to box him in a bit in jest.

He immediately picked up on the angle I was working and like a true seasoned vet handled my question with grace and poise.

"I see what you're going after Finley," Melendez laughed. "In all seriousness there are some talented women on the season and even more so because they were handpicked by the UFC to be involved. There were no tryouts like in other seasons, and I think that's going to make for a higher quality of fights throughout the tournament. Some of these fighters are champions or have been champions in Invicta so they are coming in with a good amount of experience. I wouldn't want to be in that house though, bro," he concluded with another slow rolling chuckle that Keri instantly agreed with.

After finishing up lunch we slipped over to the end of the patio to shoot a quick video interview for the road trip blog and pretended as if we hadn't been shooting the shit for an hour or so prior, which I failed at miserably because I referenced a joke we had been cracking throughout our entire sit down. Either way the "official" interview went off smooth as Melendez did his due diligence to talk about Pettis and coaching the upcoming season of TUF, He wore both his fighter and business man hat with little effort.

"Hey bro, let me know if you need anything while you're up here on your project," Melendez said as Scully and I were about to jump back into the car and make our way to San Jose. "Just give me a call or shoot me a text."

While his words were just a simple and polite gesture, it's that type of genuine sincerity that told me who Gilbert Melendez was from the very first time I met him, and I was grateful he was still the same man all these years, fights, and interviews later. That's something that set Melendez a part from so many others in my eyes, and those were qualities I knew in my heart would always be present within him.

Chapter 19

What Do You Say AKA?

"Does Khabib speak English?" Scully muttered, as we sat in the lobby area of American Kickboxing Academy.

A few seconds earlier the young Dagestani wrecking machine known as Khabib Nurmagomedov marched down the hallway into one of the workout rooms, and Scully's mind was trying to work out how an interview would play. I didn't answer him in the moment because I was admittedly caught up in the sense of presence the Russian's stoic gaze provides.

"I'm pretty sure he can speak enough to do an interview."

We confirmed that notion when Luke Rockhold, who was rolling in to put in his own evening session, pulled up in one of the chairs for a quick conversation. Since I'd seen the former Strikeforce middleweight champion turned UFC contender just a few weeks earlier, the entry into conversation was easy, and Rockhold was never one to be far from humor on any day, so he wasted no time busting some balls around AKA.

"You guys talk to D.C. yet?" he asked, while shaking a plastic bottle filled with a purple goo that was probably filled with protein and some magical key to his Baldwin good looks. Daniel Cormier emerged into the hallways just as his name was mentioned, almost as if he was summoned, and right on cue Rockhold jumped at the chance to finish the joke.

"I'm sure he'd love to do an interview because he's never doing anything anyway. Isn't that right, D.C.?"

With a shirt half-soaked with sweat and a hustled stride that pointed to him having somewhere to be, Cormier didn't slow down to respond, just effortlessly launched his rebuttal without missing a beat.

"That's funny coming out of Rockhold's mouth because some of us fucking work around here."

A moment later Cormier was through a set of doors and transformed into a wrestling coach for his youth program, and Rockhold kicked back with laughter knowing he'd landed a successful jab on his longtime friend.

While it had not always been the case around AKA, Rockhold and Cormier, along with Cain Velasquez, were the reigning kings of the San Jose-based collective. During the early days of the gym's rise to prominence names like Josh Koscheck, Jon Fitch, and Mike Swick were the superstars who drew spotlight to the facility, but that era eventually gave way to a new generation filled with a collection of mega-watt talent in a manner the natural cycle of a team provides.

That said, the very foundation of AKA's success was forged by guys like Koscheck and Fitch, and their respective ghosts didn't feel too far away. This was especially true where Koscheck was concerned. Several months before I was on my way to San Jose like Too $hort said on his tenth album, one of MMA's most notorious villains had publicly parted ways with his longtime gym and coaching staff to start up his own operation in Fresno. The split made its way around MMA headlines for a bit with both Koscheck and coaching staple Javier Mendez doing interviews to share their perspectives on the matter.

There certainly didn't seem to be any love lost between the two, and with a crew of rising stars either in title hunts or already achieved champion status the way Cain had, the powers that be at AKA had plenty of other things to focus on rather than get caught up in a pissing match. Things didn't appear to be hurting on Koscheck's end of things either.

Despite whatever labels the MMA fan base ever put on the Pennsylvania native, Koscheck had made the necessary moves to become a success in a business that crafts a low percentage of them. This was due in large part to his financial savvy beyond the cage because of the guidance he'd received from his mentor Dwayne Zinkin and coach "Crazy" Bob Cook. By the time the split with AKA came to be, Koscheck reached a point of his career where he could afford to do things his own way, and that seemed just fine with everyone I encountered connected to the gym.

Perhaps that had something to do with his personality, but I'd never experienced anything other than decency when dealing with Koscheck in the past. That said, I'd seen on more than a few occasions where the former welterweight title challenger had snapped off at a member of the media for asking a question he deemed to be asinine.

"I'm his friend and I don't even like him," a fighter once told me in regard to Koscheck, and while it was funny in the moment—and still is to this day—those words made a bit more sense in my mind while sitting at AKA waiting for some interviews to materialize.

While Rockhold and Nurmagomedov were rocking their way through a striking session on the mitts, I walked over to watch Cormier instruct his youth wrestling program, and was instantly hooked by his mixture of sincerity and intensity. Although Cormier only had a handful of years as an MMA sensation under his belt, wrestling was the lifeblood that pulsed through the former Olympian's veins. He walked across the mats in between numerous pairs of kids of various size and age, all working hard for his acknowledgment like a general who was at the same time larger than life yet present and tangible.

When one particularly scrappy Latino youth didn't take kindly to how hard his training partner applied a collar tie and slammed him to the mat, Cormier was right there in his face making him regret and understand the loss of composure.

"You can't lose your head in here," Cormier's voice thundered. "You lose your head in here with people who are working to help you? You're better than that. What do you think is going to happen out there? What is going to happen in a match against someone who is really trying to work you over? You have to keep your head at all times, because when the pressure is really on you, it's crucial to keep your focus. I don't want to see that junk from you again, you got that?"

In the midst of receiving the education D.C. handed out, the young lion had been leveled and rebuilt. He returned to his drills with humility, but continued to work with intensity that became absent of emotion for the remaining 20 minutes of practice. Witnessing that type of connection was impressive, but even more so was the demeanor of the parents who were standing beside me on the walkway above the wrestling room.

As a parent of children heavily involved in youth sports, with one of those sports being wrestling, I'd seen parents go nuclear when a coach came down on their kid numerous times. Whether deserved or not, parents of my generation seem to come apart at the seams when anyone other than them speaks to their child in a disciplinary tone, but here was D.C. raining down fire for a few seconds, and every parent down the line nodded in agreement.

It was as if they understood how fortunate their sons were to be working with a coach as credentialed and cerebral as Cormier, and that too gave me hope about life in general.

Once his wrestling practice wrapped up, I commented to Cormier about how impressive the entire scenario was, but he just nodded and shrugged it off. The sport of wrestling changed the very fabric of Cormier's life, and it was clear he was shifted into a higher gear on the mats. He'd yet to fully downshift by the time we crossed paths, but his briskness was something I understood.

I could see his mind working free of the youth practice and into something else entirely as we stood and talked, but that didn't take anything away from his polite and accommodating nature.

"I have some running to do, but let me know if you need to talk to anyone for your project," Cormier said as he wiped huge beads of sweat from his forehead. "There are a few guys working out today, and I'll make sure you talk to everyone you need to."

After a firm handshake stamped by his powerful paw tapping me on the back, Cormier was off to fight a battle of wills against a treadmill located in the bowels of the gym. A month prior he'd made a successful light heavyweight debut against Patrick Cummins at UFC 170, and his campaign for a shot at the 205-pound title was in full swing.

He'd been calling out pound-for-pound great Jon Jones during his final few fights in the heavyweight ranks, and now that he was actually cohabitating the same division as the dominate champion, the beef between them was developing some real flavor. Less than an hour after speaking with Cormier, I was told he would be fighting fellow wrestling icon Dan Henderson in May in a bout that would only serve to accelerate his quest to meet Jones inside the Octagon.

I passed by him one final time before making my exit to shoot some interviews outside the gym and watched as his brick house silhouette held a steady rhythm while the belt of the treadmill skipped under his feet. He was already 45 minutes into his preparation to fight Henderson, and those minutes were immediately piled onto the thousands he'd already spent mentally sizing up "Bones."

As I walked through the doors of the gym, Rockhold was back outside and waiting to do his interview before taking off for the night. Despite being taxed from the workout he'd just concluded, Rockhold was in tremendous spirits. The Santa Cruz native had blistered veteran Costas Philippou two months earlier to pick up his first victory inside the Octagon, and was a month away from his eventual steamrolling of Tim Boetsch at UFC 172 in Baltimore, Maryland.

Standing on the walkway with the AKA sign hovering just a few feet behind us, Rockhold was the portrait of confidence. His fight with "The

Barbarian" was coming up on the horizon, but in his mind he'd already defeated the divisional staple a million times. When the fight did transpire and Rockhold made making another man quit look simple, his self-belief would skyrocket, but he wasn't quite to that point that March day in Northern California.

Nevertheless, his confidence levels were miles above where I'd seen them on a previous visit to Santa Cruz.

My wife and I came to visit Gray Maynard and his family shortly after they made their official move to NorCal, and Rockhold made an appearance while we ate fish tacos and drank a few pitchers at a local eatery. He was in solid spirits during dinner and through another stop at a marina bar where we toasted to life a few times, but on the way back to Maynard's place it became clear something was eating at him. And that thing was Vitor Belfort.

After dominating Strikeforce's 185-pound division for two years, Rockhold finally got his long-awaited chance to jump to the UFC roster in 2013. Much like Melendez, the rangy striker with a slick submission game was one of the fighters fans most wanted to see test themselves against UFC talent, and Rockhold hyped their anticipation at every turn by calling out the best the biggest stage had to offer.

While he could have easily taken an easier fight for his first venture into UFC waters, Rockhold backed up his talk by signing on the dotted line to face one of the most established names in MMA in his official promotional debut. Fighting "The Phenom" is a tough task under any circumstance, but with the approval of a notoriously shady TRT (testosterone replacement therapy) program, the once back-sliding

Belfort had been reborn into a resurgent lion.

Following Belfort's failed attempt to coral the lightweight title away from Jones, he decided to make the drop down to 185 where he stamped his arrival with a blistering head kick knockout victory over Michael Bisping. To say Belfort looked back to form against "The Count" would be an understatement, as the Vitor that salted Bisping that night in Brazil was a newer more vicious model of the 36-year-old legend.

Even though talk of PED abuse amplified following Belfort's win over Bisping, that didn't affect Rockhold's decision to fight him in the slightest. Rockhold was eager to prove he could topple anyone inside the Octagon and doubled down on that belief by his willingness to go to Brazil where the crowds were wild and the commission sketchy. In his mind the fight with Belfort would be his moment to shine and launch him into a shot at the UFC title, but that's not how things would work out for Rockhold in Jaragua do Sol.

After an emotional back-and-forth in the lead up to the fight, Rockhold wasn't able to shake his anger or nerves once the fight got underway, and that forced him to come out stiff and hesitant. Those elements, pitted against a Belfort surging with power and confidence, created the perfect storm of misfortune as Rockhold mistakenly circled out with his hands low as Belfort unleashed then planted a spinning wheel kick. The strike landed on directly on Rockhold's chin and sent a shockwave through his six foot three inch frame before he crashed to the canvas.

Belfort would pounce to pound out the stoppage victory, and Rockhold was forced to deal with the pain of being bested by a man he didn't believe was better than him on any night.

That sting was obvious as I sat and talked with Rockhold that night in Santa Cruz and multiple times during our two-hour conversation he repeated, "I'm fucking better than him," over and over at various volume levels. And while I initially thought it was something he was telling me at random intervals, I came to realize it was something he was telling himself over and over.

Not in a way that seemed as if he were psyching himself up, but more in the fashion of someone who made one mistake that led to something he couldn't redeem immediately.

As we joked around in front of AKA, those previous hindering elements had all but vanished, but I knew the entire situation hadn't faded completely. Somewhere tucked in the back of his brain, Rockhold was saving that experience for motivational purposes that he could tap into whenever a push was needed to get through training. While he never said so vocally, I could tell he was determined to make sure Belfort wasn't a ghost that would haunt him forever. Come Hell or high water he wasn't going to let that happen.

Where most of our visits required trucking long distances between gyms, the Bay Area had allowed us to gather plenty of material for the road trip blog in a day's time. That left Scully and I feeling accomplished and our spirits high but bodies weary by the time we sat down for dinner at a sports bar a few miles from AKA. My companion uploaded the video interviews to appease the massive reader base for the sports site while I polished off a large mug of Miller Lite for good measure.

In the moments between the glass hitting the table and the waitress popping back to deliver a fresh one, my mind wandered off to the better things in my life. I was sitting at a table with Scully twenty-two hundred miles from what mattered the most to me, and by that time a week had gone by since I was actually able to touch and kiss their pretty little faces.

Sure…the phone calls, texts, and Face Time sessions served to dull the sting of not being able to directly feel their love, but nothing can duplicate what it feels like to be hugged by people who truly love each and every fiber of your being.

With Team Alpha Male and Sacramento just a hop, skip, and jump away and the sun already tucked away under the western horizon, there wasn't much we could get done in the "City of Trees," therefore we decided to make San Jose our home for the rest of the night. Funny how people always assume a career that involves travel comes with crazy nights and skeleton bones to pile up in the closet down in the basement, but such was rarely ever the case during my time on the road in MMA.

Certainly there were some escapades that would've made Jim Morrison or the great Hunter S. Thompson throw a nod of approval for the chaos, but those nights were few and far between for this husband and father of two. This rang especially true on the road trip project because we never quite knew what would happen from day to day. My lack of scheduling talents, on top of a back going further south by the day, and a mind floating between periods of sharp contrast, left a small comfort window with one or two cold beers and a few hours of sleep as the only allowances.

Since we weren't pushing into Sacramento until the morning, Scully and I took a bit of time to up our interactions on social media in regard to the road trip. It excited me that fans and readers were so pumped up and tuned into what I was doing out in strange lands. The tumultuous events that led us to make two stops in Palm Springs had taken our focus off the live blog, but that night we doubled down our efforts to make up for that gap.

Once again the comment section of the blog was alive with MMA crazies, and my personal Twitter account lit up with fans eager for more. I updated my Instagram with pictures from a cluster of different gym visits and found wonder in the connective magic that is social media. A mind as reflective as mine often gets caught up in stretching out seemingly mundane things or those widely accepted as normal, but every once in awhile that process yielded some shiny new perspective.

It's a crazy thing to know, in my brief lifetime, that relationships once kept alive by expensive long distance phone calls could fail to miss a beat because of cameras embedded in cellular phones and wifi connections. Just north of a decade earlier I had to buy a calling card just to make calling my future wife in Indiana from Illinois affordable, and that night I was able to talk to her and both of my children sitting more than two-thousand miles away in a hotel room free of charge.

The world has plenty of coldness and cruelty to offer, but it also has some pretty awesome things up its sleeve as well. We just have to find time in our crazy hectic lives to appreciate them, and even though that can be a tough thing to do, it's a necessity in the world according to Finley. It is something I'd always known, but the great big world and craziness of driving across the country to tell an MMA story locked it away as an unshakable truth.

Chapter 20

Absence

My eyes popped open and rolled blurry out into the void of darkness above my head. There was no point of focus so they remained that way, and the only way I knew I was awake in those initial seconds was the sound of ticking somewhere to my left. Panic started to set in and my breathing turned rapid as my mind raced to locate where I was.

I convinced myself I was stuck in some psychological limbo between dreaming and being awake and spent the next moments trying to unconvince myself of anything like that at all. Was I going crazy? Had I slipped off the tracks entirely? Or was this flutter of emotion and loss of traction just another nasty side effect of traveling thousands of miles and working at a breakneck pace?

A throaty gargling sound from Scully provided the anchor that pulled me back to reality as I came to grips with where I was at and what was going on. I had simply woken up, and while unprovoked and strange for my particular sleeping habits, that was the case nevertheless. Unfortunately the split-second state of panic got my adrenaline pumping and that made it impossible to slip back into the sleep from which I came.

I was wide awake. It was not yet quite four o'clock in the morning, and I felt at the opposite end of the spectrum from where fantastic dwells.

It didn't take long for the fog to lift and my bearings to return to normal. The room was pitch black which meant I must have fallen asleep somewhere in the middle of *The Other Guys*, and Scully had the good sense to turn the television off before he crashed out. Some people are room dead silent and dark to sleep people, but I had never been one of them. I could fall asleep in the middle of a train yard if my body decided it was time to do it, which was something I'd always considered as some type of strange gift.

Even though I knew I could not go back to sleep that didn't stop me from trying to lay back down, but after a few quick tosses and turns I waived the proverbial white flag and decided to get out of bed. Scully was CSI episode worthy dead, and I sat for awhile in silence looking out into the night through the hotel window. From where I was sitting I could see the fluorescent white and blue lights from a gas station on the corner, and watched as a maroon Caprice with the left headlight out turned away from the pumps and back into the San Jose night.

Since turning the television back on would most likely wake my travel companion, I decided it best to get some fresh air and grabbed my jacket before quietly heading out the door. Growing up in a small town in the middle of nowhere initially made me fearful of big cities, but after spending a decade living in the greater Indianapolis area, those fears had fallen away. That said, any place can become dangerous in the odd hours of the night, and my guard was on high alert as I made the walk down the block to the station.

The cool air of early Spring before dawn bit at my neck, but I avoided putting up my hood because of the time of night it was and to avoid looking as if I was out lurking in the darkness. That is the type of thinking required of one shuffling out for a stroll at 4:00 AM in a strange city in modern day American because people have certainly been killed for less.

While MMA was the catalyst for my road trip adventure, it wasn't the only reason I decided to drive across the country. I wanted to see and feel life in places other than my own and did whatever it took to do just that in the most genuine way possible, even if that meant taking a twenty minute walk in the hours when things hit an obtuse angle.

You can find out a lot about a place by watching how it acts when things slow down. In that sense people are no different, but a city never really sleeps, there are just shift changes for the creeds that inhabit it. From what I could tell shortly after entering the light the gas station's canopy provided, San Jose's night shift is for speed freaks.

There were two twenty-somethings hanging by the glass doors of the convenient store and they were both talking a mile per minute. Having been asleep no less than 15 minutes ago my mind was still a bit sluggish and hearing them talk sounded as if someone had taken a self-help tape and held down the fast forward button just enough to chipmunk the audio.

The man standing on the left saw me approaching and asked for a cigarette, which is something a man at an airport bar once told me is code in the drug dealing world. I told him I didn't smoke, which was true, but that didn't stop the other man from asking me the same thing after I made my exit a few minutes later with a cold Sprite and a box of semi-stale donuts for Scully to wake up to.

"I love the UFC," the man with a neck tattoo who was now standing to my left said as I started to make my way back to the hotel.

His comment threw me off and I turned around to investigate further. The road trip and the work involved had my gray matter so far out of whack, and I wondered how exactly it was the strange man outside the gas station knew I was working in MMA. I remembered the waiter in Gallup, New Mexico, so thinking the riff-raff before me had been keen to the road trip wasn't out of the question, and suddenly a bit of ego surged through me.

"Have you guys been following the road trip project?" I asked in a voice squeaky and cracked.

The men shot one another a strange look and the one with no neck tattoo quickly cleared up my confusion and tossed a slice of humble pie into the box of breakfast pastries I carried under my arm.

"What road trip?" he replied. "I just noticed your shirt."

Sure enough I was wearing a gray tee with the Octagon symbol emblazoned on the chest, and the turn of events was enough to pop a laugh out of me.

"Yeah man, I watch a ton of UFC and MMA in general," I returned as I took a few steps back in their direction. "I work in MMA so it kind of comes with the job."

"Oh for real?" the kid in the stocking hat said in the exact way a kid in a stocking hat standing out in front of a gas station would. "That's gotta be pretty dope."

"It's not bad," I said. "Keeps me busy and pays the bills, so I can't complain."

Apparently 4:00 AM was Cliché Hour in the Finley mentality, but that's all my brain would allow me to give. Anyone who has ever spent time with me in person knows I'm as chatty as they come, but it had come to question in recent years just how much was worth talking about. Small talking had been one of my favorite pastimes for the majority of my life, but right at the point where my life became interesting on a larger scale is exactly the point where I stopped talking about things so much.

Initially I chalked this change up to growing older and becoming more reserved in a sense, but had revisited that theory toward the end of 2013. The day before the last day of every year, I sit down and write two lists of goals for my personal and professional lives. When I was crafting my list for 2014, I was going to write an entry about cutting out talk for the sake of talking, but then scratched that idea when I recognized that was the method by which some of my most enduring relationships had been forged.

And while it didn't make the list, it did force me to take a closer look as to why the topic had been swirling in and out of my mind, and I came to the conclusion my job was one people just wouldn't easily understand. For starters: most people don't know or care to know that much about MMA and explaining what it is takes a considerable amount of effort, especially if that person is over the age of 40.

There are few things worse, from a conversational standpoint, than explaining something you are passionate about and dedicated to only to have the other party shrug off interest somewhere in the midway point of what you are saying. Secondly, even if the person you are talking to does know a bit about MMA, the chances they care enough to connect to my particular role in it is another stretch.

These are the things that made me trigger shy when talking about my work or the sport my life revolves around, and that is what scanned through my frontal lobe when talking to the two men outside the gas station in San Jose.

"There are a lot of good fighters here in San Jose but my favorite fighter is Cowboy Cerrone, man," the kid with the neck tattoo said as he added emphasis with a slight fist pump. "That motherfucker bangs hard."

"Oh fuck Cowboy," the other man blasted in dispute. "That pretty boy Pettis liver kicked his ass. Boom. One shot. That was some slick shit."

With the exact recall of what transpired between Cerrone and Pettis in Chicago, there was no doubting the two men standing before me were in fact MMA fans, and the idea of conversation became much more appealing in that moment.

"I actually just saw Cerrone awhile back," I said. "I interview fighters for a living and I'm doing this road trip project that took me through Albuquerque. It's what brought me here."

The man with a stocking hat laughed in stuttered laugh that sounded like a doorstop flopping and said, "Why the fuck would anyone come here on purpose?"

"Right?" his friend returned with a similar laugh. "Why don't you go to Oakland and make sure you hit all the scenic spots?"

I had to give it to them in that moment as I'd set myself up well for them to tee off. I'd never once in my life heard anyone ever say they wanted to travel to San Jose and here I was being that guy and there was no reason to explain any further.

"So you're a writer?"

"Sure am."

"You write for magazines and shit or on a website?"

"I do a little bit of everything."

"Which site do you write for? I probably know it," the man with a neck tattoo asked.

Two seconds after I told them where my work could be found the one with the stocking hat interrupted with conviction, "Aw damn man. I hate fucking slideshows."

Even though the site I wrote for had broken away from the infamous slide show approach, it was the stigma that followed it everywhere. Back in the days before credible writers filled their roster, everything they posted was a slideshow, and they embraced this embarrassment with some sort of backwards pride.

Eventually better writers and better articles would fill that space, but the stain of a cluttered past could never be fully erased, the way a sex offender can never be truly reformed. Even though they've received counseling and no longer are slaves to the impulse that once caused harm, the actions of their past will always be present in some form or fashion.

So much was that the case around the website's roster, that every now and then one of the lead writers would jump out on social media and try to defend slideshows like they weren't really this terrible thing. Moves of that nature were a difficult thing to watch and were the equivalent of pissing into the wind where public opinion was concerned.

What made it worse was how other major sites recognized how efficiently slideshows generate traffic and added them to their regular content delivery, but only our sit wore the scarlet letter. The justice scales of life are a fickle thing.

I stood talking to the delinquents about MMA for a solid ten minutes and covered a wide array of topics that included Ronda Rousey and how one of them still believed Chuck Liddell could beat Jon Jones. The latter validated my notion they were on drugs because it would take a man under some chemical alteration to truly believe such a feat possible. Nothing against "The Iceman" and all, but Liddell in his prime wouldn't have wanted anything to do with the long-reigning light heavyweight champion of this day and age.

I eventually found my way out of the conversation and back into the hotel room where death still had its clutches on Scully. I was too wired for sleep so I sat down at the computer to wax poetic on the road trip blog and would do so for the next few hours until the sun came up. Once light began to poke its way through the window, I jumped into the shower to get an official start on the day. We had planned to get an early morning start on the trip to Sacramento and I figured the sound of the shower would be enough to stir my companion from his slumber.

By my calculations he'd gotten a solid ten hours in before he eventually rose out of the pile of blankets and pillows. That was an enviable number on an adventure of this ferocity.

Chapter 21

The Tao of The Stockton Slap

Having been at a ton of gyms around the country, watching fighters spar is typically uneventful. That's not the case at Team Alpha Male, and especially so on Wednesdays.

The entire back mat space at Ultimate Fitness in Sacramento was filled with fighters paired off with one another, all going balls to the wall wearing headgear and small gloves. With the Alpha Male roster consisting of fighters all coming in at 155 pounds or under, it was impossible to tell who was who out there in the fray, but that really didn't matter due to the ferocity of it all.

After sifting through the bodies flying about, I was able to locate Joseph Benavidez off to the back, and he was getting and giving hell to a sparring partner whose identity I couldn't decipher. The only thing I could tell for certain is that this was a no fuck around session for both parties involved. Benavidez circled right then landed a left to the body followed by a cracker of a shot to the head, but was immediately stunned with a crisp return shot from the man who was previously on the receiving end of things. While Joseph was able to shake off the shot, his nose couldn't stay the same as a trickling crimson river began to spill down onto his lips.

Both fighters would keep this strange level of intensity going for another two minutes before the horn sounded and the group sparring session came to an end.

Benavidez peeled off his headgear and walked over to greet Scully and I. After spending a bit of time with him on the initial leg of the trip, we had stayed in touch and in those conversations the former flyweight title challenger urged me to make Sacramento a destination on my journey. Since the TAM squad had always been one of my favorite collectives to work with, that was an offer I simply couldn't pass up.

"Damn dude! You boys were cracking out there," I said as I backed up to give Benavidez room to get to his water. "Holy shit that was intense."

"I know right?" he smiled with panting breath as he collected his senses and gained his wind. "We don't mess around in here."

As the other fighters came spilling out from around the half wall barrier that separates the mats from the rest of the gym, veteran lightweight Danny Castillo swung by to say hello. Where the majority of his teammates competed in lighter weight classes, "Last Call" was one of the few TAM fighters to register over the 155 mark. That Wednesday afternoon Castillo looked to be pushing the welterweight mark, and despite coming off a hard sparring session himself, had his signature sense of humor intact.

"Out here fighting for titles," Castillo joked about the level of intensity that pulsed throughout the gym before putting a welcoming tap on my shoulder. "Good to see you Duane. Glad you guys could make it up here."

Castillo was another one of the fighters I had an ongoing rapport with, which made things comfortable in a face to face setting. While he wasn't as naturally gifted as some of his TAM teammates, few could say they worked harder, and that work ethic had paid dividends in recent years. Where he had been an undercard-level fighter throughout the majority of his time under the Zuffa banner, Castillo had begun to find traction in recent years.

Several big wins bumped him up the lightweight divisional ladder, and even in the fights he would come out on the losing end of, Castillo's performance was gritty and exciting enough not to cost him all too much in the bigger picture at 155. While his rise in the rankings would be enough for Castillo to be excited about, that afternoon the thing that had him jumping with the most energy was the new yoga studio he'd recently opened up.

Every fighter who rolls the dice in this rigorous sport knows they are working within a very limited window, and all hope to have something to show for their careers. The yoga studio was the beginning of Castillo's next chapter, and he had every reason to be proud of it.

"You think you're going to stop by before you roll out of town?" he asked, standing in the front lobby of the gym.

"Hell yes I will," I replied. "You think this body can resist a good sweat?"

After highlighting my robust waistline, my attempt to fish for a laugh at my own expense was successful. Every fighter in the TAM family looked to be chiseled out of marble while my shape more gelatin. It was a reality I was more than comfortable with because what would ever be the point of competing with men who work non-stop to keep their bodies in shape?

By the time the chat with Castillo wrapped up, Benavidez re-emerged from the locker room looking dapper for a man who had just spent the past two hours giving and taking punches to the dome. Joseph's fashion sense had always been ahead of his peers in the fight game, and his decision to rock a cardigan button up sweater with cut-off jean shorts wasn't something I was fit to question.

While Benavidez finished up talking to his teammates, I worked in quick interviews with TUF winner Chris Holdsworth and Coach Duane Ludwig. "Bang" had been brought to TAM-land to improve the squad's striking, and the results were showing in the form of knockout victories. Every fighter he worked with was suddenly merking fools inside the Octagon, and the overall energy throughout the gym was thick with the type of momentum that comes with progress.

During our talk, Ludwig was passionate about his craft and the work being done in Sacramento, but seemed to be somewhat uneasy for a reason I couldn't put my finger on in the moment. Two years later the reason why would crack wide open as a few tumultuous turns between the former UFC fighter and TAM leader Urijah Faber led to a nasty split.

Faber's protégé T.J. Dillashaw would leave with the coach that took him to a bantamweight title, and "The California Kid" would go public with his feelings about being burned by both. For a man who had crafted a tremendous legacy inside the cage and a solid reputation for being a reasonable and sound businessman, Faber dragging the dirty laundry of the situation into the public realm would seem out of character, but what did I know?

Money makes people do strange things, and with never having much of it to call my own, those matters always seemed foreign to me. Then again…what's ever really a team in a sport where the individual makes or breaks their own career?

It was a beautiful afternoon and Benavidez suggested we hit a local bistro he loved to frequent. The New Mexico native was getting closer to his return bout against Tim Elliot and decided for a light lunch while Scully and I put the hammer on a few plates of our own. Over lunch we talked about our favorite movies and Benavidez's love for all things Robert DeNiro. "Bobby D" was an artist that Joseph truly admired, and it was refreshing to sit and talk about mutual passions that had nothing to do with face-punching.

We finished up at the bistro and made our way over to see Castillo's place as promised. Danny gave us a guided tour of the studio, and I was impressed with how sharp the entire operation appeared to be. I was also happy to see such a good guy have a bright avenue to travel beyond the fight game, and we sat and talked about such things in the two hours before his evening classes started. It was in those moments I truly started to feel the wear and tear from the road trip starting to accumulate, and my eyes grew heavy from the lack of sleep from the previous night.

Sacramento was the final planned stop on that section of the trip, and my brain started to piece together what it would take to get back to Indianapolis. We were a world away from Albuquerque and getting back there alone was going to be a pain in the ass. On top of that, I still didn't have a return flight booked and that detail only added another level of stress.

As we pulled out of Castillo's place, Scully recommended we stop in Fresno on our way back to New Mexico. He'd been working with Dwayne Zinkin and his public relations agent Heidi Seibert for quite some time, and was adamant about getting some face time with them. I'd also known Heidi for a good clip, so everything was cool with me, and our adventure drug down the interstate en route to scenic Fresno.

We briefly considered attempting to make a stop in Stockton to see if we could miraculously coral the Diaz brothers, but neither of us had the energy or mental space to put any real substance behind that plan. Even the UFC itself never had a true guarantee either Diaz would ever show up for things they were contracted to do, so what chance did I have of locking that down?

The only time I'd ever had any type of success when interviewing a Diaz came through absolute chance and dumb luck, and none of it would ever make an article of any sort, which is a shame because it was a grand night of adventure.

I built my name in MMA media off of my "Fighting Life" series and from its inception I wanted to feature the Diaz brothers due to the feeling no one had ever really gotten it right. While I didn't know them personally, I knew enough people close to them to get a pretty good vibe of who they were in and out of fighting. For a handful of years the Diaz brothers interview became my Holy Grail, and I worked hard to figure out how to put myself in a position to lock it down.

Back in the summer of 2013, I was certain I had done exactly that. Rather than chasing down managers or flaky PR types, I went straight to Gilbert Melendez who had known both Nick and Nate for as long as he'd been competing as a professional. Gil assured me that Nate would be good to go, and if I got Nate then Nick would most likely be cool with meeting up as well. He was also clear to point out that anything involving the Diaz boys outside of training can go up in smoke in a heartbeat, therefore I should be cautious on my approach.

That's easier said than done when deadlines and magazine expense accounts are involved, but I decided to roll the dice anyway and took a shot at tracking them down in their home town. Just to make sure the trip wouldn't be a total waste if they decided to blow me off, I had the wife accompany me on a vacation of sorts up to Northern California. The way I saw it, we would go visit some friends, hopefully get the Diaz brothers to sit down for an interview, then make our way to Las Vegas to chill for a day or two before International Fight Week festivities got under way.

To no great surprise there wasn't a Diaz to be found in the 48 hours I cleared out for them. Phone calls went to voicemail and texts went unanswered as we hung around Santa Cruz waiting for a green light that never came. Thankfully the serenity of waves crashing on the beach and good fun at the boardwalk, where the timeless Hollywood classic *Lost Boys* was filmed, kept my mind occupied and on an even keel.

In this modern age where vampires sparkle in the sun and get Drake levels of emotional, it's important to appreciate the fangs Keifer Sutherland once rocked and a young Corey Haim once eluded. Damn what a film. It's cliché as hell, but they just don't make em' like they used to I suppose.

My ever-present optimism and chipper nature wasn't going to allow being blown off by Nick and Nate to sour my final days of peace before the Vegas crazy set in, and it turned out Renee's knack for all things Groupon fetched us delicious sushi lunch for a reasonable price. By the time we reached Vegas I'd made peace with the Diaz debacle, and we enjoyed a few lively nights in Sin City before she left on the jet plane back to take care of our babies.

A few days later my good friend and former MMA photographer Tracy Lee invited me to lunch, and during our drive she made mention that she also had to pick up a friend who needed to go to an ATM. I thought nothing of it as we pulled into the circle drive at Treasure Island and made small talk on some solid people watching in the interim.

Several minutes passed before none other than Nick Diaz emerged from the doors of the hotel, and I was dumbfounded.

"Are we picking up Nick Diaz?" I asked in confusion.

"Yeah," Tracy replied nonchalantly. "He needs to go to the bank or something."

Nick's eyes floated randomly around the parking space until they eventually locked in on her car and he began to walk over. He stopped abruptly after a few steps as he realized he didn't know the guy who was sitting in the passenger seat. I noticed him take stock of that and immediately began to use the universal hand signals that pose the question, "Do you want to sit in the front?"

The more my hands flailed, the more confused he looked, and that lasted for a second before his state of bewilderment fixed into full on mean mugging.

"Oh shit, he's pissed," I whispered with fixed lips.

"No he's not," she replied not even looking up. "He's not going to go crazy on you. Calm down."

She could have said anything she wanted in that moment and it wouldn't have mattered. Not only did Nick Diaz look like he was ready to throw down, but his fists were clenched as he walked closer and closer to the car. A few seconds later and he was right up to the glass looking in on me like a tiger that so desperately wants to get his paws on the asshole kids that have been making faces at him from behind the safety glass.

I tried to get my bearings and just when I thought I'd found Zen, Diaz cocked back his right hand and fired it towards the glass just before pulling up short. I couldn't help but flinch, and then watched as the intensity faded from his face for a smile to come through.

Nick and his friend were laughing when they got in the car, and it took a few blocks before the joke dissolved, but his ire would flare once more a short time later when we stopped at the bank branch of his choosing. Apparently Nick was without picture I.D. and the branch manager wasn't willing to break protocol just because he had some type of celebrity status. This of course angered Diaz, but he managed to keep relatively cool despite the man repeating over and over that he could not and would not help him out.

I sat off to the side watching the situation unfold and thought for sure Diaz would lose his shit if things continued at that pace. Fortunately for all parties involved, one of the tellers was a fight fan and had the communication skills to explain to her manager that she was willing to handle things and vouch for his identity. This made Nick happy in the moment, but I listened to the bank manager's name take a repeated lashing on the drive back to Treasure Island.

Listening in, it was obvious Diaz held back his primal instincts to bust the poor dude's chops, and I somehow imagined those types of interactions were a common occurrence in Nick's world. Somewhere along the way we decided to stop and get lunch at a Thai restaurant, and my opinion of the elder Diaz would take an entirely different turn.

We were seated next to one another for the meal, and he was quick to pick up on the fact that I had no idea how to navigate Thai cuisine. After confirming that notion, Diaz spent the next 10 minutes thoroughly explaining the menu and making suggestions as to what items would be best to make a proper introduction to the flavors available.

I was taken aback by his attention to detail and even more so by his sincerity. Due to his well documented social anxiety, Diaz can come off as a livewire in public media settings, but with just the five of us sitting down for a quiet lunch, I was able to see a much more normal side of the longtime Strikeforce welterweight champion, and I dug it.

Our conversation about the menu led to broader conversations about a wide array of topics, and he impressed me at each and every turn. Here was a guy who had been painted as the uber villain in MMA, but was decent enough to show me how to hold and use chopsticks correctly. Granted, I knew he was still the guy who was one incident away from posting a "Fuck your mother!" rant on Youtube, but it was good to know a much different side of the Stockton fighting legend existed.

On our way out of the restaurant, he suggested we all meet back up for dinner and then hit the town for a bit, and I was down as down gets for that adventure. A few days before I was lamenting the interview I wasn't going to get, but standing there with a belly full of Thai, said interview was nowhere to be found in my head. I know the majority of my peers would have jumped for the chance to get him on record several times during the stretch I was with him, but I decided to play it a different way.

I wanted to keep media out of the night entirely, because that's the only way I could see him with his guard down, and that was the Nick Diaz I was interested in writing about. But in order to get that version it was going to take work, and thankfully I had an entire evening free to set about doing so.

Our group reconvened a few hours later at Cesar's Palace for dinner, then hit one of the thousand clubs Tracy Lee has hook ups in. Everyone says Vegas is a place where networking and connections make all the difference, and there are few people more wired in there than Ms. Tracy Lee. The woman knows how to move through the hectic webs of the city, and one would be hard pressed to find a club promoter or nightclub owner who hasn't worked with her at some point. It's truly fascinating to watch her do her thing as she manages to get everyone to the party without coming unglued.

Once we hit the spastic scene at the club, Diaz went about his roaming ways. I hung back with his buddy from Stockton and had a few laughs at other people's expense. The hours flew by quickly as did a storm of overpriced beers, but a good time was had nevertheless. Around midnight, Tracy hit her breaking point and decided to bail on the night. With her being my ride, she politely stopped by where we were sitting and asked if I wanted her to drop me off at the hotel.

"You should stay out with us, bro," Nick shouted over the music. "We are going to hit a few more places and you should come with."

My mind flashed forward to a wild night of craziness that would make The Hangover look mild, but those thoughts were interrupted by the cold blade of reality. There was no doubt Nick was having a blast and seemed to be doing so in my company, but I didn't kid myself for a second that I wasn't expendable in the grand scheme of things. That dude would have no problem leaving me in Mexico if the whim hit him just right, and that was enough for me to make the call to go home.

"Well at least finish your beer, man," Diaz urged. "That shit is like nine bucks here and you don't want to just waste it."

He had a point. He had a damn good point.

Tracy floated off to say her goodbyes as I finished the last of my drink and conversation with Nick. I told him I'd love to do a longer interview to which he assured me we'd get done in the coming months. Having my confirmation, there was no need to press further, and I spent the final moments of my night enjoying the philosophical insights Diaz provided.

"Do you know why I always talk about slapping people?" he asked leaning in to talk around the music.

"I have no idea, but I'd love to know."

"It's not some bullshit I just say," Diaz fired back. "I have a reason for saying it and doing it."

"Yeah?"

"For real," he returned. "If you are sitting over there with your boys eyeing me or some shit, I'm not going to sit there and just take it. I'm gonna walk right up to you while you're sitting there and I'm gonna slap the shit out of you."

His eyes lit up as he spoke and mimicked the gesture of busting someone across the chops.

"Do you know why I do that?"

"Because he was mean mugging you?"

"Well there's that but that's whatever," Diaz stated. "If you are a grown man and another grown man comes over and slaps you in the face then you have a decision to make. You are either going to just sit there and take it and look like a bitch in front of all your boys, or you are gonna try to do something about it and get your ass kicked. Either way you lose, but slapping them forces that bitch to make a decision."

Suddenly everything made sense to me. Diaz certainly was fond of doling out the slaps, and had either done so or threatened to do so to numerous people during my stretch covering MMA, but sitting there in the back of the club, under the lights and building beat of the dubstep music, his reason for making that his go to move materialized. The slap, for all intents and purposes, was the Diaz version of the roulette wheel.

You play aggressively and you lose. You sit and watch it spin while the house takes gobs of your money…well then you're not just a loser but a bitch. And in the world of alpha males and testosterone there is nothing worse than being a pussy.

Chapter 22

There is Nothing Outstanding About Fresno

"There is nothing outstanding about Fresno."

That was the thought flipping around in my mind as I scanned the outlines and structures against the raspberry bubble gum backdrop of the evening sky. Every city I'd traveled through during my time in California had produced at least one notable feature, but Fresno registered one big blank in that department. So much so, the lack thereof became its prominent feature in my mind, but then again that mind was one warped, twisted, split, and bent as the result of weariness and extra-strength prescription drugs that kept my back in check.

The changing lights of every intersection we passed blurred and merged into the previous one. It wasn't long before I gave up on trying to make something out of it all. I was beyond exhausted, but Scully was amplified and wired for sound behind the wheel. His motives were the only reason we were in Fresno to begin with, and Scully had a tendency to get a bit animated when anything of his doing came to fruition where the road trip was concerned.

For the past few days he had been messaging back and forth with Heidi Seibert, and we were on our way to meet her for dinner. While I was always excited to see Heidi, my proverbial tank was on empty with a gas light pushing the 30 mile mark. I knew I could fall out at any minute, and putting on the energetic front was going to be a chore I wasn't sure I had the juice to pull off.

Nevertheless, once we pulled into our booth with Ms. Seibert, any worries I had of being able to be present in the moment quickly dissolved, as her natural energy was contagious. The Zinkin PR rep has a natural charisma that is impossible to miss, and the good natured vibes she put off quickly elevated my mood up a few notches. She was as chipper as ever and happy to see us, which put our ragtag collective into "aw shucks" status in a snap.

Scully kept the opening stages of the dinner conversation in the MMA media realm, and my fellow road warrior seemed downright giddy reminiscing about old interviews and such. It had been a good minute since Scully worked on the writing side of things, but Heidi had been one of his biggest contacts during those times and he had plenty of real estate to revisit down memory lane. I listened in from time to time as the appetizer sampler demanded most of my attention, but got a chuckle or two out of Scully going all high octane on the petite blonde woman sitting across from us.

My companion eventually ran out of steam, and Heidi turned the focus of the conversation to the road trip project. She had been following along throughout and dug how interactive it was due to our tying in social media platforms. Heidi had been working in the fight game a very long time, and getting her kudos for the innovative approach we took was a solid feather in the cap moment.

She also mentioned how impressed she was that so many fighters had been willing to give me their time and chalked that up to the way I handle the interview process.

"My guys all love working with Duane," she told Scully across the wooden steakhouse table. "He always does such a good job, and they all really enjoy talking to him."

Another feather added to the cap.

While extremely flattered, my state of mind was so shot that not even my ego could jump up for a quick spin on the dance floor. I just sat and nodded in appreciation, and she seemed to take note of how tired I was because she cut to the chase before our entrees were served.

"Would you guys like to go over to Dwayne's house and do some interviews?" she asked.

By Dwayne she meant her boss and longtime MMA staple Dwayne Zinkin, and Scully jumped all over that opportunity like an eager dog as soon as a biscuit hits the floor.

"That would be awesome," he replied all wide eyed and upbeat. "I've talked to him a bit in the past but it would be great to sit and pick his brain for awhile."

Admittedly I didn't know much about Zinkin beyond his involvement in MMA. For the better part of a decade his roster was filled with some of the biggest names in the sport, and he was responsible for getting all of them paid. Names like Chuck Liddell and Forrest Griffith helped elevate the UFC to the global force it is today, and Zinkin was the man behind the scenes making their deals.

Furthermore, despite being a successful manager in MMA, his time spent in the fight game was a secondary hobby for the Fresno-based entrepreneur. Dwayne had made his bones in the real estate game long before he ever heard of mixed martial arts, which meant he came to the table with seasoned savvy and lacked the unique sense of desperation that most managers in MMA wore like cologne.

Those elements topped with a bit of mystery were more than enough to entice me to speak with Dwayne, and my curiosity shifted into high gear when we pulled up to his sprawling estate. It was far from my first time being in a gated community, but Zinkin's setup was the first time I ever felt the presence of a gate was warranted.

Zinkin's house was flat out gorgeous on the outside and even more so once we walked through the doors. The first thing I noticed were the thirty-foot ceilings in the living room area which gave the interior of the house a chapel-like feel. The floor tiles were hand crafted out of marble and just standing on them made me feel like a second class citizen. In moments where the financial shock is so strong that it blasts me back to my trailer-heavy upbringing in Arlington, Illinois, the urge to drink a beer or two comes on strong.

"Do you think I could trouble you for a beer?" I asked Zinkin as I put my shoes near the door. Asking for a drink so soon after introduction could certainly have been a faux pas of sorts and made me look like a raging alcoholic, but Zinkin showed his salt by nodding and obliging with a noticeable cool about him.

He led us down into the bowels of the living area and directed me over to the bar. Much like the floors it too was carved out of a smooth polished stone, and he opened the cooler to reveal a wide variety of beers for me to select from.

"What will it be?" he asked as he handled a few different bottles and waited for my response.

"I don't drink good beer so I'll take the Miller Lite you have there, if that's okay," I answered doing my best to make a stock line not sound too cheesy.

Much to my surprise, the quip actually produced a laugh from Zinkin, and he encouraged me to help myself to all I wanted, which was a dangerous offer to put on the table to a man who has the pilsner pedigree I come from. The first drink was as delicious as any beer I can remember, and sitting beneath that epic ceiling drinking a five cent beer was the perfect metaphor for my entire life's journey.

Scully and Dwayne were shuffling through small talk when all of a sudden Josh Koscheck emerged from a door to the back of the living room. I was shocked to see Kos stroll in and even more surprised that he seemed to be in a good mood. We hadn't been given the full tour yet, so I had no idea what was sitting out back of Zinkin's property, but from the set up of the community I scanned on the drive, it was my initial though that the house nestled up to water of some sort.

"Did you drive over?" Zinkin asked Koscheck as he sat down beside him on the huge mantle of stone that jutted out from the fireplace.

"I came over on my boat," the former welterweight title challenger replied and simultaneously checked off one mystery on my list.

Upon noticing Scully and I in the room, Koscheck hopped up to his feet and came over to greet us with a proper handshake, and I knew for certain in that moment that he wasn't in one of his notorious moods. He was actually quite talkative as the four of us jumped into conversation, and said he was down to shoot a video segment to put up on the sports site for the followers of the road trip to enjoy.

A media friendly Josh Koscheck? I didn't know what to do with myself and secretly wondered if we'd fallen asleep and met a fiery end before strolling into Fresno.

While Zinkin fascinated Scully with his stories from the MMA vault, I put all of my attention on Koscheck. We'd done numerous interviews in the past, and he recalled enough of them to create some familiarity between us, but until that very moment had never been given a chance to talk to the man behind the bleach blonde locks. I was more than happy to get such an opportunity, because Koscheck had always been a fighter I was drawn to for some unknown reason.

That pull always seemed strange to me because I've never been a fan of abrasive types, in either my personal or professional lives, and Koscheck was that to the umpteenth degree. Anyone with any amount of time following MMA was keen to this, and Koscheck's track record of villainy was lengthy to say the least.

Who doesn't remember the abandonment-based emotional pistol whipping he put on a drunk Chris Leben in the first season of The Ultimate Fighter? Or using his post-fight interview to provoke the entire Canadian MMA fan base? Those moments of opportunity helped build the very platform Koscheck rose to fame upon, perhaps even more so than anything he ever did inside the Octagon.

That said, I'd always suspected there was a different version that emerged around his friends and family, and several minutes into our conversation that notion was validated. While he was quick to admit he loves getting underneath people's skin, Koscheck assured me that pissing people off for the sake of pissing people off was never really his bag.

"Making a name for yourself is what gets you paid in this sport," he laughed. "You draw attention to yourself, and once you get enough spotlight, the UFC gives you the big fights. And that's when you get paid. Yeah, I love beating people up as much as the next guy, but I'm in this sport to make money, and the only way to make real money is to be in the high profile fights."

In those regards, Koscheck had seen plenty. After a handful of no name matchups coming off the reality based fighting program, Koscheck found himself in one big fight after the next. While guys like Donald Cerrone and Benson Henderson are the current version of the "anytime, anyplace" fighter, Koscheck was the first competitor with that mentality on the post-TUF landscape in the UFC.

He stepped up and took any fight he could get his hands on, and those decisions were fueled by the formula he laid out to me sitting at Zinkin's bar. While making greenbacks was a believable enough motivation, I couldn't help but think there weren't a few people he duked it out with for no other reason than wanting to punch that person in the grill.

"Oh hell yes, there were plenty of those," he thundered. "I'm a smart businessman, so financial gain was always the driving force, but I'm also a fighter through and through, and there were definitely a few people I enjoyed beating the shit out of."

Over the next hour or so Koscheck broke down a handful of the opponents he particularly liked smacking inside of the cage, with Paul Daley, Anthony Johnson, and former welterweight king Matt Hughes being the most prominently featured in our exchange.

"It felt fucking great to crack that guy," Koscheck recalled about his knockout victory over Matt Hughes.

His eyes lit up as they floated off in the memory replay of his mind.

As Koscheck navigated the ins and outs of his career for the sake of storytelling, he did so with a very grounded sense of realism and perspective. This was especially the case when talking about the current chapter of his career, which was a far cry from the dominate force he once was. A string of injuries and generally growing older were definitely culprits in the matter, but Koscheck wasn't willing to shuck his personal responsibilities whatsoever.

He'd lost his past three fights inside the Octagon and seemed to have found peace with that reality for the most part. The only point of contention he took in regard to anything that went down over that stretch was his split-decision loss to Johny Hendricks at UFC on Fox 3 back in May of 2012. In that fight Koscheck took "Bigg Rigg" to the wire, and the judges' decision was an immediate topic of debate upon conclusion of the three-round tilt.

"I don't care what anybody says, I think I won that fight," Koscheck blasted as he shook his head in disgust. "Yeah, Johny was able to land a few good shots during that fight, but I believe I fought the more complete fight and it should've been my hand raised at the end. I got screwed and it still pisses me off."

Although he didn't agree with the Hendricks outcome in New Jersey, there wasn't any dispute offered when his next two fights were brought up. Both Robbie Lawler and Tyron Woodley earned first round knockouts over the former perennial contender, and he wasn't going to go into the excuse bag to try to make those performances anything other than what they were.

With the setback against Woodley being his third consecutive loss, it would have been understandable for Koscheck to be somewhat concerned for the security of his roster spot in the UFC, but if he had any nerves on the matter they weren't showing. Koscheck looked Steve McQueen-cool while talking about his future in the UFC, and I was a bit surprised about how he saw things playing out with the biggest promotion in the sport.

Where he'd been a major player in the welterweight fold's rise to become the most competitive division under the UFC banner, Koscheck wasn't fixed on finishing his career there. The majority of fighters I'd worked with throughout my career spoke of the UFC like the end all be all, but Koscheck had a different tone entirely, and it all came back to money.

"Would I love to finish up my fighting career there?" he pondered aloud. "Yeah…that would be pretty cool, but I can't say that is going to happen. Young guys coming up or veterans looking to get their careers back are all over the UFC's nuts, but not a situation I'm in or ever will be in. I still have awhile before I'm healed up and ready to go, but I definitely see myself fighting several more times before I retire. If the money is better somewhere else and I have the opportunity to take advantage of it I won't hesitate."

The conversation continued to flow smoothly like the Miller Lites I crushed at a rapid pace, and I believed every single word Koscheck offered up. He was dead set on convincing me he would jump the Zuffa ship if quality dough emerged somewhere else, and he would live up to those words two short years down the road as he left the UFC to sign with Bellator.

A pair of losses just three weeks apart following a two year absence from the cage would eventually make that split less newsworthy, but Koscheck was still able to fetch a solid contract despite having dropped his last five. That's a strong turn for a 37-year-old fighter whose best days are clearly behind him, but then again Koscheck has always had a knack for the business end of things.

Eventually we joined Scully and Dwayne on the other side of the room to wrap things up before hitting the road once more, and they used that time to tell us about signing Aaron Pico to the management's roster. In the world of talented young prospects, Pico was widely acknowledged as a super prospect and for good reason.

The 18-year-old Californian had already forged a highly decorated wrestling career before jumping over in his spare time to earn accolades in the boxing world. With Olympic gold on his mind, MMA was going to have to wait, but Zinkin assured us that's the sport he would be dominating in a few years. To cement that notion and paint an even clearer picture of Pico's future as a superstar, Zinkin shared that his young client had just signed a huge deal with Nike, and was going to be inking a contract with Bellator, which would be the first of its kind. It's not out of the norm for a promotion to go after a fighter they know will pay dividends in the future, but with Pico still several years away from competing inside their cage, Bellator signing the talented wrestler/boxer felt a little bit strange.

Granted, if they had the chance to snatch him up before the UFC could get him, then more power to them, but the timeline of things just felt off in my humble opinion.

Nevertheless Koscheck and Zinkin were both crazy about what Pico could become one day, and that was the note we ended our time in Fresno upon. We bid them farewell and then realized that we'd made no plans on where to rest our eyes for the night.

"I'm totally juiced up right now and could probably make it back to Albuquerque tonight if we really needed to," Scully said as he shimmied his way to the vehicle.

"There's no way we can make it that far," I replied in total shock. "I'm beat like a broke dick dog and wouldn't be able to help you on the drive. The last thing we need is to get out there in the darkness and neither of us have anything to give behind the wheel."

In addition to the picture my own words created, I could see the image of the deep dark void of the desert taking hold of Scully's mind. He knew I was right just like he knew when Butta tried to pull a similar card on me back on the first leg of the road trip. We were all undoubtedly excited to get back home and have a safe sleep in our personal creature comforts, but it wasn't worth risking our lives to do so.

"Where should we set our sights on then?" Scully asked, noticeably more tired than he was moments earlier.

My mind scanned the mental map in my head of our route back to New

Mexico, and one town and one town alone stood out as the perfect option for our dilemma.

"You want to hit Palm Springs one mo' gin?" I asked with a shrug.

"Palm fucking Springs," he replied. "Here we come!"

Despite the volume of his voice, there was a noticeable lack of enthusiasm in it. Somehow we were going to land in the former Hollywood starlet oasis for a third time, which was a fact all the more impressive considering how we never planned to stop there in the first place. It was as if the sprawling line of windmills were beckoning us in at every turn in a hypnotic and seductive trance that comes with sleep deprivation.

And therein came the worry. We had been up and at it from the crack of dawn and neither of us were free of the signs of wear and tear from the road. Scully looked as straggled as I'd ever seen him, and I knew my tank was empty as well. The lack of conversation between us was the primary indicator, and flashbacks of the ride through Northern Utah came sputtering back. A few hours of interstate sat between Fresno and our destination for the night, and the silence that hung through the vehicle was worrisome.

The desert is a cold and treacherous thing in the dead night, and the idea of making it anywhere other than Palm Springs became overwhelming. We made fruitless attempts during the first hour of the run to rally our collective moral, but the failure in doing so only further indicated the reality of our position.

It was about survival now, and I prayed the fates would allow us to find safe passage.

Chapter 23

Baseless Overconfidence in ABQ

Where the neon signs of the littered string of motels in Palm Springs once appeared celebratory in nature, they loomed ominous in the night as we entered the city limits. We'd somehow managed to find our way back, but it didn't come without several stop offs on the side of the road to find the fourth and fifth winds that were eluding us.

It was about fifteen miles from Palm Springs when Scully and I had our first tense exchange since the initial run of the project. He was tired and beat like a one-legged dog, and I the same, so diplomacy was a short stick at the ready for some clubbing action.

"Can you pick up this room," he asked with scrambled eyes lit up by the green tint of the dashboard glow.

This was a funny question in the thinness of the moment, as my card had already bounced with a thud at a gas station an hour back, and since my wife was already sleeping three hours ahead on Eastern Standard, there was no way to remedy the situation. This meant Scully had to search on one of those money saving sites from his phone, and it quickly became a Herculean task that got his dander ruffled in a big way.

"I can't fucking read this shit, man!" he bellowed with impatience. "My eyes are shot and there is nowhere open to pull over and grab wifi."

My answer to this was to pull over anyway, which I did shortly upon crossing over the city limits. As Scully raged against the technology in his hand, I took notice that all of the motels and hotels seemed ghostly and a far cry from the Spring Break carnivals of debauchery they were on our previous visits. The party was over in that sense and it seemed all the more fitting considering our situation.

"There we go!" he thundered as he slammed down his phone. "There is a place right up the road and I got us one for the night. Fuck that was hard."

Our spirits shot to the roof as visions of a comfortable pillow and a decent few hours of slumber charged our engines. I flipped the vehicle into drive and cruised down the street until Scully directed me to turn in according to his map. The car wheeled up under the canopy for check in, and my companion jumped out with haste to head into the front office.

Unfortunately, he was greeted with locked doors, and whatever good had been stirred quickly evaporated.

Scully pulled at the doors once with some form of humanity still pulsing through him before going full on Ultimate Warrior on the handles for the next 15 seconds. Curses seemingly in a foreign tongue drifted out into the thick night air before he finally realized his outburst was going to have no effect. I watched as his head dropped in despair just before he turned to head back to the vehicle.

Just before he reached the car door a man appeared from behind the desk in the front office. I pointed to him, and Scully whipped around in a manic frenzy as if the small bowl-legged man had the antidote for the poison within him. My partner shuffled back to the door on the fringes of sanity just as the desk clerk cracked them open.

As they stepped inside I slid into the seat as far as I could muster in hopes of taking some pressure off of my problematic disc. I hadn't been able to take any medicine during that stretch of the drive due to my state of awareness, and it was almost time to kick back and slip under the warm blanket of relief for the night.

I glanced over in Scully's direction from time to time, and when I saw his hands fling into the air and the old man's face twist, I knew the shit had hit the fan. I feared my frenzied companion would push the situation into the felony realm if I didn't act quickly, therefore I sprung out of the car and into the office to intervene.

While it was difficult to translate through the barking, the one thing absolutely clear is that we wouldn't be sleeping at that dive motel. As it would turn out, that was entirely due to a squinty eyed Scully choosing the next day on the calendar rather than the one we were in. Fair enough mistake for even the most alert individual to make, but Scully wasn't going down without a fight.

The man attempted to explain to him the site he used for booking was a third party so the refund would have to come from them, and if we wanted a room for the night we would have to pay another fee. That was before Scully flipped out and went Bates on the poor son of a bitch. The aftermath left us out sixty bucks and without a room to crash in.

In a fit of defiance to the universe, Scully committed to sleeping the night in the backseat of the vehicle, but that was only because his mania had fully taken hold. The man I'd traveled over ten thousand miles beside was no longer the man sitting to my right, and for some crazy reason it was understandably so.

We pulled into a Motel 6 where the lady behind the desk was more than willing to help a few ruggedly handsome strangers. She gave us a super reduced rate on a room because it was five o'clock in the morning and check out would be coming quickly around the bend. She also added that the Coachella Music Festival would bring in tourists by the scores the next two days, and the establishment would benefit greatly off of their nearly tripled rates.

That too was fair enough from where I stood.

By the time we hit the room, Scully was no longer making audible words. Rogue sounds and the occasional grunt followed by a head shake were all he could muster. Leading up to our return back east, he'd talked about stopping off to visit the tattoo parlor in Cub Swanson's gym. Yes…you read that correctly. Cub Swanson has a tattoo shop setup in his gym where he gets all of his work done. Upon learning that tidbit several days back, Scully was thrilled to lose his tattoo virginity, but I knew better to bring it back up to him again.

The man who wanted that small piece of ink real estate was long gone, and only a shell of him remained. We were halfway through Arizona the next day before Scully snapped back to form and he did so well enough to get us back to Albuquerque in one piece. I've never been one to believe in miracles by any stretch of the imagination, but having survived another insane installment of a project that was deemed as scrapheap material, and said project being touted as another success across the MMA community, brought me closer to believing in such things than ever before.

While the Almighty I Am was fresh in my cerebral cortex, I took the time to silently thank the universal powers of mercy and justice for my return to Indianapolis coming via airline. The California run blitzkrieg'd the dusty shores of Ole Bocephus Island and anything Californ-IA-related in regard to affection was torn asunder.

All was lost without even the faintest hint reconstruction would someday be possible, but as it's been known to do, time heals most things, and there were several notable survivors. The west coast gangster rap Mount Rushmore of Dr. Dre, Snoop, Tupac, and Ice Cube endured, but poor Merle Haggard was lost to the fates.

Haggard's Bakersfield sound was strong enough to penetrate the high walls of Nashville, and some argue revolutionize country music, but my love for the former Folsom Prison inmate turned hard-livin', string pickin', whiskey sippin', song sangin' country star couldn't survive the rigors of a two-week run on the MMA Road Trip Project.

Then again there were plenty of things that left with me on the trip but never made it back, or at least didn't return for a few trips around the sun. The largest item on the tangible side of things was my luggage. That's right…two week's worth of clothing that accounted for roughly 70% of my total overall wardrobe would remain in Albuquerque while I jetted off homeward bound to Indianapolis.

How does one lose the lion's share of clothing they've amassed in 34 years of life in an eight-minute drive from your friend's house to the airport? Outside of being an unfortunate soul stricken by an act of God, having a buddy named Scully is the best avenue toward accomplishing such a monumental fuckup.

Having been a resident in the home of hot air balloons and green chile for close to a decade, and being an avid traveler on top of that, when Scully adamantly told me the standard early arrival time to check in at the airport didn't apply in Albuquerque, I took his word as bond.

"Our airport is never busy," he laughed like a man in the know, as he kicked back in the comfort of his living room the day prior. "It's not that big compared to other cities its size and getting through security never takes more than a few minutes."

"Usually better to be safe than sorry," I replied too tired to avoid clichés and too well-versed in the chaos of the brand of air travel shenanigans that had always found its way to me any time my wife wasn't involved in the booking or holding my hand. "I just want to get home and don't mind waiting for a bit at the gate."

The words that came out of my mouth had a faint veil of truth covering them as I did my best to mask my eagerness to end my time with Scully and be on my way back to the land of Hoosiers. My tactics had nothing to do with getting back to being in my own company for a bit and everything to do with simply starting out on the path back to my wife and kids. I didn't care if I had to sit at the airport for ten hours and ended up jammed between a heavy set and a teething infant once the flight finally boarded, just knowing I would eventually make it to Indiana was enough for me.

Or it would have been enough had some strange part of Scully's ego not surfaced on the final night of our time together. Upon our return to "The Berque," my non-alcohol drinking vegan companion immediately began to revel in the comforts of his home coming. His fiancé was once again waiting at his house when we pulled into the drive, and it didn't take long for Scully to let his proverbial hair down and scrub the grime of two weeks of being on the road out from under his fingernails.

By the time our airport security debate rolled around a few hours later, he'd already showered, shaved, and was good and sunk into his Lazy Boy recliner for the evening. On the flip side of the equation, I was still two-thousand miles from home and looking as if I'd been calling the benches of the Little League baseball fields tucked in behind Burger King at Montgomery and Juan Tabo for the past two weeks. There was a weird power struggle at play.

Not only did Scully have the home field advantage when talking about the city he called home, but having returned to the warmth of his personal dwellings while I was still on the road in all regards, stacked a few more chips on his side of the table. Therefore I submitted to his suggestions and agreed to have him drop me off at the airport less than an hour before my boarding time.

That same self-assured smugness from the previous night was still hanging thick on his face as we strolled down Route 25 on our way to the airport the next morning. I tried not to make my constant glancing at the clock on the dash obvious because it would only amplify his bravado, but anyone who flies with any type of regularity has embedded time barriers that come equipped with internal alarms when marks are not hit.

When he pulled up to the curb to drop me off there was less than forty-five minutes on the clock for me to make my flight. In that small window I needed to print my boarding pass, check my suitcase, go through the TSA check, find my way to my gate, and board the plane. Feelings of anxiety were swelling on our drive to the airport and as soon as the tires stopped rolling I forfeited my efforts to keep my emotions in check. I jumped out in a flash and skipped the sentimental goodbye to make up whatever time I could.

I burst through the double doors like a man on a mission and my heart nearly exploded when I saw the mass of people crowded around the Southwest Airlines portion of the hub. The line to check bags bent and stretched down the hallway so far I couldn't make out where to jump in at, and a hasty decision needed to be made.

If it weren't for airports being so touchy about people just up and abandoning a bag in the middle of the terminal, I swear to Jehovah I would have dropped the suitcase right there and began sprinting toward security. I mean what could have possibly gone wrong in that scenario? A scruff-faced drifter type drops a black suitcase ready to burst at the seams, then takes off in a mad dash toward the only men in the airport carrying pistols. I'm sure it wouldn't have even made the evening news.

With the drop and go a non-option and fighting through the swarms of people at the check-in counter just not going to happen; I frantically dialed Scully's number on my cell phone.

Five rings later he picked up.

"You fucked me dude!" I shouted before he could get whatever greeting he was going to sludge out of his mouth past his teeth. "The line is fucking atrocious and you have to turn around and come get my bag."

"What's going on?" he asked.

"I don't have time to sit and explain just turn the fuck around and come get my bag!"

Thankfully he stopped asking questions and recognized the urgency of the moment. All of the assured self-confidence he wielded in his living room was replaced by a chaotic stutter as he repeated over and over that he was on his way back.

"I'm on my way back," he thundered. "Just walk outside and leave your suitcase on the curb and get going. I'll get it."

"I can't do that!" I fired in return. "If I walk outside, set it down and walk away security will tackle me and I'll be even more fucked. Just please hurry up."

I could hear the wind whipping past Scully's driver's side window in the background of the phone and watched like a hunting dog—neck cocked to the side, eyes wide and fixed on what's coming up around the bend—until I finally saw his car pop into view. I ran down the sidewalk to meet him, and once I was within throwing distance of his vehicle I chucked my suitcase toward his passenger side door.

The last thing I saw of Scully was him flying around the trunk side of the car in a rush to grab my bag as I turned and began to sprint back toward the terminal.

"I'm sorry!" I heard him scream as it echoed down the corridor off the tin roof and hollow pillars of the loading area.

"Fuck you, asshole!" I replied without turning back to see if it landed.

While I've never checked to see if they keep records for such things, I'm fairly certain I would have at least broken a few regional marks with the time I made in what seemed to be an impossible gauntlet to overcome. Pride was nowhere to be found as I sprinted, grunted, and yelped my way across the entire airport in utter refusal to miss my flight home.

Fortunately I made my gate in the nick of time and was able to board just before they closed up shop. I spent the next two hours in sheer discomfort as my sweat-soaked self was cramped between two portly old gals who not only took every centimeter of elbow room available, but somehow managed to dominate the available oxygen as well.

By the time I hit my connecting flight in Charlotte, I was a ghost of my former self, and was certain my appearance resembled Jack Nicholson's in *The Shinning*. The picture of Jack stalking Shelly Duvall with a baseball bat in tow as the gaunt waif futilely held a butcher knife and pleaded for him to stop flashed through my mind as I made my way to my seat, and stranger's refusal to make eye contact with me provided validation for what I was projecting in my own mind.

Thankfully I was able to find strands of my sanity before landing in Indianapolis, and patched up just enough of my mental structure to avoid my wife dropping me off at the institution on her way back home. All the craziness would evaporate the moment I looked into her eyes and she threw her arms around me outside the Indianapolis airport.

She was the one thing in my life that felt like home more than anything else, and it had been this way for 14 years.

I landed on an unseasonably warm night for late March, and the warm bursts that hit in the occasional wind gusts allowed us to hold our embrace for a few solid moments as we stood next to her white 2005 Scion XB. I took my time loading my luggage into the back. Standing there looking into those stormy blue eyes, all the bullshit of the travel day slipped out of my mind, and her smile reminded me of what was important.

All the stories and MMA experience I brought back raw could be processed and delivered at a later date down the road. Nothing in the lot required my immediate attention. In all honesty, I didn't really care if anything did need to be put out in the coming days because it wasn't going to happen. One of the biggest mistakes I made, in a barrel of them after my first run, was not allowing myself the proper time to slip back into my regular life.

Instead I tried to keeping charging forward full steam ahead, and that decision caused a shitload of problems in a variety of categories. Renee, being ultra-tuned in the way women magically are, was several steps ahead of me in the acclimation process, and had set each of our children up for sleepovers with friends. That meant we were two kids in love with no pressing matters on our schedule, and this was music to my weary ears.

I wanted to hug and kiss my two little ones so bad it hurt, but being surprised with a wide open night where we didn't have to rush home was one that landed pleasantly on my mind. That meant we were going to be able to stop off at a local watering hole and enjoy one another's company over a few laughs and cocktails.

Even though Renee and I had been together for more than a decade, our love was stronger than it had ever been, and the reason for that is due to our friendship never having chipped away in the slightest. I'm not saying our particular formula is for everybody or that it would even work for another couple, but our marriage had stood the test of time, the chaos of starting a family, and the uncertainty of chasing dreams, because our availability for one another never took second place to anything or anyone else.

At least a dozen of our friends had called it quits in their relationships over the course of ours, and there was one common element we always located in them without fail. All individuals and the way they handle love and relationships are different, but ramping up a section of your life without your other half involved is always the first crack in the foundation. Let me be clear in what I'm saying here.

Some partners are possessive, controlling, and jealous to the point they refuse to allow any sort of freedom or space to the other side of the relationship. When this is the case there is usually some form of insecurity eating away the romantic bond like a cancer that was either born of some incident where trust was broken, or past baggage where a former boyfriend or girlfriend used that little bit of space to pull some heinous shit.

The other side of that psychological profile is the partner that allows total freedom. The partner that wants to do their own thing while their significant other does theirs. In most cases such as this there is a certain amount of selfishness or collegiate Greek mentality involved, and a situation that starts with distance never gains any true traction. Again, to be clear, I'm not talking about catching a poker night, or a girl's night one night a week, or having a solid sense of independence, because those things are healthy.

What I'm talking about is the priority of hanging with the bros and hitting the club all weekend when your wife and kids are at home or raging with the two single girls from the office who are a decade younger while your man is sitting at home watching Baby Einstein. Rolling with people who have their own agendas and are at different points of their lives is a slippery slope, and Renee and I had seen more than a few friends lose their marriages over mistakes made on a Saturday night that should have never happened.

Nevertheless, to each their own, and our relationship has always been about spending our free time together. We both have plenty of good friends in our respective lives, but I've never once had more fun without her being there than I've had with Renee by my side. And the same applies for her as well. We enjoy one another's company in our mid-30's the same way we did when we met in our super-early 20's.

Granted, we are no longer running three-day benders and disappearing on a friend's boat for a weekend, but we still know how to have a good time. With no kids for the night we headed back toward the northern suburbs of Indianapolis where we live and set up shop for a few hours at a local place we find entertaining.

All the driving of the past two weeks and a turbulent day of air travel had me fried to the max, but I couldn't think of a better way to spend the night than sitting down with Renee and talking about how beautiful life is over a pitcher of cheap domestic beer. And that's what we did….several pitchers in fact…and by the time the third one arrived I had all but forgotten about Scully's grievous misjudgment of traffic at his local airport or an entire day wasted in Los Angeles.

We were midway through the fifth pitcher of beer when she leaned in and told me how proud she was of what I'd done, and I could feel the emotion of that moment well up in my throat. Renee had been supportive of my creative endeavors since the inception of our relationship, but she was referring to something else as she leaned in close to give me a kiss.

"I don't know what I did to deserve that but I hope there is more where that came from," I joked as gave her a kiss in return. "You say you're proud but could it be you're just happy to have your long-trip trucker of a husband home?"

"Well there's always that," she laughed. "But I'm so proud of you for creating this vision and executing it no matter what type of circumstances you were up against. Was it super-fucking dangerous for you to drive out into the worst deep freeze to hit the Midwest since we were kids? Absolutely, but you knew what this thing could become, and you literally had the courage to go out after it. The majority of people don't have the balls you have, and even fewer could have pulled off the type of stories you've written out of these trips."

Seeing such a tiny, typically laid-back woman get fired up and put some conviction in her voice had me jazzed up, and I dug what she was saying in the moment. Furthermore, it was exactly the type of message I needed to hear. The first leg of the road trip was an absolute roll of the dice because MMA had never seen a type of project like that before, and the feedback from the overall community scored the initial run a success.

By those measures, the second installment had been a victory as well. Each and every fighter who contributed to the cause was delighted to have done so, and there wasn't a single stop on the entire second run where I wasn't 100% certain the door for a return project wouldn't be wide open. That means I was able to accomplish my goal of telling an entirely unique and completely honest story with every stop.

Renee was right. I should feel proud. I had set these crazy lofty expectations for myself and pushed the envelope far beyond the point of where I thought I was capable of going. I proved to the sport I love I was far beyond driven to do the work to find the stories no one was telling and do the very best job I could at getting those stories out in a way that connected to MMA's passionate fan base.

Once again I had allowed myself to transform into Captain Ahab to chase down this mythical demon beast. Rather than the vast and open sea, I put my sanity and safety on the line up and down the asphalt strands that bend, twist, and dip up and around the backbone of America. And while the comparison to the fictional Captain filled my mind with terror that evoked the darkest of outcomes, those were thoughts best left for another night, because this one still had life, and I had the company of my beautiful wife to share it with.

Chapter 24

The Void Returns

"We never lie to our patients," the nurse winced, as she made no attempt to hold a poker face. "This procedure isn't pleasant, but we do our best to get you through it."

After limping through her spiel, the nurse bolted for the door so quickly there was no time for a follow-up question even if I had one. Not that this wasn't par for the course around my neurologist's office, because it was, but the lack of information on this visit was particularly disturbing. Two epidurals and several attempts to block the nerve bringing havoc to my lower lumbar region had proven futile, which left only one non-surgical option on the table.

A rhizotomy, or nerve ablation, would be performed on each of the branch nerves attached to my L-5 vertebra in the hopes of providing the first extended relief for me in nearly two years. Four months had passed since I returned home from my west coast run on the road trip project, and over that stretch, a veritable buffet of novelty-sized needles had been jammed into various parts of my spine. New promises would be made leading up to every visit, but it never took more than a week post-torture session for the pain to return.

The failure rate was so incredible my doctor began pushing hard for a surgical repair, but fusing my spine would have required a stretch of recovery time that would have eaten up the majority of what remained of 2015. Needless to say, the two remaining legs of the road trip would have been scrapped, but no matter how much seeing my passion project leveled would've hurt, that was far from my biggest worry where work was concerned.

Working in a digital media mill house requires fresh content to be churned out at a crazy rate, and editors showed little mercy for real life problems coming into play. The site I was contracted to had a well-earned reputation for clipping writers who couldn't keep up with the break-neck production required of them, and I refused to be another addition to the scrapheap.

Even though the popularity of the road trip project had raised my visibility to the elite-level of MMA journalism, hobbling off to the sidelines for a few months and putting my job in jeopardy wasn't a scenario I was willing to explore. Therefore, allowing my neurologist to inject a needle-type sensor into my spine that would then heat up and burn off my nerve endings was the only road I could travel.

The procedure sounded painful when they explained it to me back in June, but my imagination came nowhere close to doing it justice.

"You're going to feel a pinch and then some pressure," the doctor offered in a thick Cuban accent. "It's very important you remain still though."

A few seconds later the sting of the needle lived up to his words, and the pressure created was so intense it made my stomach turn. It was a relatively short window before he reached the proper depth and I could exhale to find some small relief, but fighting the urge to wiggle in those crucial moments was easily the biggest dilemma plaguing my mind.

None of the previous visits or shots created a need for me to move my legs, but nor had the doctor told me it was something I couldn't do. The brain does funky things when served with restrictions. You immediately want to do the very thing you are told you can't. The more his Cuban tones instructed me to lay still and continue to breathe, the less I cared about anything he was saying. The only thing I wanted to do was move my legs, and just when I thought it had built up to a breaking point, an entirely new level of consciousness forced its way in.

They said it was going to be uncomfortable. They said I would feel some heat and the nerves would twitch. They said all of these things about how the procedure would feel, but nowhere in their rhetoric was the word "searing" used.

What started as a slight tingle and some warmth running down the left side of my ass, quickly turned into an all-out fire that spread down my left leg from the inside. It was as if there was a trail of gasoline running from the base of my spine down to the heel of my left foot and the Cuban-born physician had just dropped the match to spark things up.

Every sweat gland in my body suddenly cut loose the perspiration fountains. It was as if my nervous system had attempted to put out the fire sweeping over my personal landscape. With the pain building up to become more than I could handle, panic began to set in, and I started to verbalize the terror surging through my brain.

"Motherfucker this hurts!" I shouted. "Sorry. I'm sorry I cursed."

"It's okay Mr. Finley," the doctor assured. "I know this isn't pleasant. We're about halfway done."

Just when the pain from the heat seemed as if it couldn't get any worse, that's exactly what it did, and I started to believe I was bringing it all on myself for attempting to set limitations and expectations on things I had no clue about.

"Oh, mothefucker! I can't take much more of this!"

"You're doing great," the doc calmly stated. "One more minute and you'll be in the clear."

With Dr. Vitto setting a timeframe I suddenly found Zen and started to tell myself there wasn't anything in the world I couldn't endure for a minute. The gut-check moment had arrived, and my sweat-soaked palms clinched into fists around the picnic table cloth-thick sheets on the operating bed.

"30 seconds," the doctor shared. "Here we go."

As the final countdown kicked in, I remembered the breathing my wife had used when bringing our children into the world. While it's commonly referred to as Lamaze, Renee used some satanic remix version, as stretches of chopped and deliberate breaths were infused with red-eyed demon screams, where my name was replaced with some version of "motherfucker." By the time I ran through that memory, the doctor had removed his forearm from the small of my back and took the 8-inch long needle out of my spine as well.

It was finally over, and the tears welling up around my eyes were proof that I'd been pushed right up to my breaking point. I managed to maintain enough dignity to make it back to the private room my wife had been sitting in until I finally broke down and let loose the cry that had been waiting to burst, and I was leveled to a blubbering mess for the next few moments.

Although the pain was the initial catalyst, the invasiveness of it all is really what impacted me the most. I'm the furthest thing from a control freak on this spinning ball of dirt and wonder, but something about how the whole procedure played out left me in shambles. Renee being the woman she is, and having the task of being my significant other for more than a decade, was used to picking up the pieces, but this was something completely different.

The spate of emotion that continued to flow from me was more than the spinal injury…it was the realization that age was finally starting to take a toll on my body. Where death is something every man and woman fears in some regard, the haunting shadows of getting older is perhaps the most underrated of all terrors, and that's because no one wants to give it the proper due.

Anyone even a day older than yourself will greet talk of aging with a guaranteed "just you wait to see how bad it is" eye roll, which magically strips away your right to feel anything at all about it. That's bullshit to the highest degree, and sitting there sobbing on Renee's shoulder I felt every bit of my 35 years, and it had been a hard lived 35 years at that.

When the nurse came around for discharge, she did so with a packet of recovery instructions in one hand and several slips of pain medication prescriptions in the other. I could see the muscles in my wife's face tighten when the words Norco and Percocet crossed her eyes, and for good reason. Those were monsters of the past whose presence were suddenly very necessary, and it's impossible to shrug off something that did so much damage in the none too distant past.

Chapter 25

On the Road Again

The dog days of summer finally gave way to Autumn, which is the one truly beautiful season in the heartland of America. The lush greens of the flatlands meld into a firestorm of amber and crimson just as the swelter breaks into a comfortable condition. My personal love for the fall months is without limitations, and for large chunks of my life, is the stretch of time in the calendar year where I'm most at ease.

A non-stop UFC schedule kept MMA ever-present in my life, but the call of the road was getting louder in my ears. The back condition had certainly put the remainder of the project in jeopardy, but being a man of gumption and stubbornness, there was no way I wasn't going to complete my vision of taking the trip to both coasts. Therefore I started to devise a plot, and once those gears began turning it wasn't long before the fires of passion were ablaze.

Where the second trip was more visible and ultimately more successful than the initial run, there was a buzz circling throughout the MMA community for another installment of the project to begin. This was due in no small part to my stirring the pot on social media platforms, but as long as there was a want for the stories I needed to tell, then I could find the motivation to bring them to life.

During my time working at a major sports site, I took a protégé under my wing in the form of a lanky up-and-coming talent named Hunter Homistek. "Big Red," as he was affectionately christened due to his height and resemblance to Malachi from Stephen King's classic tale of religious zealot bloodshed *Children of the Corn*, had a talent for the written word that was obvious. The stories he'd penned during his time in the big leagues were strong, and it was clear the only thing he lacked was true flesh and blood experience.

Sports journalism is notorious for not being kind to the next generation on the rise, but since I'd been fortunate to have an amazing mentor in Thomas Gerbasi, I felt obliged to do the same for another hungry, driven, and gifted writer. I knew I couldn't do for him what Gerbasi had done for me, but getting Hunter out on the road would at least be a start to me doing my part.

After I made the phone call and offered Hunter a spot riding shotgun in the car—one which he quickly and graciously accepted—I found myself thinking about Tom Gerbasi even more than normal.

Anyone who has followed combat sports over the past 20 years is certainly familiar with his name. Gerbasi is a born and bred New Yorker with a crisp eye for detail and an extraordinary ability to translate what his eyes see to the page. Tom originally made his name on the boxing beat before jumping over to cover mixed martial arts right around the time Zuffa purchased the UFC. It was a great move for the Brooklyn native as the UFC exploded in popularity just a few years later, with Gerbasi one of the driving voices bringing the promotion and its fighter's stories to the masses.

While I was familiar with him from his near folklore status in the game, our paths didn't actually cross until December of 2011, in Toronto of all places. After a long night and a hectic morning, I was hustling down the street to make the media check-in at the event, and in my haste happened to forget my coat. Granted it was Canada in December, but with the venue only being a handful of blocks up the way, I figured it wouldn't be such a big deal.

"Jesus Finley," came an unfamiliar voice from my left. "Where in the world is your damn coat?"

I didn't recognize the thick New York accent, but when I turned to see that it was none other than Thomas Gerbasi busting my balls, my heart skipped a beat. First and foremost, I was shocked a man of his stature in the fight game even knew who I was, but once the awe-struck feeling wore off, I quickly found comfort in being in the company of one of my own.

Coming from a long line of yucksters and humor mongers, it was nice to have a crisp exchange with another quick witted type, and we spent the next few blocks walking and exchanging small talk. I would see him a few more times throughout the night, and made sure to shake his hand at least another time or two before we parted ways.

I wouldn't see him again until six months later when the UFC made a stop in Atlantic City, and that is when I decided to take the plunge and hit him up for a job at UFC.com. I had been writing fighter features for more than five years at that point, and the work Gerbasi and his crew did for the UFC's website was in the exact same vein. Much to my surprise, he was open to the idea and told me to shoot him an email once fight week had come to an end.

I did just that and we've been working together ever since.

Aside from the additional revenue, easily the biggest gain from working alongside a legend like Gerbasi has been the guidance he's provided me. There isn't anything in the world of sports writing he hasn't experienced, and his drive to produce quality content is miles ahead of anyone else who claims to do what he does. Gerbasi is prolific as they come in the digital media world, and in him I found not only a fantastic teacher, but an amazing friend as well.

I know he's going to read this, and I can already hear the words come out of his mouth, "Yeah, yeah Finley. Just get back to the story already."

And while that's exactly what I plan to do, I needed to take time for a second to honor the man who made all of this possible for me.

This especially rang true when jumping out on the third leg of the road trip project. It was no secret the back situation had kicked my ass up and down main street, but Gerbasi never stopped pushing me to get back out there, because he knew the type of passion I possessed to launch the project in the first place. With the west coast already conquered on my quest, the next target was the east coast, and there was no way I could make that run without getting some time with my personal version of Obi-Wan Kenobi.

Two days before launch I received a call from Hunter informing me that his childhood friend and recent journalism school graduate Dan Sweeney was also up for making the trip. Sweeney was a videographer in the making and wanted to capture the trip from behind the lens. The project had become more interactive with each progressive step, and the chance to bring some quality video to the articles was an option I couldn't pass up.

What started out as a scrolling journal was finally shaping up to be the live and in living color project I'd originally envisioned, and I was excited to see what magic could be created working with a team of equally driven people. Butta and Scully were now replaced by Hunter and Sweeney and I would pick them up when I made my way through Pittsburgh in route to New Jersey.

I spent a week making phone calls and setting up appointments and was pleased to craft a list of high-profile names to feature on this go around. I had been talking with Jim and Dan Miller for the better part of two years about getting into their neck of the woods to go on a camping trip, and was fortunate neither had a fight booked so their schedules were open. My father used to take my friends and I camping back in my younger days, but "Big Joe" rocking two cases of beer while we climbed trees and looked at stolen porno mags was going to be a huge stretch to the actual outdoorsman experience the Millers would provide.

It was a rainy October day when I set out east on Route 70 to kick things off, and rather than attempt to blast straight through to the home of the Steelers, I decided to make a quick stop in Columbus, Ohio. Part of the reason was to get some time with my good friend and fellow MMA road tripper Damon Martin, who has called Columbus home for years, but the other part of my motivation was to get some material for my online journal with scrappy welterweight badass Matt Brown.

"The Immortal" originally came to fame as a member of The Ultimate Fighter, and didn't seem as if he was going to stick around the UFC too long when he went on a rough losing skid that saw him drop four out of five fights from 2010-2011. Yet, just when it seemed as if he would be cut from the ranks of the UFC, the resilient Ohio native battled back with fury and went on an unbelievable run that saw him notch seven-straight victories inside the Octagon.

By the time I rolled into town, Brown's streak had come to an end after a hard-fought war with future champion Robbie Lawler, but the 33-year-old was no worse for wear when we sat down for lunch. Although Brown is notoriously short worded, having interacted with him in recent years allowed him to get comfortable with me in quick fashion.

"I think this trip you're on is some cool shit," he said as he tapped his fingers on the table top. "I'd love to get out on the bike and take a road trip, but that's kind of hard to do when there is always a fight around the corner and I have a family at home. Maybe look me up on your next one and I'll see what I can do, but even if I can't make that happen, I'll definitely be following along with the journals."

And while Brown may not waste words, he certainly stands behind them, as that's exactly what he did. For each stop I made and entry into the rolling online journal, the newly minted contender would shoot a text to my cell phone letting me know what he liked about my journey. As a writer, it's always a cool thing to get fan perspective and feedback, but when a fighter is giving you the information about how well you are doing telling their side of a story, well that's gold plain and simple.

A few hours after I put Columbus in the rear view, I hit Pittsburgh where

Hunter and Dan were anxiously waiting. Just like Brown, they too were following the online journal and tracking my movements as I drew closer to picking them up. I pulled into Hunter's apartment complex and less than 30 minutes later we were out on the road.

While the first official stop on the trip was the highly anticipated campout with the Millers, there was still an open slot for the evening on our itinerary. Jim and Dan weren't expecting us until the next morning, therefore we decided to make a stop to see a mutual friend in Williamsburg, Pennsylvania. Host of ESPN Radio's "Rattling the Cage" and fellow MMA journalist Tony Reid had invited us to do an in studio appearance on his show. He also offered up the extra beds in his home for us to crash.

I'd personally been a guest on Tony's program more than a dozen times and was really looking forward to sitting down and rocking in an actual studio. As a member of the MMA media, you do a ton of podcasts and guest spots, but it's an entirely different experience to slip on the headphones and do your thing on the actual radio.

Due to my driving like an elderly woman, we cut it pretty damn close to making the show, but as Hunter parked the car and I put my 215-pound frame in high gear, I was able to get on set just as things were kicking off. Hunter and Dan would trickle in a few moments later, and we spent the next hour chopping up conversation and kicking out some laughs with Tony at the helm. It was one of those strange full circle moments in life. It was on Tony's show at the end of 2013 where I officially broke the news about the road trip, and there I was sitting across from him in studio talking about the end of it.

I'm not quite sure if that's poetic or anything of that sort, but it was definitely one of those rare moments where the universe lets you know you are where you were meant to be all along.

Once the broadcast concluded, we joined Tony's parents and wife Michelle for a nice sit down dinner where the beer flowed freely. It was during the ordering portion of our dining experience that cameraman Dan decided to order chicken Parmesan and was given the nickname "Parm" on the spot. Much like the universe made it clear I was supposed to be in the ESPN studio that day, so did it stamp how Sweeney's name would never be the same.

He would be Parm for the rest of the trip, and that is still what he's called to this day.

With a good buzz rolling from the drinks at dinner and my back medicine adding a special kind of high five in the mix, our crew decided to keep things shaking at another watering hole. We parked our cars at the Reid residence then hoofed it out a few blocks to a bar down the street. Shortly into our walk, rain started to fall, and I watched as the huge droplets splashed off the battered brick streets of the neighborhood.

It had been years since I'd seen a brick road, and I found comfort in knowing that some things truly stand the test of time. Granted, the middle of the streets buckled and rose into a hump, but the gloss of the wet bricks brought an element of serenity as we weathered the downpour. At one point I reached down to feel the cold wet brick against my fingertips, and the greater sense of life on the road washed over my body and mind.

My fascination with the road and all its wonders was as much a part of me as the heart that kept my body thriving, and standing in the middle of that street with mother nature whipping around me served as an instant reminder of why I set out abroad in the first place. It was a beautiful feeling in that moment.

There was one umbrella to be found in the group, and naturally that went to cover Tony's wife Michelle, because although MMA journalists are typically unsavory heathens, there was enough collective decency in that group to make sure the only woman in our pack received the courtesy.

We spent the next four hours pounding beers and sharing stories from the MMA universe. Tony and I compared notes on which print publications were late on their payments and just how much red had been racked up. We found it funny in the moment that magazines require writers to deliver on specific deadlines but then take no issue with dragging out the manner in which they pay you for those services.

Call it first world problems or flat out bitching if you will, but if you've never worked your ass off on a project then had to wait three months to get paid for it then it's just something you wouldn't understand.

The bartender shouted out last call and that was our sign to call it a night. We were going to have to shove off fairly early in the morning to make it out to Sparta, New Jersey, and a good night's sleep was in order. One of the biggest mistakes I'd made on my two previous runs was underestimating the importance of sleep, and it wasn't one I was willing to make again.

Our rag-tag bunch retired to the Reid residence, and after a quick call to my wife, I drifted off into the land of slumber. It was a good sleep and one completely void of dreams of any type, which strangely enough I prefer. My mind works in frantic chaos and creativity every second of every minute of every day. It's truly welcomed when everything goes black when I close my eyes.

Chapter 26

Into the Woods

I awoke the next morning to "Only the Good Die Young" from Billy Joel blaring out of my phone, smothered in the tentacles of confusion in regard to where I was. Somewhere toward the end of my sleep, I must have kicked on the Pandora music app, which in turn allowed "The Piano Man" to sing me back into the world. The situation in itself sparked an inner laugh, and the fact it was that particular song turned the peculiar into flat out hilarity.

Throughout my life I'd always found a curious amusement whenever I saw someone use "Only the Good Die Young" as some sort of tribute song. Social networks like Facebook and Twitter are where they are most often found. As a tribute to a late individual, a friend will post the song on the wall of someone who has tragically lost their life. I'm not sure if posting on a wall is still a thing on Facebook, but this is coming from a guy who had a Nokia phone long after it was no longer cool to have a Nokia phone.

In regard to using the Billy Joel classic as a post-mortem tribute, and the reason I find so much humor in it, is due to the tune having absolutely nothing to do with anyone actually dying and everything to do with Mr.

Joel trying to get a shot of ass. Throughout the course of the tune, he's trying to convince Virginia—the name of his object of affection and a weak symbolic tie to a young girl's virginity—to ditch her Catholic dogma and jump between the sheets with him.

Therefore trying to get into Virginia's knickers is the reason for the song and not some poor unfortunate soul cashing in their chips far too early. These are the thoughts that run through my mind to kick off a day.

After realizing I was in one of the Reid's spare bedrooms, I finally threw on my clothes for the day and ventured downstairs where the entire crew was already up and gathered around the breakfast nook. Tony had apparently got an early start to his day and went to fetch a buffet of breakfast sandwiches from the local Subway shop he owned. It wasn't until we sat around enjoying the sustenance where that particular detail of his job portfolio came into view, but I thought it a pretty cool thing for a man who I'd grown to become personal friends with to have a solid business to stand on rather having to rely on the fickle bitch that is MMA media.

Once the breakfast conversation was complete, the road trip crew was back on the road and making our way over the state line into the land of New Jersey. Although the state is relatively small in comparison to most of its counterparts, it is as diverse as they come. The section we were heading to meet Jim and Dan Miller had a scenic and rustic appeal, filled with timber and the color and vibrancy that comes with the changing of the seasons. It was country as country gets out there. Every other vehicle that passed by was a pickup truck with a trailer attached hauling something or other.

Just a touch more than an hour away sat Seaside Heights, which is the town made infamous by the MTV reality show *Jersey Shore*. The tank tops and gelled hair of the boardwalk was a far stretch from the camouflage hats that were visible in abundance as we pulled into a small strip mall to meet up with Jim Miller. That's a strange and mystical dynamic by every stretch and measure, and even though more research would be filed into that category of weirdness later on, meeting up with Jim meant it was time to punch the clock and get back into storyteller mode.

During my time working in MMA I had worked with the perennial lightweight contender on dozens of occasions. In addition to being a fan of his no bullshit love for the scrap, there was a decency about him that I always found endearing. Where other fighters were in the game to get famous or forge some persona that made them seem to be bigger than they actually were, with Miller none of those things were present, and it was something I appreciated about him.

As we sat down at the tiny little diner, I introduced him to Hunter and Parm and explained we would have a small camera crew capturing our adventure in the wilderness. Since Jim and his family were all avid outdoorsmen, he was more than prepared to guide us through, but needed to know how much extra equipment he would need to round up before we headed out.

"How much stuff did you guys bring?" Miller asked as he ordered a cup of coffee. "Hopefully you brought more than just sleeping bags."

While the tone of his voice was humor laden, it suddenly struck me that we were far less prepared than I had initially thought. When I agreed to go camping, the only necessity that crossed my mind was a sleeping bag and maybe a few things to munch on, but sitting at the table with Miller it quickly became clear I'd grossly underestimated what it would take to survive just one day in the woods.

"What else do we need?" I asked as I tried to play it off with a champion-level poker face.

"Well water is pretty important so I'd say you need enough water for the three of you," Miller returned with a laugh. "But since I don't see a cooler in your car I'm going to go ahead and guess I need to provide that for you. It also gets pretty damn cold out there at night, so you're going to need winter gear like gloves and hats, because if you guys go out in those hoodies you'll probably freeze to death."

He'd been talking for 30 seconds and I gained a profound understanding of just how quickly I'd die if the shit were ever to hit the proverbial fan in the real world.

"Dan and I have a cooler packed with meat cuts and sausage we recently smoked that we will have for dinner in addition to a batch of beer and homemade plum brandy we just made as well," he added. "That should be enough food to get us through, but if there is anything else you guys want to grab before we head out, now would be the time to do it."

In an effort to not look like a crew of bumbling clowns, I quietly informed Hunter that I would run down to a local shopping center we passed a few blocks back and grab a few jugs of water. It was going to be much but at least we would be a bit better off than just rolling in with our sleeping bags.

"We don't want to bring too much food out there because then you have to worry about bears," Miller instructed as he began pitching our bags into the back of his jeep. "A bear killed two kids not too long ago out where we are going to camp, and it's something you really have to be careful of in those woods."

Even though he was talking about furry two ton killing machines, there was a part of me that felt as if Miller was setting up the big scare that often comes on camping trips. When I was younger, my father used to tell my friends and I about an escaped mental patient who hacked up a bunch of stoner hippie types in some nearby woods that just so happened to be the exact woods we were setting up camp in. Those stories traumatized me as a youth, and it immediately felt as if Miller was setting the line the same way my old man did 20 years earlier.

I'd seen bears in zoos and magazines, and throughout all of my travels had never heard of the dreaded killer black bears of New Jersey.

Miller waited for me to hit the local shopping center before we followed him down the street to the new facility he and his brother had just purchased. Miller Brothers MMA was a dream a long time in the making for the two seasoned UFC veterans, and from the look of things they were just a few weeks away from their grand opening.

"Dan will be here in a few minutes, but our dad is inside working, so you'll get to meet him," Jim offered as we headed toward the door.

The first thing I took notice of once walking through the doors was the vast amount of mat space that stretched across the floor of the building. Having come from a wrestling background, ground fighting was something of a second nature to Miller, and his rapid progression through the ranks of jiu-jitsu made him an absolute monster when the action hit the canvas. Therefore it was no surprise to see so much work space that allowed for that type of fighting to take place, and the crisp white mats that lined the walls added an element of freshness to the gym.

Standing over to the right was a mountain of a man that could only be Jim and Dan's father. I made my way over to officially meet the patriarch of the Miller clan and was immediately impressed by the stock of his hand shake. His hands were rock hard and calloused like a man who'd made his living hammering and sawing things to form, and his eyes were easy as he immediately recognized I too was of the salt of the earth variety.

"Coming out to do a bit of camping are you?" Mike Miller asked, as he rocked back a bit to take a drink from his coffee mug. "The weather is going to be pretty nice, so should be a good night out there. Just hope those damn bears leave us be."

Again the topic of bears had come up, and the senior Miller's weathered Captain Ahab appearance actually made me believe the long-toothed killing machines were lurking in abundance out in the timber. He must have recognized the fear slide over my face as he too set about talking about the two unfortunate souls who met a grizzly demise out in the woods just a few months prior. By the end of the story, Mike could tell I was shook and threw a stiff paw to my shoulder to snap me back to reality.

"Oh don't get all worried now," he laughed. "We hunt in those woods all of the time and know where to go and not to go. Jim and Dan used to run up and down that timber every day when they were kids. We just have to be careful of a few things and the bears will leave us be."

While his words were comforting, I couldn't help but envision the internet head lines of how an ambitious MMA storyteller was drug off in the middle of the night and dined upon by a crew of black bears.

Mike and Jim walked over to look at the cage they were putting up and an alarm on my phone sounded to remind me that I had a phone interview with featherweight champion and pound-for-pound phenom Jose Aldo in two minutes. "Junior" was just a short time away from his long-awaited rematch with his rival Chad Mendes, and I spent the next fifteen minutes talking to the Brazilian wrecking machine about the matchup and the pride that comes from being one of the most dominant champions in UFC history.

Although phone interviews from Brazil can be a pain in the ass due to the use of a translator, this particular interview with Aldo was pure fire. Mendes had attempted to get under his skin in the build up to their second showdown, and that day on the phone the only man to hold the UFC featherweight strap was amped up to speak his mind. He would go on to successfully defend his title in the main event at UFC 179 a few weeks later in what was immediately recognized as an instant classic.

Aldo and Mendes went to war for 25 minutes in Rio de Janeiro, and it was great to see such an incredible champion add another definitive performance to his impressive legacy.

Just as the phone interview with Aldo concluded, Dan Miller walked through the doors of his new gym. While I'd worked with Jim plenty in the past, the elder of the fighting Miller brothers was somewhat of a stranger to me. Since I'd been working in MMA for the better part of a decade at that point, I knew all about his career as a fighter, just as I was familiar with the personal struggles and tragedies he'd suffered in his life beyond the cage.

One of the largest motivators I had for making the trip to spend time with the Miller brothers was the chance to do what I believe hadn't been done up to that point, and that was to tell their story the right away. Where the rest of the world saw two blue collar hard-nosed types who were willing to give everything they had inside the Octagon, I saw a much deeper dynamic that I simply had to know more about.

Fighting is a rigorous trade, and the Millers have been in their fair share of wars, but there was a genuineness to them that I felt had never been explained to the passionate MMA fan base.

With Dan walking in later than expected, it didn't take Jim but a few seconds to pounce on his brother with a few verbal jabs. Dan shrugged off the barbs, but that didn't slow Jim down as he continued to roll with the quips. It became clear that Jim was the quick-witted yuckster of a little brother while Dan was the over-protective big who allowed the younger to run his mouth at will.

"He's just pissed because his benches didn't turn out so great," Dan commented to me as he pointed to a row of wooden benches against the far wall.

"Oh you can fuck off with that," Jim cracked back. "That's handmade quality craftsmanship. Did they take a bit longer than I expected? Yeah, but so what? At least I got them done. How many of those bags did you get hung up?"

The two brothers would continue to banter back and forth for the next ten minutes, and in listening to their conversation, it came into scope that every part of their gym's construction was done by them and their father. Where any other fighter would pay to have all of these things built, assembled, and brought in my professionals, the Miller's hands on nature wouldn't allow them to travel such a route.

They didn't care how long anything took or the extra stress it added because having someone else do work they know they could easily do would be unacceptable. Therefore they would work the day away, installing showers and building a locker room, then train at night as both had scheduled fights on deck. They also had wives and children who needed them present as well, but the ability to multi-task ran deep in the Miller blood.

"They told you about the bears right?" Dan asked as he slapped a hand in the middle of my back. "You don't have be fast just faster than your friends over there."

I took one look at Hunter and Parm and knew I could out-truck at least one of them if I had to, but I silently prayed to a God I wasn't sure existed that such a footrace would never come to pass.

When most people think of camping, they picture a weekend at K.O.A. with the rug rats and a 60 dollar tent purchased at Walmart. If things go right, maybe you get to put that brand new Coleman gas griddle to use and rehydrate with the water backpack you purchased at Cabella's on some Black Friday sale during one of your adventures down a hiking trail. That's what most see as camping, but this is not the Miller way.

After trekking two miles deep in the eastern New Jersey woods, Jim finally found a spot he deemed suitable. There was no tent to stake, only a hole to dig, and he immediately set about carving out the earth with his compact shovel. As his son built what would become the fire pit, Miller Sr. began to rope food and a water bag from an overhanging branch. Suddenly I was standing in a vortex of testosterone and primitive knowledge, and didn't know what to do with my two empty hands.

"Start collecting some firewood," Miller panted as he was dead in the mix of the suck that is hole-digging. "Smaller stuff for a fast burn and I'll cut up some larger blocks later. We are going to need to keep the fire burning all night, so we are going to need plenty of it."

Conversation or humorous anecdotes have always known to have long legs, but few things pass the time during manual labor more than recalling some unfortunate tale of your youth. In this, the Millers and I saw eye to eye, and this created an immediate bond because of it. Most human beings—especially when looking to make an impression upon other human beings—recite some series of stories that highlight past accomplishments, but the crew of men out in the woods that day were not of this ilk.

Every story that came down the pipe was more self-deprecating than the last, and origin stories to Dan Miller's "Beefalo" moniker and my own personal "Duanger Fingerbanger" hangnail were thrown out for good measure. Preteen sexual adventures are tailor-made for shenanigans, and it's always nice when a particular incident can follow you around for a few decades. It was also during this mixture of sordid tales where the Miller family brew showed up to the camp out, which only elevated the laughter and ball busting all the much more.

Anyone who grew up in the 1980's did so with a healthy fear of the woods because of movies like *Friday the 13th* and *Deliverance*, and the latter became the primary running joke of the night. Suddenly the worry was no longer bears that would tear you limb from limb and feast on your Netflix-induced pudgy middle, but the lingering terror of hearing a banjo strumming somewhere in the darkness.

The humor stayed at a torrent pace throughout the night, but it was the Miller brother's sibling rivalry that stole the show. Dan and Jim are the definition of hands on when it comes to their approach at all things, and where every other American would take the most accessible approach to starting a fire, the brothers Miller went all-out Caveman.

"It's called a bow drill," Jim said as he took a wooden dowel he had carved 30 minutes prior then went to work on it with a bow he fashioned out of shoestring and sticks. "It's a pain in the ass to get a fire started this way, but I love the challenge.

"You're doing it wrong," Dan chimed in, knowing it would turn his brother's face a shade or two more red than his beard.

"Oh, bullshit," Jim fired back without ever taking his gaze off the process. "Dan started a fire this way, but there is absolutely an asterisk by it because he used some easily flammable wood to make it happen. That doesn't count in my book."

While it took no less than fifteen minutes and Jim sweating down to his fighting weight for the fire to start, the smoking embers eventually caught and a fire was ablaze. The ignition came at the perfect time, as the Autumn New Jersey sun slipped below the tree line and the scenery turned from jovial to ominous in quick fashion. The make-shift campsite seemed to draw closer to the fire as its flames jumped up and licked the darkness, and the half of our contingent that wasn't woodsman savvy began to throw out a nervous chatter.

No less than an hour into pure darkness, the last of the Miller's homemade brew tapped out, and it was time for desperate measures to be taken.

"I guess we kind of underestimated how much this crew could drink," Jim laughed as he took the last of the brandy into a steel glass. "It's not like we could have carried in a keg, but shit…we put that away quickly."

"It's too bad there isn't a liquor store in the woods," I returned, hoping the universe would drop a package store in the middle of the realm of killer bears.

"Actually there is one not too far down the road," Dan offered. "I mean, we'd have to hike out of here in the dark, but once we got back to the truck it's like a block or two down. If you're up for making the trip I can get us out of here."

While Dan broke down the options, my mind started to replay the amount of hassle we'd undergone just to get to our campsite clearing. There were hills, trenches, and plenty of thorn bushes that snagged and scraped arms and ankles. Just making it in under a bright lit canopy was an endurance trial, and going back in the pitch black of night was going to be a ferocious challenge.

Nevertheless, adventure has never been something I'd miss, and there was no way I could pass up the chance to take such a memorable, and perhaps fatal, excursion with one of the toughest men I'd ever known.

Although my horror movie-driven flights of fancy were visceral but still surface-level, it didn't outweigh what I knew about the man leading me through the thicket.

Dan Miller's MMA career had been filled with one bloody battle after the next. His ingrained toughness carried him to victory more times than not. Yet, what the man had endured in his personal life beyond the cage would be more than enough to shatter most. The death of one child and another born in need of a kidney transplant made hope and faith a strained and frayed presence throughout the Miller family. Through it all they stood tall, almost like an archetype for what made the middle of America so great yet passable for those looking for a prettier lifestyle.

During some time gathering wood, I had the chance to talk to Mike about the heavier topics, and despite his larger than life and bulletproof nature, it was difficult for the Miller patriarch to keep his emotions at bay.

"There was just so much suffering in this family going through those things," he said as he turned away to hack at a tuft of dead branches. "I remember seeing my son sitting in the bathroom crying because of what his son was going through just a room away, but then he'd shore up those tears because he didn't want to show anything but strength and positivity around his son. Then he'd leave to go train because he had a fight coming up and he'd spend every minute in the car crying his eyes out.

"One night I heard a sound coming from the kitchen and I came to out see Dan putting a feeding tube down his own throat. I rushed over to stop him, but he insisted on going through with it because he had to know what he was putting his little boy through."

I watched as his granite hands trembled a bit, but a few more swipes of the machete and he had pulled himself back together. Those thoughts and the picture he painted hung in my mind throughout the night, but faded to the back when the urgency of escaping the woods to get cold beer became the priority.

"I'm pretty sure I know how to get us out of here," Dan laughed in a manner difficult to read. It was either nervous or intentional, but there nonetheless.

"I hope you can get us out of here because I don't know my way back," I returned with terror showing through. "I'm not even worried about bears anymore."

"You should be," he replied with a deadpan voice.

"Why? I have you and I'm sure you'd fight a bear if it came to it."

"Yeah, I probably would because I'm dumb like that," Dan confessed. "It's just kind of in our nature. I wouldn't win though, and he'd run you down and kill you a short time later just so you know."

Comforting thoughts offered in the pitch black void of the New Jersey woods.

By the grace of the highest universal order, we stumbled out of the timber a short time later and I was never happier to see concrete in my life. We strolled over to the truck and returned within a half hour with several cases of beer in tow. If the previous hours had proven anything, it was that this bunch was a thirsty and capable one, and we trudged back toward the blazing fire like champions with seventy-two frosty brews in hand.

The closer we drew to the fire the more my nerves settled, and once I could hear Hunter's voice talking nonsense, I let my guard down fully. We were almost back to safety when a beast emerged from the nearby brush that nearly forced a full release of all bodily fluids. I hit the ground and turtle up, playing the possum dead position.

Then came the laughter. Then came a bunch more of it.

"Holy shit!" Jim's voice roared as he stood over top of me in full faux bear mode. "You okay down there?"

"Damn you, Miller."

"Gotta watch out for the bush bears," Dan added as the brothers had united in my misery. The elder led me right into the trap and the younger finished the job with flair. Even though my pants were nearly full of shit and my heart practically stopped, at least there was a copious amount of beer to ease my wounds.

Once said alcohol mixed with the regimented back medicine, I was no worse for wear, and we spent the rest of the night telling stories like people who'd known one another for a lifetime. There was something easy and understanding about the Miller family that reminded me of my own, and I found comfort in that, even though comfort in my own family was never easily found.

One by one the campsite warriors began to fall off, but myself and the two Miller brothers held steadfast. They made their respective careers by being as game as they come inside the cage, and that readiness for the fray extended into every part of their lives. My job is peculiar in the sense that I am charged with telling the stories of real flesh and blood people in an honest manner, but what has made me particularly good at what I do is my ability to get down to the human nature.

As I positioned my sleeping bag in between the two Millers—a maneuver done with bear defense strategy in mind—I found myself questioning what I did for a living. I knew I could tell their story better than anyone had done before me, but those matters of the heart are taxing. It's difficult to wear that type of emotion and then craft it for the masses to digest, only to have it passed off several days later for the next big headline.

But that stress would come later on down the line. That night all I wanted to do was fall asleep beneath the stars listening to Jim tell stories about Dan clearing out a house party and throwing dukes with a drunken crowd in nothing but his tighty whitey underwear. If that's not a good note to end a nigh,t I just don't know what is.

We woke up the next day to Jim brewing coffee over the campfire, and Hunter cleaning up the debris of the 72 dead beer can soldiers we laid waste to in the night. In that moment the surrounding grounds looked less like a campsite as it did a crime scene, and the collective hangover ratio was strong throughout. Once things were packed up, we made the voyage back to the trucks where we decided to grab a bite to eat before my crew broke off and headed east to see fellow New Jersey native Frankie Edgar.

The Millers guided us to a roadside diner that had the biggest menu I'd ever seen. Funny enough, one of the items on the menu was named after Jim, which was a point that ratcheted the ball-busting back to a high degree. With the entire table stinking of campfire, and my questionable stomach doubting I could make the two-hour drive taking in that distinct scent, I asked Mike if we could catch a quick shower and change of clothes at his place. A request he quickly and courteously obliged.

While the rest of the road trip posse were finishing up their respective refreshing sessions, I bent Jim's ear about his future fighting inside the cage. He'd been one of the best lightweight fighters in the world for most of the past decade, but with so many visible interests beyond punching and kicking another man in the face, I wondered how much longer he'd stay at it.

"That's a tough question," he replied. "I've been fighting so long and it's such a part of who I am, I can't see the competitor in me ever really letting go. On the flip side, being a fighter isn't what defines me, and I'm happy about that. There are only a handful of people who have competed inside that Octagon as many times as I have, and I take pride in that. It's not easy to stick around at the elite level of this game and I've done it longer than most.

"When it's time to go it will be time to go," Miller added simplistically. "I'm not going to be one of those guys who sticks around too long and ends up taking so much punishment that it ruins the rest of my life. I have kids and a family to think about and I don't make enough money to trade in my brain for it. I don't know how much time I have left, but you can bet your ass I'll give everything I have to give for as long as I'm doing it. That's the only way I know how to work."

An hour later the Nissan was back on the highway with a new mission on our minds, but retelling stories exchanged the night prior kept the radio off for the duration. In addition to my own experiences, it was great to give and up-and-coming mind like Hunter that type of exposure to the fighters he was hoping to make a career covering. My process had never been like any of my peers, and Hunter was able to get a front row seat to how my unusual approach can pay dividends.

Chapter 27

The Godfather of Toms River

"We are going to Frankie Edgar's fucking house?"

Although Hunter attempted to keep his excitement in check, learning that we would be spending the afternoon with the legendary lightweight turned featherweight contender at his personal abode was more than he could handle. Poor Parm wasn't quite sure what to do with that information, but feeding off his buddy allowed him to go with the joy of the moment.

And it was true. Rather than meet the "Fighting Pride of Toms River" at one of his favorite restaurants to do our interview, the iconic fighter with an over-sized heart and undersized frame had decided to open up the doors to his home for the next stop on my road trip. While I was somewhat shocked in the immediate aftermath of the phone call, Edgar and I had done dozens of great stories over the years, and there was a general easiness between us.

Even though Toms River was less than two hours from the woodland preserve we spent the night in fending off bears with the Miller brothers, that part of New Jersey felt like an entirely different planet. Gone were the jacked up pickup trucks with gun racks in the back window. They had been replaced by a rainbow spectrum of sports cars in different colors.

"I believe this is Bro Jersey," I said as I took in the scenery around me.

Neither of my travel companions disagreed. The GPS sounded that we were two miles from our destination, and after a few twists and turns, the hustle and bustle of strip mall shopping centers and heavy traffic gave way to the plush greens of well manicured lawns and huge houses definitely north of the $500k mark. I watched as the distance dwindled down to less than half a mile, and I began scanning the road ahead for the destination. Less than a minute later we had arrived and were immediately taken back by the homestead Edgar and his family were rocking.

Like a scene straight out of *The Sopranos*, there sat his house on a small slope, as a team of landscape workers shuffled about working on his hedges. Standing on the front porch under an enormous brick archway was the former lightweight champion, and his grin stretched ear to ear as the car pulled up. He walked down the sidewalk nimbly, skipping around a few of the laborers to meet me at the beginning of the drive.

After a quick hug, we exchanged pleasantries, and Edgar introduced himself to the rest of the crew. Hunter's eyes were lost in wonderland, and it was clear he was in awe of the notorious scrapper. I nudged him to make sure he knew the moment was real.

"Let's go inside. I'll grab you guys something to drink if you're thirsty," Edgar beckoned.

While we caught a quick tour of the stately Edgar manor, my mind rapidly retraced some of the times I'd spent with the surging featherweight in the past. We had one particularly hilarious encounter back in April of 2012 during the UFC's visit to Atlanta that involved pound-for-pound great and then welterweight champion Georges St-Pierre. Everyone was in town for UFC 145 which featured the long awaited showdown between Jon Jones and his rival Rashad Evans. When there is an event with that much heat around it, the nights on the town generally get a bit wild, and my fellow journo and partner in crime Jeff Cain and I felt like getting a bit rowdy.

I had received an invite to attend a pre-fight party hosted by Ryan Bader, and Cain and I decided it would be a suitable environment for us to put one on. Naturally we did a bit of pre-drinking at our hotel bar, then caught a shady cab to the club where the event was taking place. As soon as we stepped out of the cab we could hear the bass pounding from the speakers inside, and the way Cain rolled his eyes was the perfect indicator that we were both about to walk into a scene we both dreaded.

Clubs had become the equivalent of Hell to men our age, but with the need for adventure pulsing through our respective veins, the hurdles crowded rooms and non-stop dance music were going to present wouldn't be enough to slow us down. Since my name was on the guest list, we were able to breeze past the line, and Cain took up the charge of carving his way through the crowd to get us a much needed drink.

I walked over to the V.I.P. section where Bader was holding his shindig. The area was already spilling over with partiers, so I decided to shake some hands without going beyond the velvet rope. Several moments later Cain emerged from the fray with frothy beers in hand, and we decided to do a bit of people watching before deciding our next move.

While scanning the crowd, I noticed Frankie Edgar had just walked in and started out to intercept him before he reached the bar to say hello. As we met up, we exchanged a laugh and a quick hug, and then I noticed the man standing next to him was none other than Georges St-Pierre. Even though the music was too loud for anyone to be heard, Edgar properly introduced me to GSP and the pound-for-pound great laughed and threw a quick high-five.

It was clear the French-Canadian MMA legend was there to do a little partying, and bumping into him was a nice little tidbit for a story to be told later on. Someone handed Edgar a beer where he stood, and we ended up carving out the spot we were all standing to post up. As we exchanged whatever small talk we could, a server emerged with what appeared to be bottle service for St-Pierre and his crew.

"There are no V.I.P. booths available at this exact moment Mr. St-Pierre," the server shouted. "But we are working on it."

Georges shrugged his shoulders to show he could not care less and flashed a smile that solidified the notion. As a man who had spent his entire life caught up in weird positions of circumstance, I was ready to chalk this up as a top five moment, but the following two hours only got weirder and more awesome by the second. Three beers deep and our collective was having a rip-roaring time. The typically robotic St-Pierre that was constantly on display for the MMA media was as loose and fun-loving as I'd heard he was in his normal life.

The shots began to fly like Chicago in the summertime, and the same server who brought the bottles earlier returned with two bulky security guards as they informed Georges that an area was ready for him and his party. Knowing our time had come to an end, I toasted Edgar one last time and as I tipped the bottle. I was surprised when he grabbed my arm and ushered us through the crowd to the V.I.P. section.

To say I was shocked would be an understatement, and I raised a bottle to Georges to make sure it was cool we came along. He gave a warm gesture back to confirm. Needless to say, the night from there was one for the record books, as we were able to leave the MMA world behind to joke and laugh with the real people beyond the elevated profiles.

Eventually the dance floor crowd would break out into an overwhelming sprawl that velvet ropes couldn't contain, and Cain and I were split up from the group. Rather than attempt to battle the hordes of party goers just to get back to the table, I suggested to Cain that we call it a night and make our way back to the hotel. My poor companion was drowned in beers deep enough where forming full sentences wasn't an option, but being a savvy veteran of the night life, he sloppily nodded in my direction to affirm that he in fact agreed with me.

We stumbled out of the club together and made our way back to the hotel in one piece only to spend the entire first half of the next day fending off the remnants of a brutal hangover.

As Parm and Hunter set up the video equipment on Edgar's spacious back patio, Frankie and I ran a quick recap of that night in Atlanta.

"That was a crazy night, bro," Edgar laughed.

"You're telling me? I never knew St-Pierre was that much fun."

"Georges is an awesome guy," Edgar answered. "When he's doing interviews with the media he's pretty careful with his words because he has such a visible profile, but when you are out with him, Georges is one of the best dudes on the planet. He's such a great guy and just a blast to be with."

As Frankie and I settled into our respective chairs, Parm informed us that the background noise from the landscapers was going to cause a problem with the sound quality of the video. Edgar was quick to find a solution as he suggested we move inside and showed the boys where they could set up in a side room just off the kitchen.

"My boys are going to be running around in here but it shouldn't be a problem," he said with a laugh. "I stress shouldn't in that sentence."

As Hunter and Parm began setting up for the interview, I followed Frankie into the kitchen to grab a glass of ice water. From the decoration inside the house to the vehicles outside in the driveway, there was no mistaking that he had done well for himself in the fight game. Since he was a long-reigning champion that would normally go without saying, but making money in MMA wasn't remotely the same to the paychecks that came to title holders in the world of boxing. They were not even close, and it's one of those issues everyone recognizes but no one really talks about all too much.

"Not doing too bad, Frankie," I offered as I pointed to the Cadillac Escalade sitting outside the window.

Ever-modest, Edgar slyly shrugged off my comment with a smirk.

"I do alright, but my wife also works," he replied. "So everything you see here isn't all my doing. She does pretty damn well for us."

After we received the green light from the other room, Edgar and I sat down to do the interview. Over the next 20 minutes we touched on a vast array of topics, but every time we attempted to lock in on something deeper, the levity that comes naturally between us would breakthrough. The end result was a home run video segment for the online road trip blog and a sit down that opened the doors for more interviews in the years to come.

As we were packing up the gear, Edgar asked what our plans were for the evening. Knowing our next stop was going to be up the road in Long Island—a destination we could certainly hit by nightfall—we tossed around the idea of jumping in the car and hitting our next destination. I could tell from the looks on my companion's faces that a good night of rest would be a welcomed suggestion though.

"If you guys want to stick around down this way, I can definitely hook you up with a place to crash," Edgar offered. "It's the off season at the shore, and my buddy has a hotel a few blocks away. If you guys want I can hook that up for you, and I have another buddy who owns a bar on the boardwalk and they'll take care of you as well."

I looked around but didn't need to ask because the answer was evident. We were going to call the Jersey Shore home for the evening. I jotted down the instructions Frankie handed out. He had a training session to hit so he wouldn't be joining us right away, but was adamant we make our first stop at a local cheese steak shop on the boardwalk. We could walk down to the bar and get our evening off to a proper start after that.

We followed Frankie's directions to a tee, and after loading up on one of the finest cheese steaks in the history of mankind, made our way up the boardwalk to the suggested watering hole. That said, before setting up shop at the bar, we made our way over to the railing and found a great spot on the boardwalk to shoot another quick video for the blog. By reaching the Atlantic Ocean, the MMA road trip project had officially gone coast to coast, and we memorialized the moment with a quick tribute.

By the time the video uploaded and processed, the crew were already three rounds deep as Frankie's friends kept the rounds coming in fast and furious fashion. I was in ice cold heaven, but I could tell the wear and tear of a night of hard drinking and ground sleeping in the woods with the Miller brothers had taken its toll on Hunter and Parm. I also knew they didn't want to verbally tap out, so I gave them the out in a different fashion.

"Here is the number Frankie gave us if you guys want to go get the hotel room set up," I said as I handed Hunter the paper with the information on it.

"Yeah man, that is probably best," he replied. "The beers are going down great, but we are shot. A good night of sleep on a real bed would be excellent about now."

The two of them quickly finished off their drinks and made their way to the car. No sooner than they skipped out, did a husky man walk up and introduce himself as Kevin. He was the owner of the bar and came down because Frankie had let him know I was in town doing a story. I was honored he would make time to hang out, and he wasted zero time letting me know this stop was not going to be one I would be forgetting anytime soon.

"Frankie gave me a call, and I wanted to come down to personally make sure you are shown the proper amount of hospitality."

When you are a man who has made a career out of going strong to the paint in such memorable fashion where the signature label "Johnny Cash Hard" becomes your calling card, you learn to spot a few things. I wasn't quite sure what Kevin meant or what proper courtesy entailed in this particular part of the country, but I could feel a storm brewing on the Jersey shore. It seemed as if Hurricane Duane was about to hit a Nor'easter head on.

And I was correct.

Now, it wouldn't be responsible of me as a writer to attempt to recall the happenings of such an evening that quickly turned into a blur of shot glasses, laughs, and thumping house music. It's a rare feat for the control tower for my senses to be taken out, but this rebel assault was certainly effective in that matter. And while I can't paint a clear picture, Hunter's response when I came pouring through the door at 3:00 AM was a damn fine indicator that I'd managed to put in a proper night's work.

"Holy fucking shit, are you okay?" he shouted as he burst out of a pile of blankets.

I couldn't find the right words or string together enough of them to put together a proper sentence, but a strong thumbs up let my worried counterpart know that the man who walked through the doors was in fact his fearless mentor and not an extra from The Walking Dead. I stumbled over to the other bed, grabbed a pillow, and crashed out on a carpet floor so suspect that it managed to register as such even in my drunken stupor.

Not being one to break my wife's key rule of travel, I sent her a message to ease her soul. I picked up my phone, fumbled through a sloppy text, and closed it to bring an end to the madness. Just like the carpet, my stomach was in a questionable state. Tense negotiations were going down with my central command. It was my sincerest hope diplomacy would work and my brain would convince my innards to stay down, but I wasn't going to be able to stay awake long enough to make it to the verdict.

It all went black. Spinning black. A deep dark void turned vortex courtesy of top shelf vodka.

Chapter 28

Long Island is Appropriately Named

The next morning came like a charge of soldiers storming foreign shores. The screams and cries of havoc rang loudly as the chaos and horror unfolded live and in living color. It was a grisly scene to say the least and one that strung several mysteries out for me to resolve in my battered state.

My phone was lit up with a series of texts that apparently went down between my wife and I where I asked her to dump her morality and send me nude pictures. Naturally she rebuffed my advances, then decided to bring the heat for my apparent lack of control. The final text she sent was a strong indicator she did not go to bed a very happy woman, which told me there was a fire and brimstone phone call waiting for me in the hours to come.

There were several other messages as well. Outside of my work on the road trip, I also had deadlines for several other entities, and the interviews for those stories were fit to go down in the early afternoon. With our day planned to make the trip north to New York, I would be wheeling and dealing the best questions I could come up with all the while hating humanity and life itself from the backseat of the car, because there was no way I could find my bearings enough to drive.

Hunter and Parm kept the noise down as they packed up the room, but I could hear them snickering at my sorry state. My young protégé showed to be an apt pupil as he read all the signs correctly and took charge of our exit from New Jersey while I fumbled around with a face showing several different shades of death. Again…it was a grisly scene.

Over the next few hours we would make our way upstate and into a mess of traffic on the Parkway. We saw a total of five accidents happen in real time as impatient New Yorkers slammed into one another in failed attempts to weave in and out of traffic. During that time I also interviewed MMA legend Mauricio "Shogun" Rua, as we made a quick pit stop at a rest area, where despite my haggard presentation, somehow managed to pull off a great chat with the assistance of a translator.

It's also worth noting Parm ordered lunch from a Burger King we would later find out was the genesis for a rare strain of some bacterial disease. Our camera wielding friend would ultimately survive, but it was touch and go for the days after the incident. Just before hitting the multi-leveled terror that is the Veranzano Bridge, my phone lit up with a call from Jimi Manuwa and I spent a solid ten minutes hashing out a conversation with "The Posterboy."

Upon conclusion of that call, my interview work was done for the day, and a shred of happiness found its way into my life. I don't know much about biochemistry, but whatever happens to a human's ability to process alcohol after the age of 30 is a terrible and strange phenomenon. Where I was once able to shake off a ripper like frat boy tossing a condom wrapper, my current self wore a nasty hangover like a bright orange sweater. Just a hideous thing but such is life on the road.

Halfway across the bridge panic began to set in. There is no particular reason for this phobia from a clinical standpoint, but for as long as I can remember, I'd always been terrified of bridges. The Abraham Lincoln Bridge back home in Lasalle, Illinois was one of the longest in the country at the time of its construction, and each of the thousand times I'd crossed it, at least one terrible thought found its way into my brain. The Veranzano was a totally different animal. I'd never seen a bridge that carried dual decks of traffic, and knowing there was tons of weight zipping overhead broke a sweat out across my forehead. Never mind said bridge is as long as all get out, because if I were to put those two things together I could have very well stroked out right then and there.

With a full on panic attack just moments away from destroying me, the only protection I could think of was to dose one of my pain pills, but the choppy seas of my stomach were not going to allow it. I was prescribed a high level pain killer, and even on a good day, a slight touch of nausea would rear up. There was no way I was going to be able to keep it down with my personal constitution already on the proverbial rocks.

I was going to have to ride it out, and it wasn't going to be pretty, given my recent history.

Although my childhood was filled with various traumas that would later create substantial problems in my adult life, anxiety had never been an issue. For some reason or another I'd developed a gnarly set of coping skills, and my constant self-analysis, reflection, and critique methods allowed me to mature into a person with better than average self-awareness.

In simple terms: I'm a difficult man to work up. At least that had been true until my early 30's when, from out of nowhere, these strange fits of panic and distress kicked in. The first one hit on the way home from Renee and I's first ever visit to Las Vegas, and I was sure a heart attack was setting in.

My lovely wife had somehow managed to plan, book, and execute an incredible surprise gift for my 30th birthday that consisted of a five-day stay in Sin City. While surprises come with a varying degree of difficulty, this covert operation she pulled off was certainly one for the books because of the interweaving levels of sneakiness it took to get the job done.

The biggest hurdle came in the money department. When you share a bank account with your significant other, it's difficult to nonchalantly explain where twenty-five hundred dollars happened to go. Later I would learn she set aside money from our yearly tax return, but paying for the trip was just a small part of her overall difficulty. In addition to the cash, she also needed to set up a babysitter for our children, call my boss to get me out of work, pack all the necessary luggage, and orchestrate rides to and from the airport.

When I got home that day, I was already in a rush because Zoe had a soccer game, and I found it strange that Renee was all dolled up. When her step brother showed up to the house, my wheels started to turn thinking there could be a surprise dinner happening, and that theory picked up some steam when he said we needed to go to the airport to pick up their other brother. I thought a trip to the airport was weird and unnecessary, but wasn't hip to the grand scheme whatsoever.

The alarms finally sounded when we pulled into the departures lane, and once the car stopped, Renee got out and started unloading our luggage. While it was then and there I knew something was up, it wasn't until we hit the counter and the woman said, "Oh, you're gonna have fun in Las Vegas," did I finally understand the beautiful shenanigans my loving wife had pulled.

It was a memorable trip, and we had a remarkable time filled with the type of wild late night debauchery our pre-children relationship was keen to, but on the flight home something strange was going on inside of me. The air is thin in Denver as is, but sitting in the terminal waiting for our delayed flight, I started to feel my chest tighten and my brain went spastic.

Fresh air was the only option, and bright flashing signs in my mind signaled me to get outside no matter the obstacle. This would of course mean I had to go back through security and all the hassle that comes attached to such a move, but I just didn't care. I needed to get outside, or I truly thought I was going to die.

Renee looked concerned and confused as she followed alongside of me, and once I finally began to settle down, told her what was happening. By that time I had broken into a full sweat, the type that comes when a man who has stolen a six pack of beer from the package store is put under the hot lights. Did he really need the six-pack? No…but goddamn if his degenerate genes didn't tell him he did.

Having come out the other side of the panic attack, I instantly dreaded the thought of getting packed into the plane. If the wide open space of the airport terminal was enough to send me into a frenzied downward spiral, then being crammed into the middle seat on the airplane was certainly going to do it. I felt like I was toeing the line and on the verge of combustion the entire walk to my seat, and once I sat down kicked the recycled air blower full blast on my face.

Bless her heart, Renee held my hand the entire way through, and her assistance, in addition to five cold beers on the two hour flight, allowed me safe passage back to Indianapolis without another incident. Nevertheless, the next few years would see the process repeated numerous times, and the most frustrating part is there were never any clear indicators or catalysts.

They would just happen, and I could certainly feel one coming on strong as we crossed the Veranzano.

I closed my eyes and clenched my fists tight as I kept my head close to the open window in the backseat. I fixed the world CALM in big bold letters on my frontal lobe and pinched the soft spot of my hand between my thumb and index finger because I'd read it in an article I found on Google. The seconds passed like kidney stones, and my heart thumped like wild mustangs across the high desert in Nevada.

The full onset was just moments away, and I silently prayed to the universe it wouldn't be as ugly as I knew it was going to be. Then, from out of nowhere, it just passed. Like a fever breaking, it simply dissipated, leaving me sitting in the backseat with my tee shirt soaked and my eyes floating. To this day I have no idea why the fates decided to allow that storm of nerves and paranoia to bypass this poor bastard, but it sure enough did, and I'm sure enough appreciative.

Outside of the manic obtuseness of being in the grips of a bad acid trip, having your nerves frayed and splintered in a full scale panic attack is a close second to the worst things that can befall a person.

"Hope you like your s'getti and meatballs," Hunter panned in perhaps the worst faux Italian accent I'd ever heard in my life. "Because we in Long Island."

Chapter 29

Car Trouble and Lost Mentors

"This GPS is a piece of shit!"

As a native New Yorker, Thomas Gerbasi had spent his life traversing the five boroughs, but for some reason the particular stretch of highway we kept doubling back over was giving him fits. My fearless mentor had recently taken patronage at a quality Italian restaurant in this neck of the woods, and that's where he wanted to take our group during our one day stay on Long Island. The only problem was that he couldn't quite remember what exit would get us there, and the GPS he was using on his phone wasn't necessarily being clear cut with directions.

"It keeps saying to take this exit, but I know for a fact the place isn't located down here," Gerbasi said with a laugh.

"Never trust computers," I said mockingly.

"Easy Finley," he replied. "I'm old, but I'm not that old. I've been to this place a few times and I know it's further up."

Even though it was funny to bust his balls for a bit, the man widely regarded in MMA circles as "The Godfather of Combat Sports Writing" was ultimately correct, as the restaurant in question was in fact two miles North of where the GPS had initially instructed us to exit. Never being one to say, "I told you so," Gerbasi took his victory with silent pride, and it only served to solidify the mysterious notion that New Yorkers are born with a different sense of direction.

Saturday Night Live did a skit for the show's 40th anniversary that made fun of the way Los Angelinos give directions, and for as funny as that was in script form, it was as true to life as to how New Yorkers operate. Renee and I witnessed this firsthand during a visit to the big city back in 2013. Everywhere we stopped to plug in an address on our phones, someone passing by would see us and ask where we were looking to go.

It didn't matter how obscure the location, without fail, each individual that stopped to offer their help sure enough had a specific route to get there. Not only was it impressive how quickly each of them broke down the grid system, but it also went a long way to shatter the stereotype that native New Yorkers are assholes.

"You've traveled a long way to get here, Finley," Gerbasi said. "The least I can do is make sure you get some good food."

And while I knew he was referring to my trip across the continental United States in search of telling some overly ambitious story about MMA fighters, just the time in Long Island alone was enough to dictate a reprieve. Aside from suffering the trappings of a vicious hangover, the day's events were undoubtedly stressful, and so much so that I was honestly looking forward to putting down an ice cold beer to smooth things out.

The entire reason I marked a stop in Long Island on the road trip was to spend time with middleweight champion Chris Weidman and his coach Ray Longo. Over the years I'd done some solid interviews with "The All-American" and had the opportunity to get to know the Serra-Longo product in a social setting. Capping off what would be the final stop on the project with a current titleholder would be a fitting bookend to an insane adventure, but for reasons unbeknownst to me, things wouldn't work out that way.

I had previously contacted Longo a few days prior, and he set up a time for us to meet down at the gym he co-owned with Chris called LAW MMA. Thanks to the traffic on the Parkway, we were running a bit behind, but once I found the moxie to push off the effects of the previous night's bender, I took the wheel and started making time. We were less than five minutes behind by the time we hit Garden City, and the GPS showed we were two minutes away from our destination.

We were the third car back at a stoplight, and the crew began gearing up for our arrival. Parm was sitting in the backseat with his laptop downloading video footage to free up his camera for the interviews we were about to shoot, and Hunter was plugged in on his cell phone updating the Twitter account on the trip. We were three cars back when we pulled up to a stoplight and all of a sudden everything cut out.

The car was dead. Stone cold dead.

"What the fuck?" I shouted nervously as my hands frantically flailed around the steering wheel trying to figure out what had gone wrong. I rocketed the gear shift back to park and turned the key but nothing registered, and instantaneously all of my worst fears became true. We were a thousand miles from home and the vehicle we were dependent on was lifeless.

"Holy shit, is this actually happening?" Hunter asked as he sat in fear.

As I continued to repeat the steps, I looked up to notice something else equally strange was going on. Not only was our car down for the count, but so were each of the three cars ahead of us. For reasons beyond explanation, all four of the motorized vehicles sitting at that stoplight had died simultaneously. The panic began to swell and rise inside of my chest and into my throat, and I felt the urge to vomit all over the place.

Fear is a powerful master.

Just when all seemed lost, I turned the key, and miraculously the engine turned over, and the Nissan Altima roared back to life.

"Oh, motherfucker!" I shouted. "We are back in business!"

The three of us cheered as if we'd hit a buzzer beater to win the National Championship, and the car rolled forward through the stoplight, only having to pass one of the cars ahead of us, as the two other vehicles had also been reborn. The brief incident caused a minor logjam of traffic on the road, and my eyes bounced chaotic from the road ahead to the rear view mirror at an angry soccer mom in a minivan throwing me the finger.

Once the intersection equivalent of the Bermuda Triangle was several blocks behind us, we began to try to make sense of what had just happened.

"That was fucking intense," I said with wide eyes and a heart thumping strong. "I've never seen anything like that before."

"It just doesn't make any sense," Hunter added. "Mechanically speaking, the car was running fine. It didn't sputter or cut out. It just died like that," he said snapping his fingers.

"Yeah, and that just doesn't just happen," Parm chimed. "When cars break down there is usually a cause. The car went from fine to toast."

"And it wasn't just ours," I returned. "Did you guys see what happened to the cars in front of us? They all died too. This is just fucking insane."

As we made the right turn to head down the street to where LAW MMA was located, we strained to make any kind of rational reasoning to why what happened had happened. We were in collective agreement that all of the vehicles positioned ahead of us had also bit the dust, which was refreshing because I had started to think that was just a figment of my panicked mind. But it wasn't and it was clear what had transpired was clearly some type of phenomenon.

I pulled the car over in front of the gym, and after putting it into park flipped off the ignition. I took a few deep breaths before cranking the key back over, because I was absolutely concerned the car would not start again. Fortunately for our crew it did, and having the car fire back to life in instant fashion only furthered the mystery surrounding the incident.

"I'm going to post something about it on Facebook and see if anyone has any theories," Hunter said. "Hopefully someone out there will have an answer to what happened to us back there."

We sat in the car discussing the strange and curious turn when I noticed Ray Longo pull up and park in front of the gym. It was right about this time when Gerbasi text to let me know he was only a few minutes away as well, and the closer it got to doing some actual work, the more I was able to push the car dying madness out of my brain.

I had the boys remain in the car as I made my way over to speak with Longo about the project. Each gym has its own particular culture, but privacy is typically one constant thread that runs throughout. I didn't want Longo to see a pack of media reporters with a camera crew in tow come rushing across the street, so I decided to take the personal approach, because it was also the one I found the most comfortable.

Longo saw me coming from across the street and waited for me to make it to where he was standing. The striking guru is well known for having a unique personality and approach that perfectly mixes a light hearted sense of humor with a no bullshit view on fighting. He's also a mountain of a man with thick black hair and an accent straight out of The Godfather.

Outside of time with Weidman, I couldn't wait to pick the brain of the man who built two fighters that toppled legends in spectacular fashion. A light rain had started to fall just as I crossed the street, so I quickened my pace as I made my way to where Longo was standing.

"Hey Mr. Longo," I said as I extended my hand. "Thank you so much for making the time."

"My pleasure, Duane," he returned. "I appreciate you adding the gym as a stop on your project, and I'm looking forward to sitting down with you. Al and Aljo should be coming down here in a few minutes. Chris was here just a minute ago but I don't know where he ran off to."

By "Al and Aljo" he meant Al Iaquinta and Aljamain Sterling, who were two lighter weight fighters making a lot of noise on the big stage. I was excited to chop it up with each of them, but was slightly curbed to the idea Weidman may or may not be making an appearance. I looked over my shoulder to notice Tom Gerbasi had arrived and was making his way across the street. Seeing my close friend and mentor immediately shook off any frustration I had been carrying.

As previously stated, Gerbasi was an institution on the MMA scene, and he and Longo had done some incredible interviews over the years. Ray instantly recognized Gerbasi making his way over and welcomed him with open arms. They exchanged pleasantries and Ray's enthusiasm went up a few notches with his presence.

"Are you a part of this project too?" Ray asked.

"No, this is all Finley," Gerbasi replied. "I'm just here for support and the chance to see a few old friends."

"Well you know you're always welcome here," Longo laughed. "We even have heat this time."

Whatever that reference meant was a nod to an inside joke as the both cut up for a quick bit, but the rain suddenly got heavier and Longo suggested it was time to head inside. I motioned for Hunter and Parm to get the gear and follow us in just before making my way through the glass front door of LAW MMA.

Even though Gerbasi cringes at the mention of the word mentor, he has a firm understanding of what our relationship meant to me. I had never had anyone in my life take a sincere interest in guiding me through anything, so it was comforting to have him with me as I attempted to further my career in a game he'd all but mastered. In the present sense, it was excellent to have him with me in Long Island, because my association with him immediately put Longo at ease.

Not that Ray was worried I'd produce anything but an honest take, but his belief in Gerbasi automatically transitioned over to me since Tom had all but vouched for me.

We spent the next few hours cracking out a series of quality interviews with various members of the Serra-Longo team. Shortly after our arrival, Iaquinta came walking through the door and we immediately jumped into our exchange. In addition to being an up-and-coming fighter on the rise, Al also had a great sense of humor that surfaced during our conversation. Much like everyone else in the squad, Iaquinta was a New Yorker born and bred, and his jokes and delivery on said jokes were top notch. He was an easy going cat, but the same passion he fought with hovered just below the surface. This is the same guy who two years later would verbally assault a crowd in Virginia with the now infamous line, "Are you booing me? You better not be fucking booing me!"

Outside of an epic talk with Longo, the other dynamite interview of the day came from Aljamain Sterling. "Aljo" was a fresh young talent coming up through the bantamweight ranks, and we hit it off in spectacular fashion. Attention is hard to find for a fighter competing below the 155 pound mark, but Sterling had done a great job of finding traction in the early stages of his UFC career.

"The MMA world doesn't know it yet, but I'm coming to take over my division," Sterling said as we sat on a set of bleachers near the cage to the back of the gym. "I train with the best in the world every day, and I take anything I'm passionate about with the utmost importance. Most guys my age have no idea what they want to do, but I'm fortunate enough to have realized my path some time ago, and that puts me far ahead of the game."

"Isn't it the one you don't see coming that does the most damage?" I asked.

He immediately picked up on the analogy and replied, "That's exactly right, and that's what is going to happen. I'm going to keep winning and make more noise each and every time out."

As I sat conversing with Sterling, I found myself growing a slow fascination with him. Confidence that registers without arrogance is impressive by any measure, and nothing he said came off with an air of cockiness. Sterling was a self-assured individual and to have that type of constitution at such a young age is a remarkable feat.

We would stay in touch long after our interview that day at his gym, and funny enough, he's lived up to his words every step of the way. The kid not only has incredible physical gifts, but has a sharp intellect and broad perspective of the business that comes attached to the fight game. That's a dangerous combination for a fighter to have in a sport that eats its own without question or consequence.

After spending several hours at LAW MMA, I came to the realization Weidman was not going to appear. Although that was extremely disappointing, it wasn't a good enough reason to extend our stay any longer. I was hungry, and I know Gerbasi and the rest of our crew shared the same sentiment. We'd done all we could possibly do with what we were given, and it was time to hit the road and find somewhere to get our collective grub on.

The four of us all piled into Gerbasi's car, and after several trips up and down the interstate, we finally reached our destination just as the sun began to set on one of the longest days of the entire road trip adventure. The place was Passione Della Cucina and a feast was about to begin.

Chapter 30

Everybody and Their Motha

Just as Gerbasi had promised, the Italian spot was a revelation.

One of the underlying objectives to traveling around the country was to experience as much authentic culture per stop as possible. I had gone out of my way to scratch that particular itch at every other stop, and it would have been damn near punishable by law not to hit a legitimate Italian eatery whilst on the Island of Long. If not criminal, it would certainly be something Gerbasi would never allow me to live down.

Shortly after we took our seat, a wide array of breads, oils, and cheeses were delivered, and no time was wasted as we tore into the bountiful offering. Being the veteran that he was, Gerbasi took the helm as he ordered several appetizers and made suggestions around the table as to what was worth diving into, which was pretty much everything in the menu.

"You gonna get spaghetti and meatballs there, Finley," Gerbasi jabbed, which ultimately proved to be hilarious because that was the one item I had fixed my gaze upon.

I ultimately decided to go with some form of ravioli and that decision also brought a solid amount of mockery from the opposite side of the table. I also found the nerve to order a beer, as enough time had passed for the touch and go phase of my internal foundation to pass. With our order taken and the conversation flowing, all seemed right with the world, and that feeling would last until I took the first icy cold drink of alcohol.

The instant the cold liquid made its way down my throat and to my stomach, a rebellion broke out. The uprising demanded to be televised, and an orchestra of ominous sounds gurgled and squelched from within. A light film of sweat formed from the back of my neck to my waistline, and I began to fear for the worst.

My eyes scanned for an exit strategy as my internal alarm system hit a level three.

Outside of Ebola, there is no sound excuse for anyone over the age of four to ever shit their pants. Over the years I'd heard of several friends or acquaintances who'd suffered major natural disasters, with copious intake of alcohol always being the primary culprit. Soiling one's self is never an acceptable outcome and to protect myself from breaking the ultimate dignity barrier, I'd conditioned myself to operate on a five alarm system.

The first alarm is a notice that something is stirring below. Once this sounds, it's an indication that somewhere along the line business needs to be handled. There is no panic or concern in this notification.

The second alarm is where the timeline gets set. As soon as this chirp sounds, you begin to plot out the course and manner in which you are going to take care of this particular situation.

The third alarm is where things start to get serious. It's like, "Whoa!" Once this indicator hits, there is no more time for games or tomfoolery, because a storm is brewing and shelter must be taken. Yet, even with the overall tone of the moment, the panic level is still reasonably low because nearly every building has a bathroom.

The fourth alarm is a far different scenario. When this bell sounds, it means all hell is about to break loose and lives could be lost. Like the tsunami that comes raging into a village an hour after an earthquake, the villagers who aren't warned usually get swept away to a watery grave. In my personal experience, the fourth alarm is when the common decency of politeness and patience quickly evaporate and the natural order of every man for himself comes into play. Seeing a grown man sprinting through the grocery is an uncommon sight to see, but next time you stumble across such a vision, you'll know exactly where they're heading.

The fifth alarm is like Voldemort in Harry Potter as it's the thing you don't speak about. If and when you are stricken with the most notorious and diabolical alarm, then the laws that typically govern society have all broken down, and mass chaos has ensued. It's pure chaos and a scene where men will resort to Neanderthal status to avoid the suffering. In this scenario it is kill or be killed, as fight or flight kicks into overdrive. The science behind this stage is not official, but solid sources have estimated only a fifteen percent success rate when things go to the fifth level.

Several times in my journey through life, I'd been the unfortunate recipient of the phenomenon that happens when the human body magically jumps from a two to a four alarm, and sitting at the booth in that restaurant was one of those times. Fortunately for all, I was sitting on the outside so I was able to get up and make haste for the commode, but my frenzied rise brought questions from my contingent of friends also sharing the table.

Due to my elevated state of emergency, I was unable to answer any of their queries as I took the level four mentality and locked my focus on the destination. That said, since Passione was a foreign location, I had to stop and ask for directions, and that pushed the madness to the brink of the fifth alarm. Long story short, all ended without a chalk outline, but the posh ambient lit restroom of the upscale Italian eatery was definitely turned into a crime scene in the aftermath of the alarms being quieted.

It was a call far too close for comfort, and despite relief having come, my stomach was still a live wire that I was now afraid to touch. On the walk back to the table, I began to concoct my excuse for my blistering exit and was greeted with pure horror as our respective orders had arrived in mass. I retook my seat and recoiled at the sight of a large plate of ravioli drenched in marinara sauce sitting directly before me.

As the others began hacking away at their plates, I could barely muster enough interest to swirl my fork around a few times. Gerbasi was the first to notice and he curbed his normal joking manner to concern.

"You alright there, Finley?" he asked. "Dig in before it gets cold."

"I'm okay," I assured. "My stomach isn't quite feeling it right now."

"Well that might be the case but you better eat up," he added. "They are going to take it personally if you don't."

I wasn't quite sure what he meant by that, but it all became clear over the next twenty minutes as at least five people ranging from the waiter to the general manager stopped by the table to ask why I wasn't eating what was on my plate. None were malicious in tone, but each certainly wanted to know the reason I wasn't consuming the meal I'd ordered from their kitchen.

By the time I told the GM my stomach had taken a turn, I partly expected the owners to pop out from behind the red curtain to my right and begin the inquisition.

"That's too bad, and I hope you are feeling better," the general manager gruffed. "I'm glad to see the rest of your friends aren't having an issue."

The man broke his hard-boiled detective bit for a warm smile once he noticed that Gerbasi, Hunter, and Parm had murdered the food they'd ordered, and I felt like the odd man out as he finally walked away. Thankfully no one else from the establishment came out to question me because I'm sure the chef would have resorted to fisticuffs if he knew I didn't touch what he made for me.

"I fucking told you, Finley," Gerbasi chuckled. "They take food seriously around here."

Much like everything Tom had ever told me, there was a large degree of truth in his words, but I found some slight comfort in my ability to take the loss on my official record rather than attempt to stem the tide of intestinal imbalance and end up in a full blown Jeremy Botter vs. The Cosmopolitan incident. No man deserves to have his dignity stripped like that, and I wasn't going to have it happen to me. Long Island wasn't the hill I was going to die on, in a manner of speaking.

Hours later in the bathroom of a roadside motel in the northern part of Long Island, I finally was able to crack open the ravioli and dive in, and despite being a touch on the cold side, they were just as good as advertised.

Chapter 31

A Long-Awaited Homecoming

The skies over Long Island stretched out gray and broken the next morning as rain battered the windows of the motel room. Hunter and Parm were conversing about something from their college days, and I could tell from their respective tones the wear and tear of the road had set in. Immediately upon this registering, I quantified their discomfort by one-hundred to find the pulse of my own.

We had one final stop to make before my wild-eyed ambitious endeavor officially came to an end, and it couldn't come soon enough. I was sure any romance to be found to the project's conclusion would show up somewhere else down the line, because there was certainly none to be found as I rolled over on the lumpy single to get the hitch out of my back. I informed my companions we were rolling out in twenty minutes, then hit the bathroom to shower and take my back medicine, which was running on the low side.

A half hour later we were cutting through the rain-soaked highway en route to Huntington to see one of the funniest men to ever strap on the four-ounce gloves in Matt Serra, and three hours after that we finally set sail for home. In addition to cementing his place as the biggest underdog to ever make good in the history of mixed martial arts when he TKO'd Georges St-Pierre, Serra was also one of the most well renowned coaches in the sport.

After he guided a hilarious tour through his gym, we sat down to talk about several of the topics I'd also discussed with his fellow coach and mentor Ray Longo, with the most prominent being Aljamain Sterling.

"Aljo is an animal," Serra beamed. "The kid has all the talent in the world and he has the mental strength to really do something with it. The dude is a sponge, man. You show him something once and he has it down, and he'll keep doing it until it becomes second nature to him. Most guys come in with a skill set they are comfortable with, and they are so eager to add other skills that they abandon what brought them here in the first place. That's not Aljo. He works on every aspect of his game, but he continues to strengthen his greatest attribute, which is great to see. The kid is gonna be a champion just watch."

I continued to think about Serra and everything that was said about Sterling as Hunter commanded the helm of the Altima. Knowing that I had another six hours to drive after dropping them off in Pittsburgh, my young protégé took it upon himself to navigate the Nissan from NYC back to the Steel City, and it was a gesture I found respectable. By that time all of the effects of Toms River had officially worn off, but there was no way to avoid just how beaten down I was mentally and physically.

Sitting in the back seat and just listening was something I didn't get the chance to do much of during the road trip adventure, and it was great to relax and eavesdrop on what two younger gen artists had to say. Parm spent a good deal of time talking about how shitty the dating scene was for an actual good guy and Hunter proved to be the great friend I assumed him to be by offering encouragement.

From time to time I would offer my sage-like advice as a man who was once a wildcat before settling down to marry at the ripe age of 23, but it was good to know there were young kids who still believed in being upstanding, because society has painted Millenials as a generation of crybabies with the intellect of a bowl of potato soup.

Granted, the grapefruit video they made me watch on YouTube nearly destroyed anything positive I thought of them, but it wasn't quite disgusting enough to shatter the bond we'd forged.

It was well past midnight by the time we rolled into Pittsburgh, and the thought of pushing through another six hours wasn't something I was totally confident in my ability to do. The part of me that relishes a challenge was strong in thinking I could reach Indianapolis without harm, but the other parts of me that remembered harrowing drives through Utah and Missouri chimed in to overpower my ego.

Hunter offered up his couch for as long as need be, and it was an invitation I accepted graciously.

When we entered Hunter's apartment his girlfriend was waiting there excitedly, and it made me long for home where Renee and my children were waiting in the worst way. The sensation was nearly strong enough to get me to axe my commitment to crash out on the couch for a few hours and hit the open road like a man possessed, but the thought of not making it and ending in a fiery crash brought me back to my good senses.

After a brief conversation, Hunter gave me a quick hug before heading back to his bedroom, and I pulled up on the couch across from Parm who had selected a recliner to check out in. We held a faint dialogue for a few moments as we collectively headed toward a much needed slumber, and before long, my eyes closed for the final time that night.

I awoke four hours later just as the sun was creeping over the trees outside of Hunter's apartment. My senses were clear enough to get back on the road. I crept out of the room and down to the car with the stealth of a cat burglar, and a few turns of the wheel later, I was back on the interstate en route to home sweet home.

In my conversation with Renee the day prior I told her it would be two days before I reached Indianapolis, and the thought of surprising my family with my arrival made me happy. They had all sacrificed so much for me to make the road trip a reality, and I was looking forward to giving them some well deserved comfort that had been missing from their lives.

Every day I was away meant Renee was charged with the responsibility of making sure we had coverage for our children. Her work schedule was nothing close to set in stone, which made it difficult to set up any type of system for a sitter. Thankfully our friends James and Robin Morey were always quick to help in a time of need, and they had watched our children more times than I could remember while I was on the road. It was going to be great to relieve Renee of that pressure, and I was certain it was something she looked forward to as well.

As far as my children went, it was night and day. With Zoe being my oldest and the two of us having this unspoken understanding of one another, she always encouraged my pursuits of the things I was passionate about. Despite the fact she was only 10 when the project first began, Zoe's old soul mentality really showed through when things got tough and her father was gone for long stretches of time.

It was the opposite for Atticus and rightfully so. As the only other male in the family, he's particularly attached to his daddy and hated me leaving. Where Zoe always tried to make sense of it, Atticus refused to and seeing him cry the day before I hit the road chipped away at my soul. He'd jump up in my arms the moment I returned and then spend the next week sticking by my side. I couldn't make a run to the grocery store without him, because he feared I was secretly leaving again, and just the thought of having put them all through it time and time again made my eyes well up as I drove.

As the miles of I-70 rolled beneath my wheels, I tried to make sense of everything that had happened on the trip, and there was just too much to process. At that point I couldn't even remember where the initial idea for it all came from, but I was damn sure glad it was all coming to an end. I thought about Jack Kerouac and how his words ignited a fire in my soul, and hoped that somehow my quest across the United States paid proper homage to one of the few men I idolized.

My journey wasn't going to encourage a generation of readers to hit the open road, nor would I become a counterculture icon, but I would be lying if I didn't admit that change was one of the underlying motives behind the trip. The sport of MMA moves at such a rapid pace that often times the fighters and their individual stories get left behind. It seems crazy since they are a critical part of the sport itself, but that doesn't make the notion any less true.

Ever since I took up the pen to write about MMA, the fighters had always been my primary focus, and I launched out on the road to show fans another side of their story. With the project officially at an end, I believed in some small measure I had accomplished that, but only time would tell if that was the case. With Kerouac in mind, I decided to make one final stop before home, and it was one I knew he'd smile upon somewhere in the great beyond.

I was forty minutes from Fishers when I turned off of the interstate at Knightstown and guided the Nissan down a two-lane highway. I had been out in that area a time or two for one of Zoe's softball games, and in doing so, had driven by a tiny roadside diner straight out of the 1950's. I brushed the sleep out of my tired eyes and made way down the state road that twisted and turned through farmland and maple groves.

I eventually reached my destination and pulled into the gravel lot next to a beat up Ford 150. My brown shoes kicked up dust as I made my way to the front door and the smell of bacon hit me flush as soon as I crossed the threshold. Rural locales create rural scenes, and the layout of the diner was as one would expect on the Indiana countryside. A table full of old farmers sat off in the corner hem-hawing about whatever and a few 50 something men were scattered about the bar top with eyes as calloused and rough as their hands.

A woman with bright eyes that contrasted against her worn face came out from behind the rail to greet me and invited me to sit wherever I wished. Normally I would have gone to the furthest corner of the room to sit in solitude, but on this day I wanted something different. I'd spent a year soaking up everything I could about places far from home, and for the next hour I wanted to sit and listen to the sounds of Indiana—a state time has all but forgotten—fill my ears.

In addition to the comforts of being on native soil once again, there was also something special in knowing I could finally get a down home meal laced with all the proper fixins'. The bubbly waitress returned to my table where I ordered three eggs over easy, four strips of bacon, two sausage links, and a side of biscuits and gravy. Even though it was still on the short side of noon, I decided to order a celebratory beer to symbolize the end of a great adventure, and upon hearing my order one of the old timers to my right shared his enthusiasm for my choice.

"Hell yes, young man!" he coughed. "Never too early for a cold one."

His comment sent his table into an uproar of laughter and random chatter, and I thanked him with a slow nod of the head. Normally I would have used his comment as a bridge into some meaningless small talk, but I just didn't have it in me. I'd spent nearly a year talking and doing interviews and all I wanted in that moment was to sit and listen.

I punished the meal without mercy, and the beer ended up being a remarkable choice to wash it all down. After I pushed the plates away, I sat looking out the huge window to my right and watched as cars and pickup trucks floated by. They were all on the way to somewhere and I liked the idea of not knowing. I found peace in that mystery despite how fleeting it was.

With all of the great things social media had brought to the world, erasing the mystery that exists between people was one of the sad casualties. I'd met random people at different times of my life who would pop into my mind for no reason at all years later. In one case it was a girl I spent two intense weeks with during a summer of my early teens but somehow lost connection with, and the other was a friend who worked across from me in the steel mill after high school.

In both instances, I would create scenarios in my mind of the things they went on to do after in the years after our lives briefly intersected. For her, I imagined she chased her love for painting and went on to become a popular artist living somewhere on the east coast, then after finding some success, settled down with a husband and two kids.

The scene was a bit different for my former buddy Steve from the factory. Even though I'd always been as wild as they come, this son of a bitch was pre-wired on a setting a few levels above even what I was capable of, so I imagined something worse happened to him. Whenever he'd pop into my mind, I would imagine he gave it his best at whatever he chose to do before succumbing to the alcoholism that was already front and center in his early 20's.

Sometimes I would get lost in those thoughts, but the eventual rise of Facebook in all of our lives would come around and wipe out those fantasies. With one click of a button you can see where everyone ended up in their lives, and the reality never comes close to living up to what the mind has created. The girl found herself at the end of a heroin needle and died when she was 22, parked in the back alley of a dead end tavern, while Steve managed to get his shit together by entering the armed forces.

He served in the Iraq war, and from what I could gather, his service was exemplary, but a few years after returning home he was killed in an automobile accident when a drunk driver hit him head on as he drove home from work.

Life can be a monstrously ironic thing when it wants to be, and I remember feeling slightly empty when I figured out the respective fates of two people who shared a small but memorable portion of my journey.

I walked over to the diner top to pay the waitress with the kind eyes, but not before picking up the check of the table of old farmers who were sitting on the other side of me. During my meal, I overheard two of the men talking about serving in Korea, and that's what brought the strange memory of Steve flooding back. While they were a bit confused by my gesture, the same man who heralded my choice to get a beer before noon locked in on what I was getting at.

Our eyes connected and two old souls who'd seen too much but were living or had lived this thing called life to the fullest came to an understanding.

When I got back into my car, a wave of emotion came crashing over me and I broke into tears. While there were many things that could have been the cause of the outburst, I was certain there wasn't one solitary reason that sparked it. I knew in that moment as I sat in my car with streams of tears rolling down my face that the entirety of my trek across the country and all of the memories it created was overwhelming me.

This storm continued for the next five minutes until I finally got a grip on my faculties and set in on the homestretch. For the final fort minutes of my drive I turned my phone off and hit the mute button on the radio. I rolled the windows down to let the clean country air rip through the car and take all of my stresses and concerns somewhere far away. The gusting wind filled my ears and cleared out my mind in the process, until the only image visible behind my eyes was that of my beautiful wife and my two amazing children.

They were the only thing that mattered. They were the only thing that ever mattered, and every mile I left behind was another mile closer to having them in my arms. The blowing breeze wiped away what was left of my tears, and somewhere along the way I found the smile I'd lost in the storm of ambition that took me so far from home.

Not only was that distance going to be eclipsed for good, but I had done what I set out to do. I had driven through blizzards and rain storms alike to make good on a dream project. I had traversed deserts and mountain passes alike to find some elusive accomplishment my wild mind had cooked up. I'd managed to complete something that seemed so far-fetched at the time of conception that the company who employed me wanted nothing to do with it.

I had actually fucking pulled it off, and in the process, found a truth that had been buried inside of me all along. That truth was that the love of the three people waiting for me was the only thing that mattered. I also learned so many things about myself and my connections with other people, and those realizations were far greater than any amount of money that would come in because of my journey.

Some people never reach that level of understanding, and it took me driving twenty thousand miles to find the blueprint to become the person I always knew I could be. Some of the key pieces necessary for construction were already in place, the others—much darker and heavier elements—were in desperate need of removal or repair.

Chapter 32

Darkness on the Homefront

Control is such a strange and unpredictable beast.

The road trip had been over for only a handful of weeks and that brought about some difficult adjustments. Something that had originated as such an impossible dream had been locked, executed, and stamped in ten furious months, and I still wasn't quite sure what to make of it. The interviews and the experiences flashed through my mind frequently as I attempted to settle back into my normal life, but there was a much larger and darker cloud looming.

Going back as far as I can dig through the chasms of my mind, I've been pre-wired to some form of addiction. I was raised in a household where those elements were on constant display, and although I didn't come up in a crack house or a den of debauchery, that doesn't mean the subtle and not so subtle projections don't stick in some form or fashion. Make no mistake about it: both of my parents are lovely people, but particular demons have haunted my family for generations.

It had always been my sincerest hope not to carry those troubles into my adult life, but that was a quest I'd failed in at previous junctures. Renee and I were basically kids when we got married back in 2001, and it took some time for me to shake off some of my lesser qualities. Nevertheless, I faced up, dove in, and did the work to correct those issues, but addiction is something that never truly goes away.

It is a monster that runs on a parallel timeline and has the endurance of a Kenyan runner. It's always there looking over and checking in to see if it is needed or free to enter. Addiction is the neighborhood kid your parents never allowed you to play with because he has been known to steal, and even though he knows your parents hate him and never let you play with him, he still stops over from time to time to see if you can go for a bike ride.

Coming off the road trip, I was mentally and physically exhausted to a point that is beyond explanation, and those circumstances are dangerous for someone with my predisposed nature. This is where the control issue came to the forefront.

By November of 2014, I had been dealing with the back issue for two years and had been heavily medicated for at least half of that time. As I attempted to settle back into my family life and return to being the loving father and husband I've always prided myself in being, I found an incredible shortage of energy and this evoked a unique type of sadness. The low rising winter sun ran cold for long stretches, and I began to lose track of whether or not I was taking pills to remedy the constant pain in my back or smooth out the rugged thoughts of my tattered mind.

After a few days of this, I was able to call bullshit on myself, but it just didn't matter. I had slipped back into a full-blown situation and absolutely allowed it to happen. Anyone who has been through recovery understands the amount of fight that is necessary to remain standing clear on their own two feet, and because I had overworked myself and failed to take care of myself mentally, the will to fight was non-existent.

I've never been a man to make excuses, but the mask of addiction is a villainous thing. Once it is slid down, you begin to view things differently, and it's almost as if you're watching your own life from the passenger side of a bus window. The outcomes are predetermined, and you know how much hurt is going to be caused by it all, but something inside of you just doesn't allow you to care. I'd put Renee through it once and it nearly destroyed our marriage, and here I was on the brink of doing the same thing all over again at a time where things in our life had never been better.

Although I was in the grips of such things, that didn't mean I acted entirely without conscious. The universe blessed me with a remarkable woman, and I've been grateful every single day of our life together for how much joy she's brought into my life. Unfortunately for her I've always been what is classified as a "functioning drug addict," which by and large is what made it next to impossible for her to tell things had taken a terrible slip.

When most people think of drug addicts, especially of the opiate variety, they think of dirty-faced junkies floating around the streets hungry for a fix. The more realistic level of the populous may see a different scenario, but there is always the assumption that drug addicts don't work or function in normal society. Perhaps it's my wiring, but drugs or no drugs, I've always been able to get where I need to go and do the work that needs to be done. Granted there were plenty of junk sick days where long stretches in physical detoxification took the best of what I had to offer, but it never stopped me from being reliable.

The day my sobriety officially started the elimination of those dark days was the first thing I was grateful for, and I kept the memory of such things fresh in my mind during my eight years clean and clear. When my back issue came to call, it made Renee extremely hesitant because she knew we were going to be playing with fire on a different level, but the options available were few. I either had to suffer through a crippling disability and deal with the mental storm that would create, or I could attempt to navigate a treacherous minefield.

While she was diligent in keeping me accountable, the fast-paced chaos of the road trip project made things on my end difficult to monitor, and it was something I was certainly aware of throughout. Once I officially slipped and lost the sobriety I once held dear, I further used that scenario to my advantage. I knew it would take awhile for the true picture to take shape and simply hoped I could regain my footing on my own before the truth of my dilemma ever came to light.

My entire life I had excelled under pressure, and this was just going to be another one of those things. At least that was the plan. Until it wasn't anymore.

It was two days before Thanksgiving when the bottom of my little secret world fell out and everything exploded. Since the federal laws had changed and narcotics could no longer be called into pharmacies from doctors over the phone and hand written scripts had to be given, that meant I had to make an appointment every month to see my neurologist to refill my medicine. And while the road trip and travel made that difficult at times, I was typically able to keep a schedule that allowed a mid-month visit.

I usually kept the bottle in my travel bag, but for some reason or another, I had left it on the bathroom counter that day, and that's when she noticed the problem. It had been less than two weeks since my appointment and already the bottle was half empty, which painfully exposed the excessive amount I had been consuming.

I turned off the faucet and opened the shower curtain to see her standing there with a look I'd only seen a handful of times in our life together, and never had that look preceded anything pleasant. Her eyes were filled with tears and I could hear the pills rattling in the bottle as her left hand was trembling. In that moment she knew what was going on and the reality hit her so hard in the chest it made it difficult for her to breathe.

She didn't say anything because she didn't need to say anything. She knew. That was all that mattered. And because she knew and was a realist well-versed in the art of Finley, she was also now aware of how whatever this was wasn't just beginning. It was the tip of the iceberg, extending out of the pitch black depths of an ice cold grave, and there was no reason for me to sit around and rearrange deck chairs.

I grabbed my towel and as I wiped the water from my face let out a long exhale because I was well aware of the conversation that was about to happen. In those vulnerable moments there are always choices to be made. You can be outright honest and accept fault or you can try to dance around the issue and misdirect the blame.

In my younger days, I'd developed somewhat of a mastery in the art of deflection, but sitting there on the edge of the bathtub, I just didn't have it in me. In a flash I could see it all happen before it happened. She would cry and scream. She would ask how I would put our marriage and family in jeopardy after what happened all those years ago. My heart would break with every tremble and crack in her voice, knowing I was the source of her pain, and then she would tell me that this thing we had…this beautiful, wondrous, magical thing we'd shared for so long, was over. And it would all be my fault.

That was my vision for how things would play out and things started out exactly to plan. She unloaded a tear-filled barrage of questions I couldn't or didn't want to answer, and I sat there staring off into space. Anything I said in that moment would just make things worse, and I wasn't about to deny her the right to be angry with me. With every word things got heavier and heavier on my head, to the point I started to look at the floor.

"Fucking look at me!" she shouted as she launched the bottle off of the wall. "Goddammit Duane, look at me right now!"

I turned my eyes back to her but remained silent. This scene had played out every day in my mind since I gave into the same demons I'd been running from for years, and I was just waiting for the other shoe to drop so it could be over. But that's not what she had in mind.

"The man I fell in love with and married was and has always been a fighter," she screamed. "You are NOT giving into this. You are better than this and WE deserve better than this."

She was absolutely right but there was just so much more to what was happening than some guy who decided to dive into a pill bottle for the fuck of it.

"What do you want from me?" I fired back. "I've tried everything those fucking doctors asked me to do. I've had needle after needle jammed into my spine with no relief. I've had my goddamn nerves burned off on both sides and still nothing is fixed. I drove all the way across this fucking country chasing this thing that I'm not even sure why I ever started chasing and the only thing that takes the edge off and allows me to stand up right is in that bottle over there."

"That's bullshit and you know it."

"What's bullshit? The fact that I can't get out of bed in the morning without hurting? Or that a guy who has been happy 99 percent of his life can't find a reason to be happy anymore? This thing is zapping everything I find joy in and I can't stop it."

"Those are not the answer and you fucking know it!" she said as she forced herself far into my personal space. "We are not going back to how things were. I won't allow it."

I could feel the hostility flowing from her but couldn't find the words to make anything better. I knew it was only going to get uglier from there because that is how it had to play out.

"Well there you go," I offered feigning nonchalance. "I fucked up and broke the one promise I swore I'd never break so you have your out. I'll pack up my shit and go."

"Why would you ever do this? Why?"

"Because I'm fucking stuck, Renee," I returned. "I'm caught under it all, and it's all so heavy that I don't know how to get out from under it. I'm tired and hurting and that makes me so fucking sad that I can't stand it. I'm surrounded by all of this love but I can't feel any of it. I'm numb, and all I want to do is close my eyes and make the world go away for awhile. I just want some peace."

While my wife was once somewhat timid in the face of conflict when our union first began, more than a decade spent sparring with me had toughened her up in a few areas. Furthermore, her tiny frame had bore two healthy babies with minimal medication, and those collective experiences had forged a lioness out of a house cat. By all measurable standards, I may have been the visible rock of our family, but she was absolutely the ring leader of the Finley family circus, and I had just pushed the big red button to launch a nuclear attack.

It would be a disservice to this narrative and sully Renee's finely crafted art of chaining together curse words if I were to attempt to recall the exact quote, but never before in my life had I heard someone use the words "pussy" and "motherfucker" so poetically. It was a vicious verbal assault, yet so gracefully executed that a defense could not be rendered.

This tiny woman stood two inches from my face and passionately explained to me that there was a fight coming, but it wasn't going to be between her and I. Standing in that bathroom, she was not only demanding I begin to battle my way out of the hole I'd crawled into, but was proving she was in the hole right alongside of me.

And as the rockets and mortars hit their mark, there was simply no reason to reveal anything further, because her mind could make up the rest. My copping to the existence of a problem was all that needed to be known, and anything else in that moment would have been lost in the fire fight. If I were to tell her about how a text from a friend led to a friend of a friend getting me what I needed in Las Vegas, or how a random conversation at a bar in Fresno resulted in some extra assistance on my drip down the west coast, it wouldn't have mattered. Renee wasn't the fickle type. She just wanted results.

Most women fear their husbands will cheat on them while out on the road, but that wasn't a discomfort she had to endure. Instead, my wife had to watch trust destroyed in a perfectly legal way, live and in living color. Even though I knew there were more elements at play than she could understand, nothing bore explanation. What I did was wrong, and the center of my once in a lifetime love was hurt by my actions.

A grown man crying is one of the worst things in the world in my humble opinion, but that was the end result of a woman who stepped up to show her shattered husband he wasn't alone. The emotions would continue to fluctuate for the next hour or so, but once the cabin pressure returned to normal and logical minds shook off the insanity, solutions started to surface. Since I'd made a full recovery years earlier, I knew the way back, but my jaded state of mind wouldn't allow me to take any steps in that direction. The only answer for this problem would be checking back into rehab, and as much as it embarrassed and shamed me to do so, it is what needed to be done.

We made the necessary phone calls and started to establish a timeline, because it wasn't going to be as easy as simply running down to the rehabilitation center and checking in. Pills or no pills, my back issue wasn't going anywhere, and that topic had to be addressed before anything else could be done. What good would entering a program do if my chronic pain situation would just lead me right back to where we were standing?

By all definitions we were sitting on a slippery slope, and as cliché as it all may sound, just acknowledging the problem was the first positive step I'd taken in a year. I love my family more than anyone who has ever existed has ever loved anything, and knowing I nearly lost them because of the situation made my chest hurt. That said, I had always been able to find some strange comfort in despair.

The answers to life's problems were consistently and easily within my grasp, but sitting in my own self-doubt and darkness felt more like home to me. The same inner-voice that drove me to chase my passion was the same one I allowed to break me down. The human condition is a strange and fragile thing when left in the hands of the remarkably unstable. I'd witnessed it firsthand throughout my childhood, and it was handed down like a well-worn sweater for when I was ready to crawl inside.

Renee had always jokingly called me "The Patron Saint of Good Intentions," and there, in that stripped down moment of weakness, with all of my flaws and scars bare, it was never more appropriate. I sat back and let the skin of my neck touch the ice cold tiles of the shower stall and attempted to slow my brain down from the manic spin it was in. I'd never intended to do anything to hurt anyone, but I also could no longer deny my awareness of my own actions.

I'd driven over twenty-thousand miles to chase a dream, but in that moment I started to think it possible I had driven twenty-thousand miles as an attempt to outrun something I knew was catching up to me.

Control is a strange beast indeed. In fact, it's a motherfucker.

Chapter 33

One Last Go

The day after the confrontation in the bathroom the mood around the house was calm but spacious. Renee wore the disappointment of our situation with heavy eyes, and I did my best to give her room to move without creating friction. I had already agreed to seek outside help, but having to deal with the back situation was going to be tricky, because pain management doctors don't operate in the fast lane by any means.

After placing a few phone calls to the medical offices in question, it seemed the quickest I could be seen would be early January. This left nearly two months worth of time in question, and that gap meant I would need to stay on pain medicine to finish out the year. Renee was by no means enthused by this turn, but did her best to act like she understood. We'd been together a very long time, and one of the benefits of spending a decade with someone is knowing how they are really feeling without it being expressed.

She was hurt and there was nothing I could do immediately to change this, but that didn't stop me from trying.

Due to different sections of our past, I knew nothing I could say would change anything. Addicts by nature are manipulative and crafty people, but when you add in my unique penchant for wordplay and ability to tap emotional lines, it creates an individual who can be extremely convincing. Beyond the sadness I felt for causing the most special person in my life grief, I also battled the internal struggle that came from letting myself down.

Losing a long stretch of sobriety I had fought for and earned was a reality that kicked me in the teeth every single day, and the pain of it all just piled on with the rest of the disappointment. Nevertheless, all the self-loathing in the world wasn't going to repair the situation at hand, and if I wanted to save everything that mattered to me a solution needed to be found.

All I knew for certain is somewhere along the way I went off track, and rather than retracing the steps to figure out where that had occurred, the proper thing to do was to turn things around in the here and now. I gave her what was left of my pills and instructed her to distribute them as they were meant to be taken. That would create days where the pain in my back left me unable to get out of bed, but it was a suffering that couldn't be managed because I abused the method.

When those stretches came to call life was hard to face. Anyone who has dealt with chronic pain understands how easily it can change ones perspective, and there were plenty of days I wanted to call the whole deal off. The condition I suffer from not only locked up my back but also made my left leg one giant burning nerve, and any irritation would ignite a pain so severe it leveled me. Having those fits strike several times a day quickly add up to make joy and happiness a distant memory.

I'd spent my entire life being optimistic and happy despite circumstance, but my condition was taking those things away from me. Something had to be done, and I wasn't sure if I could make it another month before that solution was found.

Fortunately my doctor's office called and they were able to move my appointment up to the first week of December. This was fantastic news on several fronts, as I would be able to address the medicine issue but also stress the importance of taking a step toward finality. There would be no more injections or nerve burning. We needed to move ahead to surgery.

Renee's big stipulation of going to see my doctor was that I be up front and honest about what had happened with me and the pills. At first I was hesitant about it, thinking the doctor would just up and pull me off of them, but it ultimately didn't matter because I wanted her to be happy and if that meant having to deal with my back without relief then so be it.

Much like I expected, my doctor wasn't happy to hear about the amount I had been taking, but he was appreciative of my honesty. The abuse of prescription medicine has become such an epidemic in the United States that doctors are extremely hesitant to even dole them out, and there I was adding my number to a growing list of statistics. That said, he'd been handling my condition for more than a year and certainly understood why they were necessary.

After some complex conversation, my doctor and Renee came up with a suitable solution for the situation. She would continue to monitor my medicine and any infraction of this deal would result in him no longer being willing to treat me. He also agreed to do a procedure that would implant an electrical device at the base of my spine that would shock the nerve whenever it acted up. I wasn't 100 percent sold on the idea of the implant, but it was at least progress in a situation that had all but stopped progressing.

We set the date for early January, and everything that could be said and done on the matter was complete. The arrival to this juncture finally allowed some levity to return between Renee and I, and the drive home was the first time I'd heard her laugh in weeks. Anyone who has ever heard my wife laugh knows just how special that is.

With a suitable solution on the table and enough medicine to control my pain in my wife's purse, life began to return to normal. Even though I hate snow with every fiber of my soul, its arrival in mid-December made Renee and the kids happy and provided the missing element to Christmas, which was rapidly approaching. Zoe and Atticus wanted to get out in the yard to have snowball fights and build a snowman, and because my back was under control I could happily join them.

Crazy as it may sound, you come to truly appreciate the small things when constant pain hovers over your life.

Nevertheless, we were all truly happy, and it was going to be the perfect end to a crazy year. At least that was the thought until one last crazy strand of ambition came to call.

Chapter 34

The Fight to End All Fights (Part 1)

Even though I had been dealing with chronic pain issues and a backslide into the grips of addiction since my return home from the east coast, those monsters didn't slow down my ability to produce content one bit. Despite everything going on in my life, I was still churning out a slab of original content on a daily basis and delivering at my usual standard of quality with each and every one. I mentioned before how I was previously categorized as a functioning addict, and my output during dark days set against the unique style of grind to stay afloat in the digital media game further confirmed it.

I have been a bright lights big game player since birth, and my ability to pull my shit together when the pressure is on certainly shined through in those two months as I bobbed, weaved, limped, cursed, and sweated my way across the finish line on nightly deadlines.

During all of my years writing in MMA, I had never second guessed or questioned my choice of solely doing fighter features. Talking to people and connecting with them is something I'd always been good at and taking that skill to a higher level was something that interested me greatly. That said, during times of personal crisis or severe pain, when all

I wanted to do was lock myself in a closet and push the world away, I started to envy my peers who could sit back and mail in an opinion piece whenever they felt like it.

There are some fine gentlemen who make a living writing opinion columns in this great sport of ours, but their jobs were entirely different than mine. All they had to do was pick an issue and then scribble out a thousand words on the topic and send it off. My pieces involved a multiple step process. In a perfect world, all it takes is one phone call to get your subject on the line, but simplicity rarely makes a great interview.

I've never been one to take myself all too seriously but I believe there is an art to interviewing. Some would say research and information are the key elements to crafting a strong exchange, but I'm not one of those people. I truly believe it comes down to the ability to create a comfortable conversation, because once someone feels at ease, they will open up a large majority of the time.

Now don't get me wrong, just because I said comfortable doesn't mean I am suggesting fluff. I've had plenty of situations where tough questions needed to be asked and every single time I've traveled the necessary route. But rather than come out guns blazing in an abrasive and attacking manner, I take a path that presents a minimal amount of friction leading up to the big turn.

While I've had interviews that have gone south in a big way, those incidents are few and far between. I'm simply good at what I do, and being a sound interviewer who is also strong on the writing side helped me climb the ladder in the MMA world at a rapid rate.

Getting to a place where people come to expect a certain type of product from you is a great accomplishment, and I wasn't about to sacrifice that just because I was dealing with some personal shit. Granted, those issues were as heavy as they come, and there were some days where I wished I wasn't who I was, but I sucked it up and stepped up to the plate to swing like a champion.

The goal with each article was to hit a home run, and I'm happy to say there were a few round trip shots during the rough stretch. If the ball didn't clear the wall I was still able to grab extra bases, which was a suitable outcome considering the severity of my situation.

Once the medical end of things got tied up and the tension on the homefront calmed, my hyperactive brain started churning out ideas. By all measures, the road trip had been a big success that struck a chord with MMA readers all over the world, and I started to examine what if anything could be done to add to the existing body of work. Since it was already mid-December, there wouldn't be time to launch off on another full run, but there was still time to do something unique that could serve as a bookend to a crazy year.

I looked at the calendar of upcoming fights, and the thing that immediately caught my eye was the highly anticipated upcoming clash between Jon Jones and Daniel Cormier at UFC 182 in Las Vegas. The top pound-for-pound fighter in the world would be putting his light heavyweight title on the line against an undefeated man who had been hunting him down for the past two years. The pre-fight build-up had been unlike anything in recent memory, as the two engaged in brawls, Twitter wars, and epic trash-talk that spilled across multiple major media platforms.

If everything lined up correctly at home, I could take the Nissan on one last journey west and document my trip from Indianapolis to Las Vegas and back. In all honesty, my mind had already committed to the trip before I had clearance from my better half, and I set about making the necessary phone calls to ensure my accommodation. The site I worked for wasn't about to start paying for lodging, but they were excited to get more road trip content, which was the only matter I truly cared about.

Everything else could be taken care of on the fly, and by the time the week of Christmas rolled around, my next adventure was set in stone. The fight between Jones and Cormier was slated to go down on January 3, and I wanted to give myself a comfortable amount of time to reach Sin City, so I planned my departure for December 30th. Christmas and Atticus's birthday on the 27th would present an ample amount of family time with my clan, and a short six-day trip out to Las Vegas wouldn't present too much difficulty for the home team to handle.

With all the mess that had been created on my downward spiral toward self-realization, it felt good to have some positive energy rolling back in the passion department. I would make one final run for the road trip series, then return home in time to get the implant put into my back and spend the first part of the upcoming year healing in multitude of ways. The stars appeared to be aligning for one last run at glory, and I was excited to hit the road.

Chapter 35

Like a Rolling Stone

The sun was beaming brightly in the sky, and the temperature damn near tipped 40 degrees as I packed up my car for the trip. Folks in other parts of the country would be bundled up in such conditions, but for a native Midwesterner who'd spent his entire life battling the severity of misery December typically brings, it felt downright spiritual to be able to wear a tee shirt outside.

The kids were home on winter break from school, so my send off, which typically consisted of just my wife, looked like a full on pier launch as I pulled out of the driveway. I flipped the gear shift from reverse to drive and slowly made my way down our neighborhood street as Atticus ran alongside the vehicle shouting a chorus of "I love you daddy" that stayed nestled in my head long after Indianapolis had disappeared from my vision.

It was nearly two-thousand miles one way to Las Vegas, and with this being the first run I'd made solo, I had to take some precautions. First and foremost was the time I had laid out for myself. Not having someone sitting shotgun would be a problem when the night grew long, therefore I made sure to give myself a big enough window to stop off to catch a few hours of sleep. Another key factor in being alone on my journey was safety, and even though it made my skin crawl to do it, I packed my .38 caliber revolver under my driver's seat.

Having already driven across the country I was well aware of several questionable spots I would be traveling through en route to Las Vegas, and the thought of doing that alone inspired me to bring protection. You never know the type of crazy that exists in the world until you spend as much time watching the ID Channel as I have or some drug-crazed prowler breaks into your house and spends two days sleeping in your attic. True stories on both fronts.

I'd never been big on guns, but after the previously mentioned home invader, my father-in-law insisted we own one. He'd taken me to the woodshed and back over the issue for the better part of a year before he finally made us take one of his before we left his house last Christmas Eve. I grew up in a farming community where all of my friends hunted deer and shot coyotes, so I was well versed in handling a firearm. Renee didn't even want to look at the thing.

Before the trip, we kept it in a safe far out of reach from the children and taking it out to put in the car was the first time I'd touched the thing since my father-in-law had handed it to me a year earlier. Taking a four-thousand mile trip in solo fashion would be no easy task, but having a gun at my disposal in case things took a horrible turn made me feel a touch on the safer side.

In addition to the more immediate reasons for my exploits, Butta gave me an explicit mission that was of the highest importance in his book. During our emergency stay caused by our being trapped in the grips of a massive winter vortex, Butta apparently forgot his pillow. Had this been any run of the mill Walmart variety sleeping device, I'm sure the charge wouldn't be given, but the pillow in question was some special order thing-a-ma-jig that cost the big man nearly two-hundred bucks.

My initial thought was: if the damn thing was so important and expensive, then why was it left in the first place? If memory served though, the morning fog from the valium taken the night prior was most likely the culprit.

"I need you to get that damn pillow if you can, man," Butta had said during one of our monthly meet ups for BBQ and comic books. "I haven't slept right since I left it there and just thinking about it makes me pissed off. I still wake up some nights thinking how we almost died out there. People think I'm exaggerating but I'm serious as fuck. Had our car went off the edge no one would have come out to help. We are lucky we made it."

While my road tripping companion was right to assume the worst could have happened on that ominous stretch of ice-covered road, I had to keep the poker face in order to not shake him further. Any time the incident had been brought up in the months after, I fully copped to being downright terrified once the sun went down but not during the drive.

Butta wanted to make the final run of the trip with me to end the year, but another scheduling conflict wouldn't allow it. Nevertheless, he wanted me to get that pillow, but I didn't have the heart to tell him straight up that finding the Roadside Shitshow Hotel wasn't on my direct agenda. All I wanted was to get to Las Vegas in decent time, and the initial night's run was taking forever.

Perhaps it is luck or perception but driving through Missouri is a painful ordeal. Outside of making the suicide inducing flatland run border to border across Iowa on Interstate 80, navigating through the "Show Me State" was the shittiest stretch of road I'd ever come across. Not only is there nothing to see, but a driver goes long clips without running into anything significant stop wise.

The latter certainly plays into my ability to pep up upon hitting a new state, and as the western skyline darkened, the Oklahoma border was still several hours away. Fortunately I had several phone interviews slated, and they helped pass the time as I chopped up some MMA biz talk with reigning lightweight champion Anthony Pettis and Titan FC owner Jeff Aronson. Both conversations had strong moments and I was pleased with the outcomes considering the scenario.

I would have certainly preferred to have proper sit down interviews with each of them, but Ferris Bueller knew what he was talking about, and my 80 mph moving office got the job done.

After checking off the work portion of my night, I scrolled through my contacts and made a few phone calls to pass a bit more time. I could always count on my old man to chat it up for a good clip, and while Big Joe claimed a strong 45 minutes, another hour was split between my younger brother and my friend and colleague Spencer Kyte. I chopped it up with that bunch for as long as I could keep them on the line, but once the phone was set down, the low-fi hum of the asphalt rolling underneath returned.

The Midwest is a tricky place where time zones are concerned, as somewhere in the middle of Missouri, Eastern Standard gives way to

Central. You lose or gain an hour depending on which direction you are traveling, but that was a slight detail that didn't matter much because it wasn't going to change the amount of time I was behind the wheel of the car. And since I had launched at a later time than normal, I wasn't going to get very far past midnight before my eyes started going goofy.

Feeling the early stages of the blur setting in, I decided to stop for something to eat in Rollo, Missouri. I've never been one to get picky while on the road ,and there was a fast food oasis located at the first exit for the city. Pulling in, I could tell it was one of those places that doubled as a truck stop but wasn't advertised as one, which typically brings a bountiful variety of riff-raff.

Those conditions make for top notch people watching, and I was pleased to find this notion verified inside of the oasis. After grabbing a sandwich and taking a seat near the back of the sub shop, I listened to two 20 somethings get into an argument over a bag of weed. What started out as a lax conversation between a greasy haired blonde draped in a flannel shirt two sizes too big and his round faced counterpart decked out in camo, quickly turned heated.

The Kurt Cobain wannabe was apparently upset about the quality of the product sold to him, and the Army Surplus store patron was adamant about the strength of his goods. I tuned in my ears and listened close, but kept my eyes down to the failed attempt of a sub sandwich sitting before me.

"This some bunk bullshit," the blonde said in a thick drawl.

"Well it must have come from someone else because my shit is fire," the fat kid replied.

"I ain't know nobody else so it had to come from you."

"Now if anything is bullshit, that is," the rotund youth barked as he puffed up his chest and cranked up the volume of his NASCAR tones. "I know your cousin Tiffany sells bud, because I used to buy from her before I started dealing."

Now things were getting interesting. Any time someone's family gets drawn into a drug dispute all bets are off. This is especially true when it takes place south of the Mason/Dixon line.

I wasn't sure how close the grungy smoker was to this mysterious cousin Tiffany, but from the clenched jaw that became exposed after he brushed all the hair out of his face, it was clear it was a mention with which he took contention. As the two men squared up, I stopped pretending that I wasn't listening and sat back to watch the fireworks.

"She doesn't sell weed! She sells pills!" the flannel man barked. "Now I know you're lying!"

"What the fuck are you talking about, bitch? You calling me a liar now?"

Not only was the latter obvious because the kid said so, but where cousin Tiffany seemed at first to be an interesting addition to the ruckus, that wasn't going to be the case. Her inclusion had caused confusion on both fronts, and the two kids wore it over their strange faces.

The next few moments were filled with nonsensical shouts and posturing from each man, and the loudness drew the attention of a police officer across the plaza who was buying a soft drink. He came shuffling over and my senses elevated as I saw the payoff I had been silently waiting for enter the fray. Movies are rarely worth the price of admission and all this late-night drama cost was the price of a Subway sandwich.

"What is going here?" the officer asked as he stepped between the two.

I figured the two stoners would downplay things once the policeman intervened, or at the worst make some vague mention of cousin Tiffany, but nothing in the world prepared me for what came flying out of their mouths. Whatever I had done in a past life to deserve such entertainment, I wasn't sure, but I was certainly grateful.

"He sold me some bad weed, and I want my money back," the kid with the long blonde hair calmly explained.

The officer's eyes shot wide as the reality of what he just heard registered in his ears, and the shock forced the lemonade I had just attempted to drink to go spraying out of my mouth across the tabletop. Had I stepped into the fucking Twilight Zone? Did I just hear what I thought I heard?

"Excuse me," the officer replied as he leaned in closer.

"He's accusing me of selling him bad weed," the chubby youth added. "But that's a bunch of b.s."

"Because you didn't sell him weed, right?" the police officer asked, almost begging the kid to give him the mercy of a layup answer.

"No I sold it to him, but it was good stuff," he replied, and all was right with the world.

A mega-watt smile hit my face as the grand human comedy had just cemented an all-time classic in my presence. Upon having heard that response, the sound coming from their squabble muffled into nondescript blurbs of noise, and I damn near floated to the trash can to dump my tray. What a remarkable exchange, and I didn't have a care to hear it go any further.

Once perfection is reached it can only go downhill.

I jumped back into my car and used my recharged tank to blast the next pne hundred miles of road with ease. Before I knew what was happening, I had crossed over into Oklahoma and it was a touch after midnight. I pulled up the GPS to check my options and making it all the way to Oklahoma City felt like a stretch. The more realistic option would be to pull off somewhere in Tulsa to catch a few hours sleep before starting out fresh in the morning.

I called Renee to have her jump on the computer and book something for me in Tulsa, which was still an hour and change up the road. Renee wasn't too keen on putting her mind to work at such a late hour, but she knew it was a better thing for her to be looking up the information instead of my tired eyes coming off the road to look at my phone.

Twenty minutes later she called me back to say she'd booked a room at a place called the Crystal Palace Inn. While the name told me it wasn't a national chain, her insistence that the spot had a good review on Yelp was somewhat comforting. She sent over the address via text, and I immediately plugged it into the GPS.

"Sounds like a murder motel like that movie Vacancy," I joked in an attempt to mask my paranoia.

"The reviews were pretty good, and the price was a steal, so that was hard to pass up," she replied with a laugh.

There was nothing comforting about that moment. It wasn't so much that my wife and I had gone through a major marital storm in the weeks prior as it was her unconscious willingness to put me in harm's way. Being a man through and through has its setbacks from time to time, and for some reason my wife viewed life on the open road like a Sunday stroll through the neighborhood farmer's market. I on the other hand was far more distrusting, and my slight paranoia had gotten me out of tight spots more than a time or two on the rough terrain I traveled through life.

It's just a simple fact that darkness lurks in abundance, but comes out to play in remote areas where opportunity is presented.

The bright lights of Tulsa up ahead did little to calm the thoughts of being murdered, but a long strip of hotels on the horizon finally did the job. I didn't know much about the city, nor Oklahoma in general (other than it was the birthplace of my good friend Brian Foster). Now it wouldn't be fair to judge an entire populous by that crazy son of a bitch alone, but it gave me a good idea of the general foundation being blue collar with a penchant for rowdiness.

That's probably the best compliment I could give Brian Foster, but even he was several hundred miles away in the eastern corner of the state as I trudged through the orange lit highway in the early morning hours of New Years Eve.

The bright yellow glow of a Super 8 caught my eye and I looked down at the GPS to see just how far away I was. The skin on the back of my next began to crawl when the weary gray matter behind my eyes added up the situation as my motel for the night was still sitting eight miles up ahead. From the best I could tell, the strip of lodgings my car was rolling past only extended for another exit or two, which meant the place I would be staying rested somewhere up ahead in the darkness.

With Renee off the phone, there was no need to curse her silently, and I let out a few healthy blasts before calling her again. The clock on the dash showed it was after 2:00 AM, and that added the fear of being locked out to my already established fear of death.

"Are you there yet?" she asked as she picked up the call.

"Normally I'd say I wish, but I'm starting to think this place isn't going to be anything I'd wish for."

"It won't be that bad. Quit your bitching."

I wondered if she'd say the same thing had she been sitting in the passenger seat with me, but I already knew the answer.

"I'm not bitching," I replied. "I just drove past a perfectly nice stretch of recognizable hotel chains that I know are open at this hour. What if the office to this place is closed up?"

"Hey," she crackled. "The Yelp reviews were good, and I'm sure it's going to be fine. Why wouldn't there be someone at the front desk?"

They are off murdering someone. They are busy pulling up the carpet from the last person they murdered. The list went on and on in my head.

"I'm still about 10 miles away and driving, so can you please call them to make sure someone is there for me to check in?" I asked.

"Duane, are you serious?"

She wasn't happy. Not in the slightest.

"It's after three o'clock in the morning here," she continued. "Why can't you call?"

"Will you just please call for me?" I pleaded. "It's been a long ass day and I don't want to hassle with it."

"Fine," she thundered.

It was a tone I'd come to know well over my decade plus with the blonde haired blue eyed vixen. She was going to do it, but the annoyance created would be tallied to some running list for things to be taken out on me at a later date.

We hung up the phone, and I rubbed my eyes to clear up the blur created as the street lights began to space out and the winter dark wrapped thickly in and out of them. The sure fire sign that you are heading out of a well populated area is the lack of lighting, and the sudden appearance of the void told me the Tulsa city limits were up ahead.

I took the exit directed by the GPS, and all of my wild-brained theories started to take shape. Most exits that have lodging posted around them have other businesses dotted up and down the street, but there was nothing to be found off of 56th Street except what looked like the house from the movie Fight Club and the flickering white and yellow sign of the Crystal Palace Motel. I was heading into a shit show and there was no way around it.

The office was located underneath an overhang, and I left the car running as I pulled up next to the glass door. Upon my exit, I was greeted by the stiff wind of a single digit temperature that put a pep in my step as I headed to check in. The metal knob on the door was cold fire as it hit my warm skin, and a quick turn produced no results. The door was locked, and my frustration meter skyrocketed.

As I rang the bell for the front office manager, I took a quick inventory of the parking lot. That was an easy task to accomplish since there were no other vehicles present, which meant there were no other guests at the roadside murder post. I was going to be the main point of focus for the group of maniacs I was sure awaited me, but I was tired enough to not give the slightest of fucks.

After a series of rings that would have woken the victims buried out back, a man finally produced himself from the room behind the counter. He was a slight man with huge frames sloping off of his face, and he took his sweet time getting to the door to let me in.

"Are you….Mr. Finley?" he asked as he read my name off a piece of paper.

"Yeah, I believe my wife called just a few moments ago."

The moppy haired stranger nodded his head in agreement as he opened the door to let me in. I did my best to not let the freeze in behind me, but that didn't seem to matter to him at all. My persistent ringing had either stirred him from his sleep or taken him away from playing games on his phone, because his annoyance with my presence was hanging heavily in the room.

After the credit card and license plate routine, the slender manager looked up with his sunken eyes and slid over my key.

"You're going to stay in room 11," he said. "That's the one right across the lot from here on the other side."

With no other guests—or at least ones with vehicles staying in the rooms between where I stood and where he told me I was staying—I felt an already odd situation become that much more peculiar. Was there a reason he was sending me across the way? Was that room rigged for death the way my mind had imagined?

"Why that room?" I asked keeping my mania in check.

"You want a different one?" he replied nonplussed.

"No….I suppose that will be fine."

As the man finished up the paperwork, my eyes scanned the lobby for any clues or things out of place. Other than the 1960's décor holding strong there was nothing that screamed for me to run, but I did notice several issues of magazines that to my knowledge hadn't been printed in a decade sitting out on a coffee table. Nevertheless, my car would go no further, and it was time to get some sleep.

I called Renee as soon as I got into the room and told her about the ominous feelings I had swirling my brain. She did her best to calm me down, and I heard about half of what she was saying as I checked the walls and floors for trap doors. I told her goodnight and sent my love, then set about taking every piece of movable furniture and pushing it up against the door. If anyone was going to try to come through that bitch I would hear it.

Furthermore, I took the revolver out of its bag along with the box of bullets my father-in-law had given me. Since they had been sitting under the driver's seat they were warm to the touch and that helped steady my hand as I slid six bullets into the steel. Once I had it loaded, I sat the gun on the night stand beside the bed. Just loading the goddamn thing made my nerves jump, and the reality of having to use it nearly made my stomach turn.

In any case, I'd done all I could do to protect myself from harmful forces, and it was time to do my best to shut off my brain for the night. I picked up the remote sitting next to the pistol and found a Rosanne rerun on TBS. The Conner family brought a slight bit of comfort as I sat in the bowels of Tulsa on Death Street and closed my eyes thinking about how much the character played by John Goodman reminded me of my own father.

"Well at least it will make for a good story."

Those were the words I was sure he would fire off when I told him about having to stop at such a place, and it was a conversation I was looking forward to having. All I had to do was survive the night, and I felt reasonably confident I'd done enough to give myself a strong chance of that happening.

Chapter 36

The Devil's Bad Luck

"What the fuck?!"

Those were the first words that came firing out of my mouth as the gritty labored sound of a diesel engine firing to life just outside of my window tore me out of the thin depths of sleep I'd managed to find. My heart raced wildly as I fumbled to find the pistol on the night stand, all the while trying to make sense of the frenzied scene.

The iron beast beyond the door continued to rev and rage loudly, and I could see two different forms slipping below the blinds on the window. One was man-made, while the other the faint glow of daylight breaking. If the sun was just coming to call, that meant I'd only been asleep for a handful of hours, and there certainly wasn't a truck parked outside of my door when I called it a night.

I grabbed the gun and put my feet on the floor as I Rambo crawled over to the wall just below the window sill. Of all the scenarios my mind had cooked up, never once did I think I would actually have to use a weapon to fend off wolves at my door. My brain dug deep to harvest any logic that could be found in the situation, but mine as I did, the reality of the scenario couldn't be avoided. I was being attacked and I was going to have to fight back with force.

My right hand trembled as I pulled back the hammer on the .38 and I took a series of deep breaths. I'd never had anything that would constitute as an out of body experience, but sitting there on the floor of that shit hole motel, I could see myself from an outside perspective. I had too much to live for to have it all end at the Crystal Palace, and just when I gathered my wits to actually aim the gun at the door, all the pressure in the room was relieved.

After one final full throttled cry, the vehicle just outside of my room downshifted into reverse and I could hear the truck backing out of the parking space. My head popped up enough to peak out the corner of the window to see a rust bucket red Ford F-150 pulling around the lot and taking a right turn back out onto 56th Street. My rubbery frame crashed back down to the crusty carpet below and I returned the hammer to its upright position.

Jesus Christ what a way to start a day.

With a gallon of adrenaline coursing through my veins, it would be impossible to crawl back into bed to catch a few more hours, so I gathered up my belongings and decided to get back out on the road. By the time I exited the room, the morning sun was on full display, and whatever cobwebs that remained from the previous day's drive were left in Room 11.

My breath fogged up the windshield in the morning freeze, and I had to let the ice cold engine blow through the vents to keep it from blinding me entirely. I was still so far from reaching my destination, but with a full day to get things done, I figured to be pulling into Las Vegas in the early hours of 2015. That town never stops, so arriving at 3:00 AM doesn't hold the despair it would anywhere else in the country, and doing so on New Year's Eve meant I would probably be able to catch a few cold beers with friends.

The hours of the day rolled by with minimal discomfort as I found various ways to entertain myself behind the wheel. Without having someone else to converse with, I had to get creative, therefore I turned to modern technology to be my companion as I entered the Southwest. Even though it ate up a shit ton of data, I queued up a run of standup comedy on Pandora, and what a decision that turned out to be.

One of the first great memories of my life was sitting with my father watching standup specials on HBO. The old man always loved a good laugh, and he wasn't the type of parent who would censor anything for his child. If he found it funny he would immediately show it to me, and I was always grateful for it. Even when the scope of the jokes were beyond my capacity, the larger than life hero in my world would always bite the bullet and mow through the awkwardness of explaining why Richard Pryor's joke about blowjobs was hilarious.

And it wasn't just Pryor—who I would later come to clearly recognize as the greatest standup king of all-time—it was all the other greats as well. Eddie Murphy and Robin Williams became immediate favorites in my household, as did Rodney Dangerfield and his protégé Sam Kinison. All the screaming and "no respect" punch lines in the world couldn't exhaust me on them, and we had some incredible nights sitting and laughing together on the couch.

In a strange parallel, it was quite fitting that I was killing time on New

Year's Eve listening to comedians, as that was the one night a year my father and I made sure to camp out in front of the television. Back in those days, HBO always rung in the coming year with an entire night of standup specials, and even though my father was the very definition of a party animal, he took that night off from his raging against the world to hang out with a son that could never get enough of his attention.

Nevertheless, there wasn't much of that life that still existed as I mowed down miles of New Mexico highway en route to Las Vegas. Nearly 30 years had passed since those people sat watching Robin Williams tear up the stage of the Metropolitan Opera House, and plenty of life had rained down over that stretch. Those rising tides waged war on us all, and not all the damage inflicted was the type where recovery is possible.

I was less than an hour outside of Albuquerque when a clip from Bill Burr came through the speakers and my spirits were back to full capacity. I loved the fiery red headed comic, and my eyes welled up with tears as Burr launched one home run after the next. Somewhere close to the ABQ, I shot off texts to Carlos Condit and Isaac Vallie-Flagg because I wasn't above making a quick pit stop to grab some lunch and catch up with the boys.

With it being New Year's Eve, I didn't expect quick responses from either of them, and my hunch proved on point as my phone chimed with messages from both long after Albuquerque was an option. By the time Carlos text to wish me a happy new year, I had already crossed over into Arizona with Flagstaff just a few hours away.

We exchanged a few more messages, but Carlos had never been much of a phone person, so I capped the conversation with well wishes and turned my focus to the angry skies overhead. The horizon of the Arizona skyline was visible for miles and miles, and it didn't look like anything pretty was coming my way. A few moments after turning the volume of the radio back up, a light snow began to fall, and I fired off a text to Renee to share my shock.

"I leave Indiana and it's 40 degrees but somehow hit a snowstorm in Arizona?"

A couple of goofy looking emojis in her response told me that she was busy doing something around the house and didn't have time to engage in meaningless banter about weather that was cooking up two-thousand miles away from her. When you have been married as long as we had, you pick up a thing or two in regard to how people react to certain things and what they are really trying to say when they don't say much of anything at all.

The Nissan pressed on westward, and the snow began to fall in a fierce bluster that cut down visibility significantly. Having grown up in the Midwest and driven through the worst conditions imaginable for the past 20 years, I wasn't shook in the slightest, but my fellow drivers on Interstate 40 couldn't say the same. Vehicles were pulling over left and right, and I was sure they all assumed me to be a moron for charging on without caution.

I continued on without worry until I read a digital road sign hanging above the interstate that informed drivers the interstate was shut down just beyond Flagstaff. My mind was blown. While the snow was falling at a steady clip, the road conditions were solid by all measures, and unless things hit Arctic conditions, I couldn't process a complete road closure. Nevertheless, if the flashing sign was telling the truth, there would be no way to get to Nevada on the course I was traveling, and a decision needed to be made.

I could either stop for the night or find some way around the road closure, and I opted for the latter. I pulled up the GPS to look for an alternate route and found only one option available. The weather app on my phone showed most of the storm was focused on the northern portion of the state, and everything down around Phoenix appeared to be decent. I'd made the run from Phoenix to Las Vegas numerous times in the past, and could manage that drive even if my energy was running low.

In order to get there, I would have to get off of the interstate and take a state road for a healthy clip before hitting I-17 south into Phoenix. I turned off where the GPS instructed me to and immediately found the road conditions to be much worse than they were on the interstate. The tail end of my car slid a bit here and there, but after a few tense moments, I found my groove and set the cruise for 30 mph as I drifted off into the darkness.

It felt as if my vehicle was literally creeping along a rough desert road, but the thought of beating the elements gave me a strong charge. I followed the instructions on the screen and after a few turns noticed that the scenery surrounding me changed drastically. Where everything was once a wide open space, suddenly jagged rocks and huge evergreen trees lined the roadside just beyond my windows. The road also became slicker, which upped my alertness considerably.

How I had managed to drive into the heart of an Arizona snowstorm was beyond me, but I'd stopped trying to figure out my questionable luck years before. I simply had to deal with the cards dealt, and it wasn't going to be a pretty run through the badlands.

Whenever the road flattened out and I could take a breath, I messaged Renee to look on Google Maps to try to figure out where the fuck I was or what I was driving through. Since the cell phone signal was choppy at best, her messages trickled in slowly, but she was ultimately able to find the answer to why my surroundings had changed as I had managed to pick a nature preserve to drive through.

In my defense, there weren't many other options as the state of Arizona is low on roads that ran due north or south for some reason. The only thing I could do was remain patient and keep my eyes keen as I plowed my way through hills and valleys.

Once my cellular signal returned, the GPS updated to show a large patch of green on the screen which confirmed the information my wife passed along. I was absolutely in some type of nature park, and judging from the amount of green showing on the trail, it's a park I'd be in for at least another hour. Rather than get caught up in the manic thoughts that led to me nearly shooting a truck driver the day before, I managed to keep calm in thinking the further south I drove the more the weather would let up.

Granted, there were thoughts of death trickled in, but for the most part I was able to keep things on the up and up.

My theory eventually proved correct as the white wall of the snow storm broke and drops of rain began to trickle off of the windshield. That meant the temperature was rising the further I drove in the current direction, and a half hour later the snow had given way entirely to the other form of precipitation. This allowed me to slam my foot on the gas pedal and do my damnedest to make up for all the time lost on the detour, which was a turn I welcomed beyond explanation.

But the darkness ahead registered deep in the chasms of my mind. Without panic or trumped up fear of death at the hands of a motel clerk, the space finally arrived for me to think about everything I had left behind in Indiana. Somehow I had managed to compartmentalize everything surrounding my situation and had placed it behind all of the trappings of making one final run across the country.

Alone with nothing but a light Arizona rain, the room had finally cleared out for me to delve into the twisted reality of how I allowed addiction to find its footing once again in my life. They say addicts throw excuses out like Kleenex, but the complexity of my situation wasn't as simple as admitting I had a problem. I knew I had a problem because I never stopped having that problem. When you are stricken with that affliction it never truly goes away, It just waits in a dormant state until you are weak enough to bring it back.

In my case it was the back catastrophe which opened that door, but even though that is pure honest truth, I would be lying if I didn't see the darkness of my past waiting out on the porch. I saw it standing there waiting to catch up and somehow managed to convince myself that things would be different this time around. Even though this thing tore me apart several years earlier, this go around I would keep a better eye on it and never let it close enough to hurt me.

As my mind played back the tape, I thought of how battered women sounded explaining why they never left to Dr. Phil, and how abuse truly is a complicated matter.

Nothing is ever as easy as I'm leaving, or I'm putting the bottle down, because everything in life has a system of roots and mine ran deep. Being a staunch believer that self-pity is the most despicable of human traits, I'd never allowed for it in my life, and my opposition to such things became the catalyst for my sense of detection to grow strong. All things had roots just as every action had a reason. Very few things under the sun ever occur at random, and my situation certainly wasn't one of them.

My relationship with drugs and alcohol went back a very long way, but every chain could be broken. I was going to beat this thing once and for all, but in order to do so needed to have my back fixed. There would be no purpose of going through the process of distancing myself from the rattle of a pill bottle only to have morphine shot into my legs and hips every time the nerve that had haunted my existence decided to wreak havoc once more.

Driving into Phoenix, I found my stance and it was the firmest it had ever been. Finding that line brought a sense of peace and clarity to my tattered mind as the windshield wipers swiped the falling metaphor clean off the glass.

I would later find out the gauntlet I traversed driving on Route 87 out of Winslow was the Apache-Sitgreaves National Forest, and I'm quite sure it would be a lovely place all day-lit and safe looking, but it was quite monstrous in the conditions I encountered on New Year's Eve. Maybe one day I could go back with my family and talk about the time their father spun a 360 while praying to a God he wasn't sure existed for help in any form.

Maybes and some days have the longest shelf lives.

While my head was in full swing heading south into the Phoenix area, I started to notice something amiss with the Nissan. During the aforementioned spinout, her ass end hit a wall of snow and ice that knocked things back on course. It was like an under-sized and overworked Barry Sanders cutting back toward the line and using a spin move to pinball off of one linebacker and break into open ground. I'd like to think it was that flawless, but I'm sure the great Mr. Sanders never had tears in his eyes.

The headlights caught a green sign that showed the exit for Black Canyon City was ten miles ahead and suddenly things began to feel familiar. My lifelong friend Joel Eckberg and his wife Carrie used to live in the pristine (if anything in the desert is ever such a way) town of Anthem for a few years, and Renee and I would visit every trip we made to Vegas.

Those were some great times with two of our dearest friends, and I found myself missing it all as my tires kicked up rain from the pavement. Joel was three years ahead of me in high school and was one of the best long distance runners to ever come out of our area. He shattered every record for an Illinois Class A school during his four years and went on to have a solid college career. Joel was the quieter half as his twin brother Jeremy excelled in other areas, but running was certainly his jam.

He was also one of those crazy motherfuckers that not only ran just for fun, but would enter those extended races that made a marathon look like a jog down the block. Somewhere in the early 2000's he ran some one-hundred mile-long race across the state of Wisconsin, and it was a concept I couldn't even rationalize in my brain. Driving one-hundred miles is an exercise most frown on, and here this crazy son of a bitch was running on his own two legs.

My memory on the matter is rather tricky, but I think they gave him some small bronze cup for his efforts, and the doctors gave him a hefty bill for the Achilles tendon that required surgery after the fact. I'd given him shit for the end results for years, but how far can one really mentally jab someone with that type of mental and physical endurance? The answer is not all too much.

My eyes scanned the GPS to locate Anthem and sure enough it was dead ahead down I-17. While the Eckbergs had moved back to the Land O' Lincoln a few years before, that didn't stop my memory from replaying the time Joel let me tear his new motorcycle around a mission parking lot and all the well-timed cannonballs I dropped on him from the pool deck. Those were certainly unforgettable times and it reminded me that I hadn't talked to either Joel nor his twin brother Jeremy in quite some time, but ours was the level of friendship that did not require maintenance.

It's a great thing to not see someone for a handful of years then pick up exactly where you left off when your paths cross again. I was fortunate to have my entire inner circle operate in this fashion and that in itself was tremendous.

Once I felt comfortable in my surroundings, I decided to make some aggressive moves to try to cut back into lost time. Rather than run 17 all the way down into Phoenix, I made the decision to exit onto Route 74 and run that state road over to Morristown. From there I could hit Route 60 and start my run toward Kingman, which has many distinctions in addition to being the halfway point between Phoenix and Las Vegas.

Somewhere in the middle of 74, I had the good sense to re-examine the GPS to see what my options were going to be. The original path on Interstate 40 that would have taken my through Flagstaff also ran through Kingman and up into Nevada. Unfortunately, it seemed 40 was also the only major thoroughfare into the state of my destination, and once again I called on my better half to do some research work for me.

Just as I had the night before, I messaged her to make a phone call for me.

"Why in the world can' t you call?" she asked, even more annoyed than the previous evening.

"Renee, I just drove through a white wall of hell and my nerves are just now coming back," I replied. "I don't know if the interstate is open at Kingman. Can you call somewhere up there to ask if they are allowing cars through?"

"Where in the world would I call to find that out?" she huffed.

"Fuck, I don't know! Google a Shell station in Kingman," I answered.

"Don't you swear at me!" she shouted. "I should be in bed. Instead, I'm playing navigator for you again. Apologize for swearing or I won't do it."

In all honesty I wanted to swear a few more times and take the intensity of the situation up a few levels, but that never would have traveled to any place good. Instead, I did as she asked and crawled through the phone with my proverbial hat in hand and showed contrition.

"Thank you," she responded in calm tone. "I'll jump on the computer and see what I can do."

A few moments after tasking her with the assignment, 74 came to an end in Morristown. I made a right turn and started to make my way northwest and hoped Renee would call back with some good news. A quick scan of the landscape showed that rain had pretty much missed the sleepy little town, but there were elements of frost visible. Even though traces of white on the ground wasn't what I wanted to see, the lack of precipitation in that area was a silver lining to be taken.

No rain meant there wouldn't be any snow, and that was a fantastic comfort.

The tiny nook of Wickenburg came up out of the darkness in quick fashion, and as I let off the accelerator, I noticed the sound coming from under the hood jump up a few decibels. Normally when a car makes a sound that is out of the ordinary it would be cause for concern, but the Nissan was a warrior through and through. She had been run hard as fuck through rigorous conditions, and I was sure the stir coming from the engine compartment was her way of letting me know she needed a break.

I had just entered the Wickenburg city limits when Renee called back with the unfortunate news that I-40 through Kingman into Nevada would be closed until the morning. At least that's what the man she'd spoken to at the Shell station had told her, and she didn't seem to take any contention with his knowledge on the subject.

"So you're not going to be able to get through until the morning. You'll have to get a room," Renee instructed.

"It certainly looks that way," I replied. "Mother Nature just not going along with my plans and wants to keep me in Arizona it seems. Thank you for making that call."

"No problem, babe," she interjected. "Since I knew the next thing you'd ask me for was to jump on the computer and find you a room, I already have that taken care of. There is a Super 8 in a town you should be coming up to called Wickenburg, and I already booked you a room there. Since it's New Year's Eve the rates are all jacked, but we aren't going to find anything cheaper."

The woman truly was, is, and will forever be my better half.

"I just pulled into Wickenburg so that will work perfectly. You're amazing to me."

"Don't you ever forget it," she returned in a voice I could tell passed through a smile before hitting the phone.

"Happy New Year, baby," I added. "Let's make this one something special."

"They're all special, but what would be even more special, is if you let me go to bed. I love you babe. Goodnight."

I gave her my love then jumped off the call to punch in directions to my new destination. While I was somewhat perturbed by not being able to make it to Las Vegas as planned, there was a part of me that found relief in being able to call it a day. Arizona had been nothing short of a nightmare for me and managed to do so in ways I could have never expected. With the car making noise and my brain fried, I figured the grand powers of the Universe were telling me it was time to hit pause on my pulsing storm of ambition for the day.

In the process of finding the release button, I also took inventory of how sad it was to be wishing the love of my life a happy New Year over the phone two-thousand miles away. There were no kisses or hugs, just more driving and the lure of a good night's sleep. It may sound crass to equate the two on the same level, but rest assured, that was the thought.

The GPS showed the hotel just a turns away, and after coming through a huge roundabout, I could see the bright yellow sign glowing in the darkness. As soon as I pulled into the parking lot, my phone chimed with the confirmation email for the booking. The hotel itself wasn't all too large, but there were only a few other vehicles parked in the lot, and I was happy to be able to grab a room on one of the biggest party nights of the year.

It was just a touch after two in the morning when I walked into the lobby and was greeted by a middle aged woman named Tammy sitting behind the desk. She drug herself up out of her chair and I placed my phone with the email confirmation on the countertop.

"How's it going?" I asked . "The room should be under Finley."

The look on her face was a mixture of several elements exploding at once. Her features were hard in the way folks in that particular part of the country are known to be, and her two pack a day habit had done a number on her skin. On the other hand, her eyes were like two live wires hovering over a huge puddle of water, which told me there was some sort of speed involved. I'd worked the midnight shift operating heavy machinery after high school, and amphetamines are prevalent in the life that exists for labors between the hours that crawl and unfold between eleven and seven.

My speed theory was solidified as I watched her trembling hands fumble across the keyboard. Despite her best efforts, she just couldn't seem to reign in her high to turn the corner, and her full out assault on the "Escape" button gave away her position.

"Computers give me fits as well," I added in hopes of taking off her edge with some small talk. "I'd rather do without the damn things."

"When was your reservation for, sir?" she asked with a shaky voice.

"Right now," I returned. "My wife booked a room here for tonight."

"Well that's not gonna work because we are all full. Are you sure it wasn't for tomorrow?"

The red tack on my frustration gauge began to rise, and I didn't know if I had the capacity to work it back down.

"Of course I'm sure. The storm is preventing me from making it up to Las Vegas because the roads are shut down, and she just booked the room. Look here," I said as I held the confirmation email up for her to see. "I already paid for the room and that's what I want."

Her beady eyes scanned the words of the email and she began to shake her head. Whatever the fuck that meant it wasn't good.

"I'm sorry, sir," she moaned. "The computer shouldn't have showed a room available because we are all full. I honestly don't have a single room available."

I felt the rage boil up from my guts and burn in my chest. I was about to explode and that wasn't how I operate. After being a reckless and whimsical teen, I'd dedicated my adult life to having a remarkable level of patience that extended to every walk of life. From her demeanor it was clear whatever mistake that had happened certainly wasn't anything of her personal doing, and I wasn't the type of person to take out my angst on an undeserving human being.

That just wasn't my way, but a small part of me wished it were as I stood there in the lobby of Super 8 with my options dwindling.

A small part of the raging river of emotions broke, and a few curse words were mumbled as I heaved the door open and angrily shuffled back to my car. In that moment, I didn't care what the Arizona Department of Travel deemed to be unsafe: I was going to get to Nevada come hell or highwater.

I jumped back into the Nissan and turned the key ready to knockout the final three hours of the drive like a force of nature. I was set to tear up the asphalt with a vengeance never before seen by the likes of me, but once again the universe had other plans.

I turned the key and there was nothing.

I turned it again and the engine gave a faint whimper before going silent.

I turned it a third time and the windshield wipers crept across the glass but nothing came from under the hood. My car was dead in the parking lot of a Super 8 that didn't have the room I had just paid for, and my mind could clearly see a handful of excrement being Nolan Ryan'd into the spinning blades.

I was fucked in every which way, and there was no way around it.

After taking a few moments to gather myself, I picked up the phone to bring Renee up to speed on the situation at hand. Not only was she going to be delighted to be woken up after she'd just fallen asleep, but she would be absolutely thrilled to learn that my car had broken down. In most people's world, that would mean a trip to the dealership repair shop for a problem that was most likely covered under warranty. In the interim, while the fixes were being made by certified mechanics, a vehicle of similar value would be given to make sure the owner wasn't put out by the issue.

That's not how things worked in our world.

With me being a writer and her a fine dining bartender, it was a paycheck to paycheck existence that didn't have the built in wiggle room for catastrophe. Granted, anytime problems arose, we always found our way through them, but this was going to be a much different story. We were resourceful people to the bone, but having the Nissan take a shit so far from home and just after Christmas nearly bled us out was going to paint a grim picture.

I dialed the phone slowly and prayed for her to have a cooler head than mine.

I can't say she didn't come unglued upon hearing the spate of misfortune, but I can give her credit for one of the quickest turnarounds in crisis history. Throughout our time together, I had held position as the key problem solver in our union, but she'd been known to step in from time to time and take the help when shrapnel from a life bomb dropped me to the dirt.

As I sat with a dead car and a mind exhausted in Wickenburg, it was fortunately one of those times.

"Even though our AAA membership has expired, they should still be able to direct us to someone who should be able to come out and help," Renee commanded. "Go back in and ask the lady for the numbers to any other hotels or motels in town, and you get on to calling them, because I'm sure it's too cold for you to be sleeping in that car."

"Yeah," I sighed. "It's cold as fuck out here and that wouldn't work."

The next hour was spent caught up in a rapid series of phone calls where Renee provided as many solutions as she could muster for the grim scenario at hand. She'd called AAA and they had given her the number of the local service they use, and I plugged said number into my phone to call for help. The young man working the operator line informed me that all of his trucks were currently out fishing vehicles out of ditches and gave me the number of another service he said could possibly help.

This game went on for a few more turns and every hurdle I jumped another rose on the path ahead. I was finally able to track down a towing service on the outskirts of Wickenburg, and the man said he'd be on his way shortly. While I waited for him, I walked back into the Super 8 to ask Tammy for the numbers to other hotels in town.

Our earlier interaction had obviously riled her up, and she wasn't quick to provide the help needed. That said, her humanity eventually surfaced, and she used her speed ravaged mind to help the cause. Unfortunately much like what Mary and Joseph experienced as the holy mother prepared to bring Jesus into the world, there wasn't a room at any inn to be found.

After asking Tammy if I could crash out in the lobby chairs for a few or if she had a broom closet I could catch a few winks in, the beleaguered night manager told me the best option was a 24-hour Denny's a few blocks up the road, and in hearing that I was certain the bottom of the barrel had been located. The thought of sitting in a booth as the late shift staff lurked about made my skin crawl, but that would be the only option available if the tow truck driver couldn't jump the Nissan back to life.

A small bit of relief was found when the big white truck finally whipped into the lot, but that relief was extremely short lived as the car didn't respond to the jump. We made several attempts, but each result was the same. My car was dead, and it wasn't going anywhere without being fixed.

"It's your starter, buddy," the old man with a big streak of grease on his cheek coughed. "As soon as you tried to turn it over, I could see the cylinder smoking. It's shot and gonna need to be replaced."

"You know anybody who can get that taken care of?" I asked in desperation.

"Yeah there is a guy here in town but he's not going to be back to work until the 2nd, so that would be Friday morning."

Once again another handful of shit hit the proverbial floor model in my mind.

"Is that my only option?" I asked already knowing the answer.

"Yeah there isn't anyone else unless you go to Phoenix and that's a haul," the old man answered. "I can give it a tow there for you tonight, and I'm sure he'll be able to get to it first thing in the morning on Friday."

"Does it have to be tonight?" I asked. "I was going to sleep in it since they fucked up and don't have a room for me here."

The old man paused for a moment before unhooking the jump cables and slamming down the hood. It looked like he was trying to stand up straight but a lifetime crawling over and under cars had done a number on him.

"Since I wasn't able to get her started for you I was going to tow it for free," he sighed. "Figured you'd had enough kicks in the nuts for the night and was going to do you a solid, but I can't come back and grab it without charging you. If you let me take it now I'll do it free of charge, but that offer only stands for the night."

As his words bounced around my head, I attempted to do a quick bit of damage control. The repair on the starter would run around the two-hundred dollar mark, and the towing company ran at a 85 dollar minimum for their services. The last thing I wanted to do was face up to the freezing scene during the early morning hours in a city I didn't know a soul, but the thought of saving a good chunk of cash was too much to pass up.

If that meant legging out a few hours at the Denny's down the way, then so be it. I asked the old man to hold tight for a moment, then ran back into the hotel to sort a few things out with Tammy. Once she found out I was stranded, the seasoned gal turned downright sympathetic, and she wrote up a card that gave me the next two days for the price of what was already paid.

"It's the least we can do for ya," she said as her hands found their steady point long enough to punch my information into the system to secure a two-night stay. It was a strong move for someone I hadn't given all too much credit during our initial exchange, and if I weren't already pushed beyond my limits, I would have felt like an asshole for storming out on her.

I shuffled back to the tow truck and gave the old man the green light to take the car. He informed me the mechanic's shop it was going to was just a few blocks down the road back toward the main part of town and that I'd hear from the guy first thing in the morning on Friday. Tammy was nice enough to allow me to put my luggage in the back office, and I gathered several other work related items from the car and put them into my backpack with my laptop.

The old man's radio lit up a few moments later, and he was called out to an urgent situation back toward Morristown. He told me he'd come back through and grab the car on his way home so I shouldn't be sleeping in it tonight. I assured him that I wouldn't and started to plot my course for the Denny's Tammy had suggested.

From where I stood, I could see a Marathon gas station a little bit down the way, and while there was an office building blocking my direct view, a yellow hue projected into the thick night sky told me the restaurant in question was located just across the way. With no other option available, I buttoned up my petticoat up to my neck and pulled the straps to my backpack tightly before making my way out of the parking lot.

Being a stranger in a strange land created the base for my foundation of caution, and being paired down to being a drifter in that strange land only made things worse in that sense. The Marathon up the way was lit up like a fluorescent bonfire in the dark of winter, but getting there wasn't going to be a gingerly stroll up the road.

Between the gas station and I sat a three block gap of the deepest dark I'd ever seen, and walking into the unknown had about as much appeal as a frightened co-ed deciding to take a shortcut through the park to get back to the dorms. I wasn't sure what waited for me out in the void, but I was absolutely certain it was nothing good, and my feet refused to cooperate with the brain that was telling them to go forth.

This lasted until the first bit of cold found its way around the rim of my wool overcoat and slipped down the bare skin of my neck. Freezing to death was an actual possibility in such conditions, therefore getting a move on was the only option on the table. I cautiously started out into the blackness, and my eyes scanned the blank canvas for anything I could find to set as markers.

Once my vision adapted I located two junked out cars sitting out in the open land about 20 yards off the road, and there was an overturned hauling trailer another few feet behind where they sat. I could hear small chunks of gravel crunch beneath my feet, and the sound of the scraping seemed to echo out into the desert.

I looked up to see the Marathon station drawing closer. Despite the dropping temperatures, there was a person standing outside under the overhang with a hose spraying down the concrete. It was difficult to tell at such a distance, but the figure appeared to be a tiny person, and I figured it to be a woman. I attempted to zone back in on the darkness to my right, but after having looked at the lights of the Marathon, my night vision had totally gone to shit.

As I turned my focus back to the gas station, I heard a faint grumbling coming from the void to my right. I stopped abruptly to let my ears zero in on the sound, and in between the cutting wind, things went silent enough for me to realize the true nature of the disturbance.

It wasn't grumbling. It was a growl. And there were several others that kicked up behind it.

The instant my mind processed what the source could be, I erupted into a dash for survival. I wasn't sure how many dogs, wolves, or coyotes there were coming for me across the rocky terrain, but they were sure enough coming. My lungs burned hot as the ice cold air rolled in and out of my lungs in rapid-fire turns, and the weight of my backpack lit up my legs as well.

Even those individuals who run for exercise underestimate the shape necessary to run for one's life because there are a variety of additional elements involved in that situation. Conditioning is one thing, but when the adrenaline that fear produced hits the central nervous system, it's the equivalent of nitrous hitting an engine, and that level of burn is difficult to sustain.

It was a balls to the wall sprint to the Marathon and my jumbled vision could see the finish line coming into view. There was only one more block to go and there was nothing that was going to stop me from reaching my goal. As I drew closer, I noticed the woman holding the water hose stand up and take notice before dropping the works all together and making her own break for the door.

Although I was confused in the moment, her move made a tremendous amount of sense in retrospect. Standing under the well-lit canopy had created the same viewpoint of standing next to a campfire, where everything lurking on the outside can see in, but you can't see out. Now imagine her terror when she halted her remedial task to hear what the commotion was, only to see a 215-pound man trucking at full speed out of the darkness toward her.

She would later say it wasn't me as much as what I was running from, but she sure enough locked the two glass doors behind her.

Blocking my entry from the gas station never truly came into play as the sudden arrival of the police just as I crossed the imaginary finish line put her at ease. No sooner than I hit the well-lit area did a police cruiser bust in with a mega-watt beam pointed directly in my eyes. I attempted to block out the laser as I caught my breath because I knew an explanation to why I was running in the middle of the night was certainly going to be necessary.

"Sir, are you running from a pack of wild dogs?" the officer shouted to me from behind the light.

I didn't have the energy gathered to properly respond and used all I had to shake my head to answer affirmatively, and before I could even pull myself upright, his tires screeched and he peeled back down the street in the direction I had arrived from moments earlier. Apparently wild dogs were a veritable threat in the Wickenburg area, and it was strangely comforting to know the growling and the chase weren't figments of my imagination.

A few moments after the police officer sped away in search of the devil dogs, the woman circled back out from behind the doors. A huge cloud of fog encircled me as my struggle for breath kicked a batch of hot air out into the night, and the sweat that poured down my face became an instant conduit for the chilled wind.

"Come on in! It is cold as a billygoat's pecker," she commanded, and her choice of verbiage instantly made her a friend.

I leaned against the counter by the register as I hit the final stages of physical recovery, and listened to the woman go on and on about nothing in particular. At first she replayed the encounter from different angles and perspectives, but once she really settled in, she bent my ear about everything that had been going downhill in her life. Being a strong listener means providing a comfortable platform that isn't interrupted by your own personal matters, and while I wanted to remain decent in that moment, I wanted to let her know her problems didn't have shit on the mountain I'd accrued.

Allowing myself to be the place she dropped the broken stones of her life for a few minutes ultimately paid off as she told me about a place she knew that rented rooms in town. Under normal circumstances such an idea would've sounded insane, but having to pick between staying in a warm room and fending off a few crazy old women or sleeping on the bench of a booth at Denny's, made it an easy choice.

She made a quick phone call and everything was set in place. The old birds were going to take me in for a proper night's rest, and the gas station gal provided all the information necessary. When she reached the moment where she realized I didn't have a car to get there, the slightly nervous and heavily weathered woman took things one step further and called someone to pick me up and give me a lift.

"How in the world did you find someone at this hour on New Year's that isn't already wasted or in jail?"

"He's the cook over at Denny's," she replied not missing a beat.

Chapter 37

Stuck in Purgatory

Of all things I didn't expect to stir me out of a slumber on the trip, bacon sat at the top of the list. With the amount of traveling I'd done, I'd gotten used to waking up in strange places as much as a person can, and it took a few extra moments to find my bearings on that particular morning, as the night prior was truly one of the longest and stressful days as I'd experienced in life.

People rarely are as advertised, but the two elderly women who took me in for the night were just as Marathon Lady had described. Both had lost their husbands some time back, and rather than give up the ghost and submit to the pressing storms of old age and sadness, they decided to squad up against such forces. It was a decision that seemed to have paid off as both were downright jubilant in the kitchen that morning.

"Look who it is," the woman who I would come to know as Rebecca shouted at a level of volume and joy that made my head snap back a touch.

"We were wondering when you were going to wake up," added the other who went by Anne.

"I didn't mean to sleep in," I replied. "What time is it?"

"Oh it's just a little after 8," Anne chimed.

My mind tried to make sense of the comment, and I suddenly began to feel as if I'd overstayed my welcome. It was after four o'clock when they opened their door to me, and there it was, just four hours later and they made it seem as if I'd been decked out for half the day. Then again, those women were remnants from a time where making the most of the day meant far more than it did on the current landscape.

Nevertheless, I put the card on the table just in case.

"Do I need to be making my way out?" I asked as I entered the kitchen.

"Don't be silly," Rebecca smiled. "We made a big breakfast. Sit and visit with two old ladies for a bit."

Their smiles were beaming back at me and it would have been impossible not to do as they asked. I've always been a firm believer that a person's eyes tell the story, and the police officer from the previous night could have used Rebecca and Anne's peepers to find those mysterious dogs out in the brush. They were honestly jumping with vitality.

"You're a writer, is that correct?" Anne asked from out of left field.

A rough mixture of shock and humility slowed my response a bit, but I ultimately gave in.

"I'm something like that. I'm not sure you'd call it a writer necessarily, because I don't write books."

"He writes about those fighting guys," Rebecca said. "Not the boxer guys but the other ones."

Her words elevated my level of shock to full blown confusion, and I came to the conclusion it was quite possible Rebecca was in fact an ancient mystic.

"How in the world do you know what I do for a living?" I asked, grinning from ear to ear as recognition is a difficult thing to come by in any form as a writer.

"I looked you up on Google," she replied in one deflating swipe. "It's not often we get a call that late at night, and I wasn't going to take a felon under our roof."

I'd spent so long in fantastical scenarios and dragging myself up and down the mountains of fortune and despair, that I didn't even see her stiff right cross of reality coming my way. It was a move well played and we filled the next two hours with chit chat. A broken down car had put my ambitious self in a bad way, but that sudden turn resulted in getting the chance to meet two of the nicest women on the planet. Life can be pretty cool some times.

Before my mad dash to the Marathon, Tammy told me the room at the Super 8 would be available after noon, so I started to shape my plans toward getting back to the scene of the crime. Neither Anne nor Rebecca were much for driving, but the latter made a phone call to have someone give me a lift. Time spent in the comfort of strangers ended up being a great start to my day, which in turn became a solid beginning to another year all the same.

The cold weather lifted and the desert sun opened up to put off a bit of the warmth it was notorious for, and that created the proper conditions for a quick stroll through town. There wasn't much to Wickenburg in general, but the city had a tiny downtown district with shops, eateries, and a few saloons. With nothing on the docket and time to waste, I decided to duck in for a sitting at one of the taverns and enacted the sacred Finley family gift of losing an entire day inside the walls of a watering hole.

Sitting at the end of the bar I became known to all as "The Stranded Guy," and that suit me just fine. There was no need for anyone in the place to know much about my story or where I was headed, because I'd never see a single one of them again, just as they'd never lay eyes on me a second time. Having grown up around neighborhood bars that didn't register on the softer side, I'd learned at an early age how to conduct myself properly on foreign turf.

While society outside of the saloon doors operates on a distinct set of rules, the laws of a dive bar don't adhere to common order. The people who frequent the low lit neon traced belly of a particular hole in the wall tavern actually take a large amount of pride in everything about it. Where most would scoff at a crock pot of pulled pork being served by a barehanded barkeep with a spoon in one hand and a Pall Mall in the other, the regulars of that establishment don't even bat an eye.

Those places have a language Harvard scholars could never decode and a sense of reasoning that would make most clinical psychiatrist deem them insane.

Example: If Banker Bob decided to shoot a bit of pool at a normal sports bar, there would be very little concern for his safety. Even if Banker Bob got a bit tipsy and shot off his mouth a bit more than he was known to do at said sports bar, there would still be very little reason to believe anything terrible would happen to him. In fact, after drinking his bodyweight in Jack Daniels and bumming a pull off of a joint from the dishwasher out back where he went to take a piss, Banker Bob would have an Uber called for him and wake up the next day feeling like he was Billy Badass King of the World.

Now for the Dive Bar Example: The moment Banker Bob walked through the doors in his shirt and tie and two-hundred dollar shoes, he became a potential target for at least four patrons in the place. That said, we're not talking about all-out savages here, so they allow him to sit down and drink his one beer—and only one beer—without incident. The moment Banker Bob decides to wander back to the pool tables, he's broken the invisible treaty between lions and sheep, and has officially become fair game. The moment Bob steps too hard in any one direction he will get the shit kicked out of him, and the men who did it will return to their barstools and continue drinking while Bob lays swollen and bleeding on the concrete a few feet outside of the door.

Every habitat has its own way of keeping order and I knew how to handle myself in a saloon situation. I would sit there quietly and enjoy my beer all the while keeping my eyes locked on whatever sporting event was on the television in front of me. At no time would I enter the billiards area, and I'd keep up a strong pace that showed all of the eyes watching me that I wasn't a pinky out sipper. This would eventually cause one of the pack to pop over and test me in a manner of speaking, and I would answer that test with stern eyes and a firm temperament.

Just as expected, two hours and change into my sitting, the vacant stool to my left became occupied. I knew what it was since there were at least seven other seats open down the way, and I handled the situation according the Dive Bar Rules of Engagement. The man introduced himself as Bobo and invited me back to "shoot some stick" with him and his buddies. I didn't entertain the thought for a second and continued to keep my eyes fixed on the "Place Your Corporate Name Here" Bowl that was playing out on the screen overhead.

Upon my decline, Bobo began to press, and that's when I turned my attention to him in full. Since he was the one they sent over to fish me out, I knew Bobo was the flake of the group, but I was sure the three men to the back were hard as nails. I didn't budge in the slightest, but I remained civil and courteous. My lips said I wanted to be left alone, but my eyes read I was a crazy motherfucker fresh out and I had no issue with breaking his nose.

In reality, smashing the grease ball was the last thing I wanted to do, but the steps taken were necessary in keeping it peaceful inside the well.

My plan worked out in stride, as the shark tank at the back of the room eventually dissipated, and the threat level was lowered to green. Once this transition occurred, the avenues of conversation were opened, and I had the pleasure of meeting a wide array of bat shit crazy individuals en route to catching the buzz I sat out to catch.

One man spent an hour telling me how he came down to Arizona from Wyoming twice a year to wrangle goats, and because he liked the people around Wickenburg so much, he decided to buy a mobile home and a plot of land to put it on. Just the thought of someone buying a mobile home and then fixing it to a specific place erases the word "mobile" from the equation, but there was no way I was going to try to explain that to him.

A few beers into his story, another man came to call, and his heavy Russian accent gave me a chuckle. Here was a man dressed like he was straight off of a Marlboro billboard but was speaking like an extra in Eastern Promises. I had just about gotten used to the paradox, when from out of nowhere, his accent flipped from Eastern Block to somewhere south of Rio de Janiero. The man in the Stetson somehow switched from Russian to Portuguese without anyone missing a beat. I was initially impressed by his performance, but when I found out later on in the evening he suffered from a brain condition that made him change accents without him knowing, my enthusiasm turned to sympathy.

That said, it was still funny as hell to sit and listen to while I wasted my stranded day away with a crowd of people I'd never see again.

By the end of the night the stranded guy became an accepted figure on the dive bar scene, and I was able to catch a lift back to the Super 8 before I lost my bearings. It's a genetic gift and curse to be able to house as many ounces of shitty beer as I can without getting the wobbles, but I was savvy enough to hear the hotel room calling.

I checked in with Renee one last time for the night, then caught an Undercover Boss marathon rolling on one of the local channels. Not a single bit of MMA or the road trip project found a way into my head that day, and despite being stranded in a town I came to the conclusion was populated by meth heads and hookers, the day wasn't all and all too shabby.

If everything went right with the Universe, the phone would ring somewhere close to sunrise, and some friendly mechanic would tell me the Nissan was fixed and ready to go. If the Universe wanted to take its courtesy a step further, the same friendly mechanic would then tell me the repair was around one-hundred bucks, and I'd be back on the road with some good news to share with Renee.

At least those were the things I hoped for as the ambient noise of a millionaire pretending to sympathize with a single mom lulled me to sleep.

Chapter 38

A Real Life Vacation

The phone sure enough rang in the early morning hours of Friday January 2nd, but nothing I'd wished for came close to being reality.

The mechanic on the other end first informed me that the problem wasn't my starter and that my engine had seized. There wasn't a cell in my body that believed his diagnosis, and I wasted no time pushing back. I'd been in two different vehicles where major engine damage had occurred, and few things are more violent than having an engine lock up at 60 mph when the timing chain snaps.

He was a bit distraught that I wasn't willing to bite, and once he dropped the eighteen-hundred dollar price tag for the repair on me, I closed the door for him.

"I bought that car for two-thousand dollars and drove it coast to coast and most of the way back again. There is no way I'm going to put that kind of money into it. I'll have someone come up from Phoenix to scrap it out then take the money and fly home."

"Now Pete told me you had somewhere you had to get in a hurry, that's why I moved your car ahead of all the others I had lined up ahead of it.

Are you telling me that you don't need to be somewhere?"

"I have to be in Las Vegas for work by tomorrow, but I'll take the fucking bus if need be," I replied. "There is just no way I'm going to pay that kind of money."

The man hem-hawed for a bit with different chatter about rods and pistons, then found enough footing to make one more play at my wallet.

"If you are going to be up in Nevada for a few days then there is no reason to make a hasty decision like having it scrapped," the mechanic said. "We were in a huge rush this morning trying to get you back on the road, but since we have a little bit of time, I'll have Tim my engine guy come in and give it a good look."

For whatever reason, Tim the engine guy apparently wasn't on duty that morning, but I agreed to let him take another look under the hood with one major stipulation in place.

"No matter what, do not pull the engine," I commanded. "You can have him look, but don't do any work to it before you give me a quote and I agree to the price. Do you understand?"

"Sure thing, Boss," he replied.

We went back over that stipulation at least three more times before ending the call, and I was confident I'd made my point. With the possibility of getting back on the road with my own car checked off the list of options, I began to shoot out text messages and search for answers online. I was sitting three hours south of Las Vegas, and it was the day before one of the biggest fights in UFC history as Jon Jones was to take on Daniel Cormier for the light heavyweight strap.

If worst came to worst, there was a Greyhound bus that rolled through the opposite end of town, but no one at Super 8 could agree on whether or not it stopped on every pass through Wickenburg. Fortunately, my good friend Jeremy Botter was unwilling to shrug off my troubles like several other so called friends had managed to do, and "Bottertron" stuck by my side until a solution was found.

Since he had to cover the weigh ins later on in the afternoon, he couldn't jump in his car and drive down to grab me, but said he'd be able to meet me in Kingman if I could get there. I called around to check cab and rental car prices and both were astronomical compared to what things would typically run anywhere else in the country.

It seemed as if all would be lost until my phone lit up with a text from my friend and former neighbor Pat Rouselle. He'd been a huge fight fan for years and wanted my take on the tilt between Jones and D.C. He also saw one of my posts about being stuck in Arizona on Facebook and wanted to know how everything was going since I'd been drinking in a bar just 20 minutes from his place of employment.

After years of living a few houses down the street from us, Pat and his family picked up and moved out to the Phoenix area. He'd said it was the best decision they ever made, and from the pictures I'd seen, the dude had never looked happier. I wasn't sure why I never thought to ask him for help, but since he reached out via text I decided to inquire.

True to his Midwestern roots, Pat didn't hesitate a second. He had to work until five but assured me that he and his wife Brandi would come through Wickenburg and scoop me up. Pat said they didn't have anything planned until later that night, and a quick run up to Kingman wouldn't be a problem in the slightest. His news rallied my spirits, and the road trip project wasn't going to come to a gruesome end in the Arizona desert.

I was going to make it to Las Vegas after all, and I couldn't wait to see the sprawling lights roll out in the valley coming over the Hoover Dam. The run had taken so many hits and suffered through all of the highs and lows that not making it to the fights would have meant it was all for nothing. The trusty Nissan would have gone down in vain, and I couldn't allow that to happen.

The show had to go on, and because of a few good friends, it was going to do exactly that.

Chapter 39

Are You There, Pussy?

When so much is put on the line to reach a specific goal or destination, other elements attached to the situation can take on a higher meaning, and UFC 181 became my vision quest.

I was just as excited as the next person to see Jones and Cormier finally settle their beef and fully expected an all-out scrap that would test the mettle of both men. They were both remarkable fighters, and who would have whose number was truly anyone's guess, but I leaned slightly toward Jones on my pick.

That wasn't to say Cormier didn't have a great chance of winning, but I figured Jones's length and striking abilities would add up and eventually take a toll on the former Olympian. That's how I saw things on an analytical level, but being able to sit cageside while those two elite level warriors waged war inside the cage registered on a much higher plain for me.

I'd trudged through such a copious amount of shit on my final run of the road trip project that not making it to the event would have been a failure of epic proportions, and one that I would have had a difficult time with coming to grips. My goddamn ambition created the twenty-thousand mile journey, and that same goddamn ambition was going to make sure it carried through until the end.

When Jones raised his hands at the end of a lopsided unanimous decision victory, the cap could finally be placed on the adventure in full. It was finally over and being able to say that was something long overdue.

Unlike coming home in October, there would be no deep retrospection because home is a place I wouldn't see for several weeks. Where my initial plan was to be gone for six days, nearly a month passed before I was able to hug my children and kiss my wife again. This was the direct result of the shifty mechanic breaking the one stipulation I put in place and then trying to strong arm me for two thousand dollars.

Even though I told him not to touch the car before giving me a quote, Captain Slim Shady decided putting wrenches on the vehicle would be the only way he could jack up the price. It was his way of calling my bluff about leaving it behind, but being a man of my word, I did just that. Since he'd put so-called work into the vehicle, I couldn't have it scrapped without paying his fee, but since he didn't have a signed written estimate there was nothing he could do to legally demand payment.

We were at a stalemate and I left it as such as I floated across the friendly skies en route to my loving home just north of Indianapolis.

Just as Botter had proven to be a great friend by coming all the way down to Kingman to pick me up, he proved our bond that much further by allowing me to live on his couch for the month I was stranded due to the car situation. We made the most of our time as we hit the gym like animals in the morning then drank and gambled like degenerates in the evening. It was a great way to spend a few weeks, but I couldn't wait to get home.

One advantage to living in Las Vegas was the access to fight gyms, and I made my way around to see several of the people and places I visited on my initial run through one year earlier. I caught up for dinner with Gray Maynard a time or two, and tested King Mo's video game skills on several 16-bit classics. He kicked the dog shit out of me shortly after every quarter dropped, but that's not something I'd ever admit on social media. The way I saw it and still see it to this day, Mo ducked me on Burger Time and that's a chapter that needs some closure.

I worked throughout my entire stay in Vegas, churned out quality content for my employer, and hit every single deadline for the companies with which I had contracts. Most people would have wilted under the weight of my situation, with being stranded and having your car stolen out from under you, but I'd never been like most people. I simply did the work that needed to be done and made the most of the time I had until I could finally go home.

Thanks to a Buddy Pass from a good friend I was able to do just that, and the snow covered Indiana flats never looked as good as they did that day. My wife lined up a ride for me from our good friend James Morey, and he was sincerely delighted I had managed to make it home safe and sound.

"That stuff only happens to you Duane," he said over and over as he shook his head, and oh how true it was.

I knew my family would be waiting anxiously by the window to see me pull in, and I had the good sense to have James capture the moment on video from my phone. Atticus was the first out the door and he sprinted out to me before jumping up in my arms. Zoe being far more composed, shuffled out to join in on the hug, and I couldn't remember ever feeling more loved. Last but not least was Renee, and her smile was the final piece of home I was missing.

Once the four of us were back together, nothing else in the world mattered, and I never let a single one of them out of my sight for the next two days. It was the type of feeling a man spends his entire life searching for, and some never find, but I had it around me always.

With everything I had gone through, my employer decided to give me a week off the clock, and that opened the door for what needed to come next. Even though I'd just returned home and the last thing in the world I wanted to do was go away for another stretch, the time had finally arrived for me to seek help for my problem.

I sat my children down and explained the reality of the situation, because I'd always believed that frank honesty was always the best method. Naturally I didn't want them to think of me as anything but their father who loved them more than anything in the world, but if breaking the cycle meant my persona had to take a bit of damage in their eyes, then so be it.

As it turned out things fell in exactly the opposite manner. My children handed down no judgments in the matter. All they wanted was their father to be okay, and that made what I had to do just a bit easier. The night before I entered rehab I laid and snuggled with each of them and felt content the right decision was being made.

Once they were asleep, I went into the bedroom to begin packing my bags. Renee sat on the bed folding laundry, and we talked about our journey. She knew the decision I'd made wasn't one I had come to easily, and her eyes were compassionate and soft. Our entire relationship she'd inspired me to push to become something greater than I was the day before, and never had it shone brighter than it did when I was at my lowest.

I had accomplished this incredible journey with a scope never before seen in my field. I had taken a wild idea and executed it at such a degree that it carved out my place in the MMA universe and exposed my writing to an entirely different segment of the sport. Despite what happened with my back and the pills, what I achieved was something that wouldn't be lessened because of my shortcomings, and that was one huge positive I took into the next week.

Most importantly, my family was proud of everything I'd done. Seeing their father and husband pursue his dream was something I knew they'd never forget, and somewhere in my mind, I hoped it would be a time they'd revisit somewhere down the line when their passions roared to life.

Early the next morning my wife pulled into the rehabilitation center and gave me a kiss before I exited the car and made my way toward the door. They were the same doors I'd walked through a broken man nine years earlier, and the same doors I walked out ten days later determined to conquer the world.

While it hurt to be returning to a place I swore I'd never see the inside of again, there was a triumph to be found in that moment as well...even as dim and bleak as it was. I'd never been the type to back down from anything, and returning to rehab simply meant it was time to put on the gloves once more.

If writing about fighters and getting a glimpse at their lives had taught me anything, it was that nothing has the right to keep you from being the person you want to be. And while my personal struggle didn't involve going toe-to-toe with another human being inside of a chain-linked cage, it certainly involved a fight.

There wouldn't be a paycheck on the line, but waiting in the wings would be my ability to dictate my freedom in life. Professional fighters are born into this world a different breed, and the course they travel is one where resistance waits for them around every corner. Every step forward is earned in their world, and that was a reality I'd come to see with clarity. Every accomplishment comes from being willing to go beyond the limits that previously existed, and the discoveries made in the aftermath of those moments were the lessons that last a lifetime.

That is what the fighting life was all about, and it was the only thing I'd ever known.

ABOUT THE AUTHOR

Duane Finley is a journalist/writer who has covered combat sports for several major publications. He is currently the Senior Editor for FloCombat. He is a proud father.

Printed in Great Britain
by Amazon